Women Poets on the Left

Lola Ridge, Genevieve Taggard, Margaret Walker

Nancy Berke

University Press of Florida

Gainesville · Tallahassee · Tampa · Boca Raton

Pensacola · Orlando · Miami · Jacksonville · Ft. Myers

05 04 03 02 01 6 5 4 3 2 1

LIBRARY OF CONGRESS
CATALOGING-IN-PUBLICATION DATA
Berke, Nancy, 1956–
Women poets on the left : Lola Ridge, Genevieve
Taggard, Margaret Walker / Nancy Berke.
p. cm.
Includes bibliographical references and index.
ISBN 0-8130-2115-4 (cloth : alk. paper)
1. Political poetry, American—History and criti-
cism. 2. Politics and literature—United States—
History—20th century. 3. Women and literature
—United States—History—20th century.
4. American poetry—20th century—History and
criticism. 5. Ridge, Lola, 1883–1941—Political and
social views. 6. Taggard, Genevieve, 1894–1948—
Political and social views. 7. Walker, Margaret,
1915– —Political and social views. 8. Right and
left (Political science) in literature. I. Title.
PS310.P6 B47 2001   811'.5209358—dc21
2001027905

The poem "Ann Burlak" by Muriel
Rukeyser reprinted by permission of
International Creative Management, Inc.
Copyright 1987.

Frontispiece: 1775–1936 by Rockwell Kent is
reproduced courtesy of the Rockwell Kent
Legacies and courtesy of the Rockwell Kent
Collection, Rare Book and Manuscript
Library, Columbia University.

The University Press of Florida is the
scholarly publishing agency for the State
University System of Florida, comprising
Florida A&M University, Florida Atlantic
University, Florida Gulf Coast University,
Florida International University, Florida
State University, University of Central
Florida, University of Florida, University of
North Florida, University of South Florida,
and University of West Florida.

University Press of Florida
15 Northwest 15th Street
Gainesville, FL 32611–2079
http://www.upf.com

Contents

For Laurie Berke Segal, Terri Steiner,
and in memory of my poet-colleague Marcia Lipson

Acknowledgments

Lola Ridge once said of writing poetry that "anything that burns you" should come to light. *Women Poets on the Left* grew out of my "burning" frustration that no critical books on the poetic vision and practice of American leftist women of the modern period seemed to exist. Had it not been for Jane Marcus and her unwavering support, generosity, critical expertise, and brilliant insights, my burning frustration would have remained just that. Her confidence in me and her belief in this book's importance made writing it one of the most rewarding experiences of my life.

At every stage of writing, from the first sentence to the last period, Shuang Shen was there, eager to read and comment. I owe a tremendous debt to her. Her friendship, support, and interest in this project helped keep it moving forward. Wayne Koestenbaum, Florence Howe, Page Delano, Ethan Young, Carol Deletiner, Lillian Robinson, and Cary Nelson read all or part of the manuscript at various stages of completion and offered invaluable criticism. Jean Pfaelzer and Sharon M. Harris, editors of the *Legacy* special issue "Discourses of Women and Class" in which my article "Ethnicity, Class, and Gender in Lola Ridge's 'The Ghetto'" appeared, provided me with excellent editorial guidance. I am grateful to Marcia D. Liles for checking dates and other biographical information in my chapter on her mother, Genevieve Taggard. Susan Fernandez, my editor at the University Press of Florida, has shown great support of this project. Jackie DiSalvo, Ann Lauterbach, and Carla Capetti took time out from their busy schedules to talk with me about some of the problems and challenges of my subject long before I began to realize them on paper. Laurie Segal brought the exhibition catalogue *Alice Neel: Paintings from the Thirties* to my attention.

As this book required much foraging in archives and libraries, I owe thanks to the staffs and librarians of a number of institutions: the Rare Book and Manuscripts Library, Columbia University; the Manuscripts Division of the New York Public Library (Genevieve Taggard Papers); the Sophia Smith Collection, Smith College Libraries (Lola Ridge Papers); Rare Books and Special Collections, Princeton University Libraries; the Beinecke Rare Book and Manuscripts Library, Yale University; Special Collections, Dartmouth College Library; Van Pelt Library, University of Pennsylvania; Tamiment Library, New York University Libraries; Wexler Library, Hunter College, City University of New York.

A Friends of the University of Wisconsin–Madison Libraries grant-in-aid allowed me to read through many wonderful little magazines in the Marvin Sukov Collection—my thanks to John Tortorice and staff members of Memorial Library, University of Wisconsin–Madison. I would also like to thank Karen Carlson for housing me during my stay in Madison (in addition to Mom, Dad, Laurie, Dean, Rebecca, and Adam, who entertained me on weekends). Support from the City University of New York Graduate School and the Adrienne Auslander Munich Dissertation Prize helped defray the costs of what seemed like endless photocopying.

I am also grateful to the following individuals, institutions, and estates for permission to reprint material from Lola Ridge, Genevieve Taggard, Margaret Walker, and Muriel Rukeyser: Elaine Sproat; Marcia D. Liles; University of Georgia Press; International Creative Management, Inc.; the Rockwell Kent Legacies, as well as the Rockwell Kent Collection, Rare Book and Manuscript Library, Columbia University; and University of Nebraska Press, publishers of *Legacy,* for permission to reprint the portion of chapter 2 that appeared as "Ethnicity, Class, and Gender in Lola Ridge's 'The Ghetto.'"

Finally, I would like to thank my friends (you know who you are) for being there for me, and a special thanks to Emmy for suggesting that we celebrate.

1

Introduction

"The Buried History within the Buried History"

I was a Communist when I painted Nazis Murder Jews *about
a Communist torch light parade in about 1936. . . . I showed the
painting at the ACA Gallery. A critic wrote, "An interesting
painting, but the sign is too obvious." But if they had noticed
that sign, thousands of Jews might have been saved.*
Alice Neel

What's in the men nowadays—the women *have the fire & the
ardency & the power & the depth?*
Genevieve Taggard in a letter to Josephine Herbst, early 1920s

In her landmark anthology published more than twenty-five years ago, *The World Split Open: Four Centuries of Women Poets in England and America, 1552–1950,* Louise Bernikow reserved a special mention for a group of women poets who represented "the buried history within the buried history." As she explained, "Women on the left in America have been banished from contemporary consciousness by the slow erosion of neglect" (45). Bernikow draws attention to two particular poets whose work had been buried twice. Despite their inclusion in Bernikow's collection (as well as one other influential second-wave anthology), these poets, Lola Ridge and Genevieve Taggard, and their poems, continue to be buried history.

Bernikow's landmark anthology is a product of second-wave feminism's dedication to reinstituting women's history and culture. It also coincides with the ascendency of academic feminism in the 1980s, albeit still oppositional, and the rise of a distinct set of feminist critical values. Academic feminism's critical intervention became particularly evident in literary studies of the modern period. Yet while the male biases of the modernist canon are well known, the biases in feminist criticism of the modern period present an additional challenge that requires the creation of a more complex, fully articulated gender of modernism.

The modern period (roughly 1915–1945) examined in this particular study became the subject of a number of influential feminist literary critical projects. Given the number of women who participated in the modernist movement as either artists, polemicists, editors, benefactors, or simply muses, it is not surprising that a new critical movement dedicated to correcting male biases, challenging stereotypes, and recovering women's creative contributions would fashion new sites of investigation.

In the 1980s, feminist literary critics such as Susan Stanford Friedman, Shari Benstock, Carolyn Burke, Sandra M. Gilbert, and Susan Gubar surveyed the rich territory of a gendered modernism and recovered important white female writers such as Gertrude Stein, Djuna Barnes, H.D., and Mina Loy.[1] Studies of women writers of the modern period overwhelmingly focused on those American (and British) women who became expatriots largely due to a climate inhospitable to their creative concerns. Shari Benstock's influential *Women of the Left Bank* chronicled the interwoven worlds of dozens of women writers who made Paris their home between the two world wars. In contrast to the aesthetically radical sensibilities of a number of the women in Benstock's study, criticism by Celeste Schenk, Cheryl Walker, Gloria Hull, and more recently Suzanne Clarke, examined the challenge to modernism by emphasizing the genteel, conservative, or sentimental aspects of women's poetry of the modern period. Yet the majority of modernist literary scholarship as it succeeded in recovering women writers who were aesthetically acceptable tended to ignore political radicals. As a result, the work of American women poets who wrote socially motivated verse has suffered almost complete neglect.

Bonnie Scott's important *Gender of Modernism* anthologized the work of significant modernist women such as Nancy Cunard, Zora Neale Hurston, Nella Larsen, Marianne Moore, Jean Rhys, Dorothy Richardson, Sylvia Townsend Warner, and Rebecca West. Scott's anthology is extensive in its characterization of what constitutes a gender of modernism. She includes English poets Charlotte Mew and Anna Wickham as modernists, yet the absence of American social poets like Lola Ridge, Genevieve Taggard, and Margaret Walker suggests an unwillingness (or perhaps ignorance) on the part of feminist scholars of modernism to reenvision what the gender of modernism looked like in the American context.

Celeste Schenk has pointed to a particular problem regarding the gender of modernism. She contends that a kind of "[m]odernist hegemony that fetishizes formal experiment" (231) is perhaps responsible for the marginalization of certain modern women poets (notable examples are feminist Anna Wickham and marxist Sylvia Townsend Warner). This obsession with experimentation has brought about an "inadvertent feminist adherence to a politically suspect hierarchy of genre." While American women poets on the left lived abroad as well as used formal experiments, the "modernist monolith" embraced by many feminist critics has managed to ignore these women's contributions and has thus shrunk rather than expanded its notion of the gender of modernism. American women's social poetry with its focus on the external forces that shape human consciousness, as opposed to the individual psyche of the artist, has not been examined closely enough to understand its potential to reshape our appreciation of modern American poetry as a multiplicitous practice. As studies of modernism continue to benefit from important critical interventions on behalf of women writers, the sidestepping of radical women poets, their contributions, and their complicated relationship to the modernist movement leaves a rather sizable gap in the gendering of modernism.

In the 1990s, thanks in part to the enormous influence of Cary Nelson's *Repression and Recovery,* American literature scholars have focused on the problem of neglecting radical and/or socially motivated poetry. Susan Schweik's *A Gulf So Deeply Cut* looks at American women's war poetry about World War II in order to "locate intertextual links and political alliances between . . . women's poems and male-authored war poetry, as well as breaks between feminine and masculine traditions" (24). Mark Van Wienen also assesses wartime poetry culture. His enormously important *Partisans and Poets* examines and complicates the popular poetries produced during a time of fervent political debate and repression. He looks at the movements and groups that utilized this poetry and also recovers forgotten black, women, and radical poets. Walter Kalaidjian's *American Culture between the Wars: Revisionary Modernism and Postmodern Critique* examines a good deal of radical poetry, reading it together with the visual and political culture of the time. He then rather ambitiously links radical interwar culture with postmodern art and poetry. While all three of these books offer substantial arguments about the importance of political poetry in the making (and remaking) of modern American culture, none look comprehensively at individual poets as part of the larger argument about the neglect of what Alicia Ostriker refers to as a "third style" of twentieth century (women's) poetry (55).

While it cannot be denied that since the publication of Bernikow's classic anthology, now itself out of print, much exciting scholarship on women poets has appeared, one crucial question repeatedly comes to mind. Why is it that no literary historian or scholar in the last twenty-five years has written a book devoted exclusively to American radical women poets? The answer is complicated. The modernist poetry canon is extremely narrow in its construction. Modernist studies have tended to focus on right-wing rather than left-wing poets and writers. Feminist projects to recover women writers have had an apolitical or antileft bias. One other important consideration is the marginalization of both the left (contrary to what the conservative media have led us to believe) and modern poetry in academic studies.

Bernikow's book, and a handful of others, certainly suggest a rich tradition of verse that women wrote as witnesses to both the twentieth century's vast waves of repression and its fertile grounds of dissent. With the Feminist Press's 1987 publication of *Writing Red*, Charlotte Nekola and Paula Rabinowitz revisited perhaps this century's most significant decade of radical literature. In this anthology, the editors include fiction, reportage, and poetry by a number of significant, albeit forgotten, women writers. The poetry section, edited by Charlotte Nekola, includes a variety of verse: from black poets including Kathleen Tankersley Young and Gladys Casely Hayford, to blues lyrics by Susan McMillan Shepherd, to labor ballads by Florence Reece and Aunt Molly Jackson. In an essay accompanying the poetry, Nekola reminds us that poets like Genevieve Taggard and Margaret Walker were active left voices. While *Writing Red* reintroduced readers to radical women poets of the 1930s such as Taggard and Walker, there were no ensuing books devoted to these women or to the social poetry genre they helped create.

Women Poets on the Left takes up the neglect where Bernikow's and Rabinowitz and Nekola's anthologies left off. It explores the socially conscious verse of radical women poets and the contributions they made toward a multivalent political poetry produced as one of many competing poetry projects of the modern period (1910–1945). While this is not a comprehensive study of women's social poetry, it is the first book to look at a group of radical women poets who were active during the 1930s. It explores women's political poetry by examining and recovering the work of Lola Ridge (1873–1941), Genevieve Taggard (1894–1948), and Margaret Walker (1915–1998). In addition to reassessing the work of these three writers, *Women Poets on the Left* joins the ongoing discussion of modernism's contested terrain and responds to Cary Nelson's contention that the canon of modern American poetry tells only one side of a more complex literary history of the poetries of the period. Though Ridge, Taggard, and Walker were not alone in their interest in writing poems bearing witness to social and political repression in America, they are nonetheless representative of a neglected poetic discourse; left-oriented poets and poetry have been historically marginalized by literary histories that classify either the poem as object popularized by the New Criticism or the abstract disinterestedness found in the traditions of canonical poets such as T. S. Eliot and Marianne Moore. It is the alternative social spaces that Ridge, Taggard, and Walker created in their work that is the central focus of this study.

By "alternative social spaces" I mean the creation of poetry not based purely on aesthetic values. Although poets like Lola Ridge, Genevieve Taggard, and Margaret Walker were interested in the formal processes involved in making poems, they were decidedly more interested in how poems could represent human suffering and struggle to a diverse audience. Genevieve Taggard first achieved acclaim as a poet for her complexly worked love lyrics, but the searing social lyrics she composed in the 1930s and 1940s have never been sufficiently appreciated. It should be said that although Lola Ridge and Margaret Walker were no strangers to personal crises—ill-health, poverty, sexism, racism, and other forms of alienation affected each writer to a certain degree—neither poet wrote what might be classified as personal poetry. Their social observations and representations of specific historical moments—defining points in American social formations such as labor unrest and slavery—signify unique perspectives in modern poetry. As exemplars of a social dialogue in verse, these three poets redirect the modernist focus on the "revolution of the word" to a socially encompassed "revolution in the streets." While social and political oppression and the resistance to it have always had a place in national poetries, their place in modernist poetry has always been suspect. Using a language that is decidedly modern, while at the same time engaging with its reader rather than distancing her from its subject, Ridge, Taggard, and Walker emphasize social commitment and radical, political consciousness as a poem's primary, although never exclusive, goal. Much modern poetry criticism has written off socially directed verse as propaganda without looking at its deeper nuances or its social and historical position within its culture. Thus, the different set of poetic values that these radical women explore in their writing has not been considered poetic value at all. But their work gives the political reader a viable alternative, an oppositional poetics that is useful, as Nelson, Kalaidjian, Schweik, and Van Weinen remind us, in telling a different narrative about modernist poetics. It is necessary to open up a dialogue on the place of women's political poetry within the study of literary modernism. Such work offers a challenge to the primarily aesthetic attention of feminist literary modernism. The work of Ridge, Taggard, and Walker renders the gender of modernism differently. It suggests that other voices besides the canonical women poets that we have come to know through the aesthetic biases of their critics also represent modernism's gender differences.

Women Poets on the Left confronts two important aspects of revisionary practice within modern American poetry. The epigraphs with which this book opens indicate new social formations in aesthetic production. First, painter Alice Neel recalls the importance and problematic reception of social messages as they began to appear within modernist discourse in the first half of the twentieth century. Second, poet Genevieve Taggard suggests that the woman writer in the 1920s would change the literary landscape by asking new questions about art and society. Alice Neel's and Genevieve Taggard's remarks serve as reminders of what Bernikow has termed the "buried history within the buried history." Postwar criticism, particularly the New Critics with their antihistorical, antisociological bent, was successful in rooting out the "obvious" artistic projects that reminded their audience of urgent social meanings. That same critical attitude was also successful in silencing women artists whose "depth," "power," and "ardency" went into constructing a socially conscious aesthetic. What happened to that political female poetic, that fire, that ardency, that power, that depth? This book considers such questions and opens up a new dialogue for all those interested in continuing the search to answer them.

As noted, *Women Poets on the Left* is not a comprehensive study. It focuses on three radical women poets of the modern period whose work is representative. Through social observances and historical witnessing, Ridge, Taggard, and Walker establish a poetry of praxis. Their work demonstrates the much contested idea that poetry can be used to address societal problems as well as record for historical posterity the social and political culture of its time. It also reveals to later generations of progressives and feminists what radical women were thinking about as they composed poems during the first half of the twentieth century.

The tradition of the little magazine, which has recently received necessary critical attention, provides a source for women's political poetry.[2] It also helps situate Ridge, Taggard, and Walker's lyrics as part of a significant radical, cultural milieu. Noteworthy are the number of excellent women poets who, in addition to publishing in the little magazines and radical journals of the modern period, also published books and had active careers as social poets. A number of radical women poets published poems and books during the first four decades of the twentieth century. With the exception of Muriel Rukeyser, none are recognized today; nor do they have books in print. Furthermore, with the notable exceptions of Nekola and Rabinowitz's *Writing Red* and Maureen Honey's *Shadowed Dreams: Women Poets of the Harlem Renaissance,* very little work by modernist political women is represented in anthologies.[3] Some readers may wonder why Muriel Rukeyser (1913–1980) is not included as a subject in this particular study. Perhaps one of the greatest social poets of the twentieth century, Rukeyser has been the subject of a full-length study by Louise Kertesz, *The Poetic Vision of Muriel Rukeyser* [1979]. Critical work on Rukeyser as a leftist poet of the 1930s continues to be published, and selections of her poetry have been put back in print.[4] While Margaret Walker's poetry and essays remain in print, little if no scholarly attention has been paid to her contributions as a radical poet of the 1930s.[5]

Numerous radical women poets provide us with a fascinating alternative version of modern American poetry culture. There are those like Joy Davidman, a Yale Younger Poets Award winner, who wrote left-wing poetry during the "proletarian" 1930s, but eventually rejected their radical pasts. Davidman consequently converted to Catholicism and married English writer C. S. Lewis.[6] Although Josephine Johnson wrote interesting proletarian poetry in the 1930s, she is better known as a Pulitzer Prize–winning novelist (*Now in November* [1934]). Some, like California radical Marie de L. Welch, showed promise early on, publishing in both regional literary arts journals and major publications such as the *New Masses* and the *New Republic,* but produced disappointingly little, and by the 1950s would share the fate of even the better known radicals such as Rukeyser, as well as novelists Tillie Olsen, Meridel LeSueur, and Josephine Herbst.[7] McCarthyism and the postwar return to home and family placed their double silence on radical women writers. The same might be said for the excellent radical poet Ruth Lechlitner, whose relatively small output (and move from the East Coast to the West Coast) seems to have removed her from the wider exposure her work deserved. Lucia Trent was a familiar name to readers of radical journals in the 1930s. She published several books of political verse, edited a number of anthologies with her poet-husband Ralph Cheney, and wrote a manifesto, also with Cheney (*More Power to the Poets!* [1934]). Trent disappears around the time of her husband's death in 1941. Other poets wrote in spurts, wrote comparatively little, or stopped writing altogether. Race conjoined with radical politics perhaps explains the fade-out of two gifted black women, Kathleen Tankersley Young and Gwendolyn Bennett. More is known about Bennett, who had trained as an artist and also wrote prose. Bennett was close to the Harlem branch of the Communist Party and ran an arts center in Harlem under the auspices of the Works Progress Administration.

During the first four decades of the twentieth century, radicalism and radical activity took on an assortment of forms in a variety of communities. Coupled with different literary movements, languages, and forums, radical women were not only separated by what they wrote but also by how they wrote, making it difficult to identify exactly how to characterize women's radical verse. Reading through a variety of little magazines in the Marvin Sukov Collection at the University of Wisconsin–Madison Library provided me with a look at the changes in aesthetic as well as political sensibilities that occurred throughout the modern period. The magazines also make it clear that there are no standard ways to classify modern poetry or separate politics from each journal's aesthetic production. While it remains difficult to characterize the very nuanced literary production of women poets in the little magazines, one might rather loosely suggest that there are two distinct styles with regard to form: a premodernist poetic sentiment, which is expressed through traditional forms, and a modernist sensibility expressed through collage and/or the imagist lyric. Yet the early modernist work is itself complicated. It includes the ballad-style labor and pacifist lyrics of poets like Miriam Allen de Ford and Sarah Cleghorn, as well as the work of anarchists Lola Ridge and Mina Loy, who employed free verse to condemn, in radically different ways, constraints on the individual. Begun in the 1910s, *Poetry Magazine,* the *Little Review,* and *Others* enlisted an eclectic group of artists, including women determined to "make it new" through linguistic and structural experimentation, and left-wing women like Lola Ridge, who hoped to "make it new" by representing urban, immigrant structures of feeling in their free-verse poems.

In the 1920s the preoccupation with alternative culture, sexuality, and personal as well as political freedom encouraged radicals like Edna St. Vincent Millay and Genevieve Taggard to alternate their poetic expression between their desire for personal satisfaction and a concern for social justice. Then there is the later modernist work of Depression-era radicals. Poetry magazines in the 1930s such as the *New Masses, Dynamo,* and *Rebel Poet* printed work in which modernist montage and socialist reportage mixed and merged, creating the pulsating lyric hybrid of poets like Muriel Rukeyser, Ruth Lechlitner, and Joy Davidman. *Poetry Magazine* continued to be a nonpartisan, but eclectic literary journal that nurtured women poets, including the three subjects of this study. In fact, Margaret Walker's most enduring poem, "For My People," first appeared in *Poetry* in 1937.

The early modernist work, roughly from 1915 to 1930, reveals an interest in a range of new cultural developments: war and war resistance, feminism and the "new woman," race and immigrant politics, new forms of technology (especially with regard to the arts), experimentation in verse and sex, an interest in European aesthetic ideas, and the creation of an American avant-garde. The new woman consciousness established by little magazine editors such as Harriet Monroe, Margaret Anderson, and feminist sympathizer Alfred Kreymborg not only supported women poets but also radical social causes.[8] While Genevieve Taggard would later refer to the 1920s as a "dark period" in American culture, a number of small journals published work by progressive women poets and attempted to resist the 1920s' zeitgeist that eschewed politics for the comfort and culture of consumer capitalism. The New Orleans journal *Double Dealer* reminded its readers of the condemned men in American prisons when it published Lola Ridge's anti–death penalty sonnet, "Electrocution," in 1921. Genevieve Taggard's editorship of the *Measure,* also in 1921, established a place for patriarchal critique. Her poem "Ice Age" draws upon the tensions of heterosexual coupling through use of apocalyptic imagery.[9] Taggard was also poetry editor of the *Liberator,* published from 1919 to 1924, and edited *May Days,* a collection of verse from the *Liberator* and its better known precursor the *Masses.* African American journals also flourished in the 1920s. The important periodicals *Crisis* and *Opportunity* published most of the black women's protest verse that is currently being revived in the recent spate of African American literary anthologies. Wallace Thurman's *Fire,* a journal "devoted to younger Negro artists," made its single issue appearance in 1926. It is of notable interest that Helene Johnson, a neglected voice from the Harlem Renaissance, and the only woman poet represented in *Fire,* contributes the most politically resonant poem, "Southern Road," about the lynched black body that had become the most ordinary figure in the southern landscape, "[a] solemn, tortured shadow in the air" (17).

The later modernist work covers the years 1930 to about 1945. The *New Masses* is probably the most influential left magazine to be published at this time, although it commenced its publication in 1926. The *New Masses's* first four years included interesting work by women, particularly the forgotten Marie de L. Welch. From 1930 to 1935 little or no poetry by women appears in the magazine, but with the emergence of the Popular Front in 1935, innovative radical work by female poets appears frequently in its pages.[10] For example, Genevieve Taggard contributed her Popular Front poem "At Last the Women Are Moving," which celebrates the complacent woman's political awakening as she moves in protest. Little magazines and reviews of the 1930s and really the entire modern period provide a significant source for lost twentieth-century poetry culture. It is important to consider what Cary Nelson has observed about American poetry in the modern period. If we survey the literary magazines, political journals, and partisan newspapers of the time we will find a variety of poems on a variety of subjects that suggest a wholly different "discursive terrain" for poetry than what can be found in individual books and anthologies (*Repression and Recovery* 199). The 1930s (and the early 1940s) was a special period for leftist women who wrote poetry. The sense of fear and anxiety and the very real social and economic devastation the Depression brought inspired women artists— perhaps like no other time in the century. While female progressive intellectuals no doubt joined their male counterparts in a shared belief in the failings of the capitalist system, many women began to link Depression-era social problems, such as joblessness and homelessness, with the kinds of domestic failures that were pertinent to American women at this time of struggle. They were hit where they lived.

The 1930s and early 1940s created a politically charged literary culture in which collage, reportage, free verse, and proletarian forms met. In addition to magazines like the *New Masses,* women poets produced verse under the auspices of a variety of Popular Front organizations. While androcentric in character, these organizations viewed women's contributions to be part of an integrative Popular Front effort to fight social injustice at home and fascism abroad. Yet despite the appearance of poems like Taggard's "At Last the Women Are Moving" and Ruth Lechlitner's "Lines for an Abortionist's Office," which were direct responses to women's experiences in a time of unrelenting hardship and sorrow, Depression-era radical journals had a masculine bias both in terms of the authors and contents they published. Jack Conroy's the *Rebel Poet*, an important journal of the period, is a case in point. It not only published more men than women but also its poems characteristically represented the brave worker pitted against the leviathan of capitalism, which suggested a kind of manly courage that excluded women and the social problems they faced. Yet the women who published verse in the *Rebel Poet* were equally adept at contriving (or identifying with) masculine personas to send out similar anticapitalist messages. For example, Gale Wilhelm, the author of the 1930s lesbian "classics" *We Too Are Drifting* (1935) and *Torchlight to Valhalla* (1938), writes in her short poem "Strange Serenade" (March 1931) of the "discordant song patterns" of American laborers. Like her poem "Strike Leader," which appeared in the radical, eclectic journal *Nativity*, labor is represented in fragmented terms, but is understood to be an adjunct of the male body.

While male poets far outnumbered female poets in the radical journals of the 1930s, and male editors overshadowed female editors on journal mastheads, important work by women appeared in the more partisan left journals, as well as those journals lacking a political agenda.[11] The journal editors even when they included women did not consider them, literally and semantically, as critical voices. Ironically, arbiter of left culture Mike Gold warns in his *New Masses* essay, "America Needs a Critic" (1926), that America needed a "strong poet . . . a man of the street . . . a man fit to stand up to a skyscraper" (quoted in Nekola and Rabinowitz 129). Yet what appeared in the July 1928 issue of the *New Masses*, under Gold's editorship, were two poems that seemed to undermine Gold's gender bias. Marie de L. Welch's "Iron Workers" and "Skyscraper in Construction" reveal not only a strong poet but also suggest that a woman was equally capable of recording the rhythms of the street and could just as well "stand up to the skyscraper." Her poem "Skyscraper in Construction" is particularly interesting because Welch takes the virility that Gold had placed in the hands of his idealized male worker-writer and deconstructs the masculinized phallic object—here as a signpost of a monolithic capitalism—she observes being erected:

> Winds bed
> with lean iron bones,
> lie with virile skeletons
> that must be marble-fed
> to an obese white impotence. (4)

As a journal closely associated with the Communist Party U.S.A., the *New Masses* editors no doubt shared the problematic attitudes about gender relations found within the party cadre. The Communist Party U.S.A. has a somewhat peripheral relationship to this book's thesis. None of the three central subjects were party members. Yet the Communist Party was certainly influential in shaping left political culture throughout the time that women's social poetry flourished. Contemporary feminist critics concur on the negative as well as positive influences that the Communist Party had on women's lives, particularly in the 1930s. While acknowledging that the party's attention to the Woman Question was grossly inadequate, Barbara Foley maintains that "the Communist-led movement . . . made the question of male-female equality a live issue; it involved women in the class struggle and addressed a number of issues of urgent concern to working-class women" (*Radical Representations* 215). Deborah Rosenfelt similarly regards the Communist movement's dual character: "The Left was a profoundly masculinest world in many of its human relationships, in the orientation of its literature, and even in the language used to articulate its cultural criticism; simultaneously, the Left gave serious attention to women's issues, valued women's contributions to public as well as private life, and generated an important body of theory on the Woman Question" (quoted in Foley 216). Constance Coiner does not disagree about the Communist Party's overwhelming masculine rhetoric and biases, but she also suggests how much we still have to learn about women's rights by studying the party's rank and file female membership. "The CP's work among women in the '30s should be carefully evaluated as part of the struggle for women's liberation in the United States" (*Better Red* 70).

The left's contradictory stance vis-à-vis the Woman Question can be found in its revolutionary journals of the 1930s. In a number of interesting instances tokenism prevailed. The symbolic status of certain left-wing women poets, while allowing a presence for female radicals, also reinforced the left's hypocritical perspective. It advocated a democratic, people's art, yet it continued to put women artists in figurehead positions. While quite a few women poets wrote about the crisis conditions in America at the time, it was often the case that left journals included the work of only one or two women poets, and often no women contributors are found at all. The power of women's radical verse as it appeared as token representatives of left culture from a woman's perspective is present in a number of examples. The *Left*, a short-lived journal from Davenport, Iowa, published two issues in 1930–1931. The journal was, in many ways, at the forefront of Depression-era modernist radicalism. Edited by a disparate group of writers such as V. F. Calverton, Norman MacLeod, and Joseph Kalar, the *Left* published essays, poetry, photography, and was one of the first little magazines to publish criticism about experimental and documentary cinema. Lola Ridge is the only female contributor in the magazine's short history; a badly edited version of her long poem about the Italian anarchists Nicola Sacco and Bartolomeo Vanzetti, "Three Men Die," appears in its premiere issue. While contemporary critics of modernism such as Peter Quatermain have found Ridge lacking in the prerequisite modernist technique and sensibility, the *Left*'s editors seem to have been less preoccupied with what constitutes modernism and more interested in building an aesthetic critique of capital based on artistic variety.[12] In the same issue they published marxist poet Louis Zukofsky, whose technical innovations had more in common with Ezra Pound than with either Ridge or the proletarian poetry beginning to surface in other leftist journals. Yet as the *Left*'s editorial policies may have included a more eclectic response to modernism, like other modernist journals it maintained a gender bias.

Just as Lola Ridge was the only female contributor to the *Left*, Muriel Rukeyser was the only woman published in *Dynamo*. Once attacked by *Partisan Review* editors for being "a poster girl . . . of proletarian literature" (Kalaidjian 161–62), it might be suggested that male jealousy amidst an atmosphere of left-wing male chauvinism put Rukeyser in the position of token female. In issues from 1934 and 1935, *Dynamo* published "Theory of Flight" and also "Poem out of Childhood," a radical and feminist look back on an adolescence from which the poet had barely emerged. Rukeyser's

brilliant poems lit up the pages of this important journal, complement-
ing, even overshadowing the work of male poets Sol Funaroff, Joseph Kalar,
Edwin Rolfe, Isidore Schneider, and Ben Maddow (also known as David
Wolff). The poems in *Dynamo,* especially those by Rukeyser, show that
poetry can be both advanced in form and politically committed in outlook.
Critic William Kozlenko addressed the *Dynamo* poet's distinctiveness. Writing in the little magazine *Literary America,* he characterizes the proletarian
poetry of the 1930s as "closer to the pulsation of life," and effectively immersed
in the "sociological verities of life" (7). Still one can't help but wonder what
Dynamo would have looked like had it included more female contributors.

While not the token black radical, Margaret Walker is the only female
poet included in the first issue of *New Challenge,* which was launched in
1937 with Richard Wright as associate editor. *New Challenge* was an offshoot
of *Challenge,* a black-oriented journal in the spirit of proletarian magazines
like the *Left* and *Dynamo.* Edited by Dorothy West, *Challenge* originated in
Boston in the mid-1930s. Walker contributed three poems to the fall 1937
issue of *New Challenge.* Two of these, "Mess of Potage" and "Hounds," have
remained uncollected.

Whether they took up token positions in the radical journals of the
modern period or were given their own special issues in experimental magazines, women poets with a special penchant for the political need to be part
of our continued recovery process in American literature as well as part of
our continued reassessment of the gender (and race) of modernism. It is
important to note that the cultural significance of left-wing women poets
extends beyond the more narrow terrain of literary magazines and discussions of modernism. Lola Ridge, Genevieve Taggard, and Margaret Walker
wrote poems that examined and condemned some of the worst atrocities in
both national and international history. That these writers participated in
other forms of social debate yet were also poets are facts that must be combined to assess their contributions to unrecognized cultural debate as twentieth-century left intellectuals. Compiled by Cynthia Davis and Kathryn
West, *Women Writers in the United States: A Time Line of Literary, Cultural,
and Social History* is dedicated to a chronological and intertextual representation of American women writers. This reference guide includes Ridge's,
Taggard's, and Walker's publications as part of a historical time line with far

greater scope than what we might glean from a purely "literary" guide to women authors. These three poets, whose names, works, and dates appear more than once, are placed within a complex social/historical nexus of activity in the United States from preconquest and colonial beginnings up to the present. This time line helps to reinforce the contributions of left-wing women poets beyond the narrow confines of aesthetic evaluation.[13]

Lola Ridge, Genevieve Taggard, and Margaret Walker come together again as like-minded social/political writers in Paul Lauter et al.'s popular revisionist textbook *The Heath Anthology of American Literature*.[14] The Heath project emphasizes opening up the canon, considers cultural difference, and includes voices on the margins. While no anthology can repair the serious neglect that radical writers have suffered in the politically indifferent literary climate of the last twenty years, *The Heath Anthology* has helped to increase the awareness of teachers and students of literature that American poetry exists in a variety of shapes and forms, and one such shape is the politically charged expression of women poets like Ridge, Taggard, and Walker. Thus the Heath project has become a useful tool in encouraging the making of other anthologies, literary reprints, and critical books such as this one.

Of course literary/historical time lines and projects like *The Heath Anthology* are important. Recovering neglected authors is not the only aim of this particular study. The work of Lola Ridge, Genevieve Taggard, and Margaret Walker gives significant insight into the kinds of human experiences that criticism of modern poetry often neglects to emphasize. These poets have much to teach and remind us about the cultural, historical, and political legacies that have brought us to where we are now, and to where we may still be going. Their work is also an important reminder of how multivalent American aesthetic expression has been. It also shows how diverse our social experiences have been, and—how tragic. These poets, who have written about world wars and race wars, labor struggles and domestic struggles and have composed poems inspired from newspaper headlines and actions in the streets, do not merely create impressions of a distant past but allow that past to be part of our knowledge of lost political and aesthetic traditions.

The poetry of Lola Ridge, Genevieve Taggard, and Margaret Walker is placed in a "tradition" of left poetry, which is itself a highly diverse tradition. I also place myself in a tradition within left, feminist criticism. My interest in the historical conditions that give rise to literary production and the social history depicted inside the literary text aligns me with certain aspects of marxist or socialist-feminist criticism. This study's emphasis on drawing upon the radical interventions of politically committed women poets and the reading of their poems within the contexts of the particular historical moments that produced them is decidedly outside most feminist critical perspectives on modern poetry. Marxist or socialist-feminist criticism is interested in social/historical processes and reading class along with, or inseparably from, gender (and race). Thus my discussion represents an oppositional, though much needed, dialogue within mainstream feminist criticism and modern American poetry criticism.[15] Yet it is not only mainstream feminist criticism and modern American poetry criticism with which my study must contend. It must also justify reading women's social poetry of the modern period in the age of postmarxism and French feminism. The left's "Jacobin imaginary," as Ernesto Laclau has termed it, has collapsed, which seems then to sever the connection between the contemporary reader and the political struggles and radical desire about which the subjects of this book wrote.[16] Yet while Lola Ridge's homages to striking workers, Genevieve Taggard's merging of picket lines and party lines into lines of verse, and Margaret Walker's evocations of African American labor may suggest an era when the "Jacobin imaginary" was alive and well (and was something on which neither of the three poets would perhaps agree), their work still gives us an idea of what it meant for a woman artist to use her art to express social outrage. We may then recognize how certain kinds of poetic expression, even if unsuccessful or ideologically flawed, could be used to assess what these poets—and many of their readers, past and present—would claim to be a classist and racist patriarchal social order. The aim here is not to engage contemporary readers in whether these writers were accurate in predicting history, but to explore how they bore witness through powerful poems. Another aim is to engage readers in what it meant to write political poetry as a woman in an era when people began to call into question the uncertainties of the system under which they lived.

    An important term for this study of women's political poetry of the modern period, and one that is currently undergoing much critical revision, is class. As Wai Chee Dimock and Michael T. Gilmore ask in the introduction to *Rethinking Class,* "[h]ow can we continue to use the word with any sense of political efficacy, when its instrumental expression—"class struggle"—has ceased to be a vital historical force"(1)? This need to rethink class and approach it with a critical distance complicates the important classed articulations that Ridge, Taggard, and Walker used in their writing. It also questions how to "do class" in a field of study that has traditionally ignored class issues. In her groundbreaking study *Sex, Class, and Culture,* Lillian Robinson observed that "the most massive and brutal attempts to deny the existence of an analytic category occur with respect to class" (66). Class issues and the representation of working-class history and politics were important tropes in the work of women social poets such as Ridge, Taggard, and Walker. Though not working-class writers in the traditional sense (Ridge, Taggard, and Walker were educated and groomed for a life beyond employment in other people's kitchens, factories, and office buildings), they identified with, lived among, protested alongside, and dreamed their creative acts through a highly diverse, disenfranchised, working-class America. Yet the idea of class as a category of study in relation to modern American poetry has suffered from severe historical amnesia. The dialogues and debates about class in relation to art were significant features of American literary culture during the 1930s. We have, for the most part, forgotten these discussions, particularly so when we address gender.

Cary Nelson's *Repression and Recovery,* published in 1989, created a landmark theoretical base on which to discuss the genre from a class perspective. Nelson's poststructuralist readings of modern American poetry, which decry boundaries, limits, or any fixed discursive practice within the genre (or any field of literary studies), may have established a platform for change in poetry studies. Scant scholarship has followed, however, which examines class as a central trope and the social consequences that accompany it. Cora Kaplan's announcement in the October 1997 *PMLA* calling for articles to reassess the role of class suggests how much the topic of class has been shoved aside in pursuit of other epistemological categories: "[C]lass is perhaps the least examined and most elusive and vulnerable of the social determinants of meaning and subjectivity, such as race, ethnicity, gender, and sexuality" (1038). Much work has been done on the categories of race and gender, but scholars have paid little attention to class or toward understanding the necessary trajectory of race, class, and gender. While there has been a developing focus on rethinking class, modernist studies continue to ignore the relationship between classed representations and modern American literature—in particular, poetry.

Reading the poetry of Ridge, Taggard, and Walker one is particularly struck by their attention to social class inequities. These three women crossed class lines, lived on the margins as writers, as radicals, as women. Margaret Walker lived on the margins as a black, female academic. Lola Ridge, born in Ireland and raised in Australia, was a foreigner and anarchist. Genevieve Taggard was a communist, and she did not stop being a communist after the Hitler-Stalin pact, or after V-J Day. All three wrote sonnets, a form disparaged by modernist critics. Not only did they pique certain modernist sensibilities by writing sonnets, these poets followed Percy Bysshe Shelley's examples from radical sonnets such as "England in 1819" and "To the Republic of Benevento" instead of continuing with the sonnet tradition as Shakespeare, Elizabeth Barrett Browning, and Edna St. Vincent Millay employed it. Ridge's sonnet "Electrocution" critiques the death penalty through a graphic description of death in the electric chair. Taggard's "Silence in Majorca" honors the Spanish people in their fight against Franco. And Walker's "Whores" examines the traffic in working-class black women. Each poet wrote about race. Ridge wrote about race riots and even identified immigrant Jews as racialized others. Taggard's early poetry and fiction pay homage to working-class Hawaii; her later poems honor the neglected cultural contributions of African Americans. Walker "races" working-class life and classes black aesthetics. Yet while the discourse of class remains oppositional within modern poetry studies, reclaiming these poets in a scholarly discipline that has buried the traditions in which they participated is very difficult. Alan Wald discusses the intentional silencing of America's radical literary culture, particularly as it developed out of the Communist Party during the 1930s: "[T]he silencing and distortion of the Communist literary tradition has turned out really to be a means of silencing the larger radical and working-class tradition in literature" (70). Insert left-wing women poets of the modern period into Wald's assertion; the reconsideration of this work informs us of such silenced traditions. It is an important historical, cultural, and political guide for many contemporary communities that have been excluded from literary discussions. Wald emphasizes that

> in literary studies [it] is the disempowerment of the population of ordinary people who are denied a genuine history of their own cultural activities through access to authors who write about strikes, rebellions, mass movements, the work experience, famous political trials, the tribulations of political commitment, as well as about love, sex, the family, nature, and war from a class-conscious, internationalist, socialist-feminist, and anti-racist point of view. (70)

In the postcommunist West, particularly in America, it has become fashionable to assume the disappearance of the class society, of working-class issues. Class has and continues to be obfuscated through a complexly wrought, institutionally mediated, historical and cultural amnesia. Ralph Miliband contended that "[i]n the United States, 'working class' has been all but expunged from the political vocabulary: there are the very rich at the top, the very poor at the bottom, and everybody else is 'middle class,' whether well-to-do-lawyers and doctors or factory workers and shopkeepers" (19). Equally important, the experiences of working-class people are radically different today than they were during the period of mining disasters, marble strikes, and steel industry massacres, which caught the attention of writers like Ridge, Taggard, and Walker. Yet, while working conditions may have greatly improved, wage-earning individuals still constitute a majority in the United States as well as in most other industrialized nations. The categories that constitute wage labor may be highly diverse, ranging from marginally employed college professors to office clerks, truck drivers, and food service workers, but grievances about working conditions, hours and hourly pay, and discrimination based on race, gender, and sexual orientation still create in working people a sense of powerlessness as well as insecurity and continue to present themselves as potential sites of struggle.

As unfashionable as it is to talk about class in the United States as we enter a new millennium, discussing gender in terms of oppression is equally unfashionable. This is particularly true in feminist literary studies. *Women Poets on the Left*, as it merges the "social determinants" of class, race, and gender by discussing work of women who wrote socially engaged verse about these determinants and their deep connection to the politics of oppression, challenges and reminds feminist literary studies that it remains a project in need of further complication as long as it ignores the importance of class—even as class, as an overdetermined category, has changed and become more amorphous. (So have gender and race, but we still examine these categories.) We must continue to acknowledge the political in women's poetry as it addresses class oppression, whether by black writers, lesbian writers, or any other group of marginalized women.[17] (Perhaps Foucault is right in asserting that one falls into the same trap arguing for a countertradition to a feminist literary tradition that wants to valorize canonical women writers over all others; alternatives create their own absolute power bases.) The point here however is not to argue for a countertradition that makes a "canon" out of marginalized writers, but to remind readers and scholars not only that these poets exist but also that their work has contemporary relevance. In addition, their exclusion from texts and syllabi has happened because of overt, covert, and perhaps unconscious, political decisions made by individuals within feminist literary practice.

One way to challenge the forgetfulness of some feminist literary investigations is to complicate certain popular tropes. One trope of emphasis here is the body—more specifically the working-class body. The body has become an important, extremely elastic, and popular theoretical site for contemporary feminism. However, what Teresa Ebert describes as "ludic" feminism—feminist theory's more recent preference for "playful meditation" over "historical explanation" (16), and in which many theories of the body are staged—removes the body from its political inscription. My reading of the body in Lola Ridge's work, for example, may appear out of sync with recent feminist theories of the body. I concentrate on Ridge's descriptive interpretations of the exploited body of workers and other individuals existing on the social margins. I am interested in how all three poets saw class relations as inextricably linked to the physical bodies of the men and women represented in their poems. Some recent feminist scholarship has recognized and recorded how working-class women writers *wrote the body.* Constance Coiner's study *Better Red: The Writing and Resistance of Tillie Olsen and Meridel LeSueur* looks at the "body" of work, as well as the cultural and historical bodies through which these two feminist, radical writers came to writing. Paula Rabinowitz's *Labor and Desire* rereads and theorizes a lost generation of radical women novelists whose neglected work embodied both the individual as well as collective concerns of working-class women during the 1930s. Barbara Foley, Laura Hapke, Deborah Rosenfelt, Suzanne Sowinska, Gay Wilentz, to name a few, have written books or contributed articles about working-class women's writing (and the bodies inside which they wrote) before World War II. Elaine Hedges and Shelley Fisher Fishkin's *Listening to Silences* asked a variety of feminist critics to rethink Tillie Olsen's classic text. In fact Deborah Rosenfelt's essay, "Rereading *Tell Me a Riddle* in the Age of Deconstruction," asks us to look at an important working-class woman's text from the theoretical perspectives feminist critics of the ludic variety have used while rejecting the classed perspectives of writers such as Olsen. Therefore it is still a viable and important question to ask, why the body as a site of political and economic struggle in American women's poetry of the modern period has not yet been addressed? *Women Poets on the Left* may ignore ludic feminism's more decentered approaches to examining the tropes of women's poetry. It embarks, however, on the more difficult task of recovering what many political readers see as a necessary political voice.

Cary Nelson's *Repression and Recovery* considers the important role of class (as well as gender and race) in modern American poetry, and is thus the work to which this study is most indebted. One of Nelson's most significant claims is his questioning of the relationship of literary history to canonicity. We need to be aware of the process of how literary forgetfulness occurs: "We no longer know the history of the poetry of the first half of this century," and he further argues that what is most troubling about this lack of knowledge is that we do not even "know that this knowledge is gone" (4). Nelson rightly claims that literary history has characteristically told "a selective story substantially constituted by its cultural presuppositions and restricted by its ideological filters" (5–6). Besides reading those poets whom the narrowly defined modern American poetry canon has excluded, Nelson maintains that we must ask "new" questions and avoid making canonical judgments: "Literary history is never written from the vantage point of a secure and stable distance"; it is always surrounded by socially determined conceptions of "literariness" (17). Nelson also asserts that "[t]he full range of modern poetries is so great that it cannot be persuasively narrativized in any unitary way" (7).

Yet what is perhaps most useful for this investigation into the politics of everyday life, which were central to Ridge's, Taggard's, and Walker's poetics, is Nelson's statement that literary history is detached from history in its broad construction, both in terms of national history and the "history of everyday life" (7). However, in order for Nelson to suggest the important combination of national and local history—which much of the forgotten poetry of the modern period explores—rather than offer the traditional close reading of individual poems, he surveys a broad array of neglected verse, largely from little magazines. He purposely truncates poems, choosing to focus on lines, phrases, images, and even dust-jacket design "to suggest the range of voices, styles, and discourses at work in the period" (19). He also hopes to undermine the temptation to see particular works as representative and thereby feeding into the conventional arguments with which canons are made.

My interest in women's political poetry and my frustration in finding so little critical access to poets such as Ridge and Taggard has required me to use a more conventional methodology. Whole poems are emphasized as I work with individual poets in separate chapters. While none of these poets can present an accurate portrait of women's political poetry in the modern period, by focusing on a select group as I do here, we can learn at least something about how left political culture influenced the work of women poets. The book's focus also encompasses a wide range of issues, observations, and experiences, many that have been, like the poets themselves, buried away and blotted from our cultural and historical memories. Unearthing these poets' work is restoring some of this memory. The reader who explores these chapters encounters labor strikes and race riots, the Depression and particular aspects of the Great Migration, lynchings (legal as well as clandestine), immigration, and prostitution. While these events may not be in themselves new subjects, they are still unfamiliar tropes in most studies of modern American poetry, as they are in most studies of feminism and modernism. *Repression and Recovery* has brought to light dozens of poets whom we have forgotten or whose work we never knew existed. It is my decision and desire that three of the poets mentioned in Nelson's important book have their own broader spaces in which to emerge from the relative obscurity they have suffered so far.

As Nelson makes his argument about the neglect of radical poetries through an extensive (and exhaustive) survey of eclectic verse, Betsy Erkkila also attempts to complicate the writing of feminist literary history as it pertains to women's poetry by doing a selective study of American women poets. In *Wicked Sisters: Women Poets, Literary History, and Discord* Erkkila argues that feminist literary history has so far only told the story of modern women poets as a totalizing discourse. Her study situates itself directly inside particular debates within feminist theory to aid her in historicizing the work of Emily Dickinson, Marianne Moore, Elizabeth Bishop, Adrienne Rich, and Gwendolyn Brooks. Through a comparative analysis of these poets, Erkkila contends that "the emphasis among many white feminists on both patriarchy as the primal oppression and psychoanalysis as the primary mode of conceptualizing women's experience has tended to reduce all women writers to an economy of the same, transhistoricizing and universalizing the lives and works of women writers across race, class, sexual, and historically specific bounds" (3). While Erkkila offers an important debate on modern women poets and literary history, like other feminist critics whose work she hopes to challenge, she does not emphasize in significant detail specific political or historical events. Nor does she examine political poetry and its articulations of class. While her goal may be to destabilize and deconstruct the universalizing tropes with which feminist criticism has come to assess women's poetry, she does so by remaining inside the canon: her subjects are canonical poets. What would happen if Erkkila had chosen noncanonical, neglected, radicals to collapse the hierarchies of feminist criticism within modern poetry studies? How might a feminist critic challenge such hierarchies by exploring and historicizing the work of women poets who put class before gender? A case in point is the countertradition that Erkkila suggests when she mentions Muriel Rukeyser and quotes from her early work "Poem out of Childhood": "'Not Sappho, Sacco / Rebellion pioneered among our lives' [Rukeyser] declared . . . to signify her break with traditionally female poetic modes and her commitment to a politically engaged . . . poetry" (8). Although Erkkila acknowledges Rukeyser's choice of Sacco over Sappho, and she does want to deconstruct Sapphic Modernism, she does not tell us about what the embrace of *Sacco* meant for American women poets in the modern period. This is where *Women Poets on the Left* enters the discussion of "women poets, literary history, and discord." The class inequity and social injustice that the mere mention of the name *Sacco* suggested to radical poets like Rukeyser (and Lola Ridge, as discussed in chap. 2), is an important critical point that feminist literary history still needs to explore.

Although one cannot so simply state that the choice of Sappho or the choice of Sacco has determined how women poets have been received in the annals of American literary history, the absence of a significant conversation about the influence that radical politics and culture had on modern women poets has left us with an incomplete picture of the complex choices that American women writers had to make. I call upon these lines of verse, "Not Sappho, Sacco" as a sign of the problem of writing class back into a poetic discourse and literary history that has so far remapped the territory of gender and race, but has yet to draw sufficient attention to class.

Lola Ridge, Genevieve Taggard, and Margaret Walker come together in this study as important examples of what it meant for a woman to write political poetry during the first half of the twentieth century. While these poets share an "aesthetic" sensibility to write socially motivated verse, it is essential to maintain how different these three authors are on several constructive levels, which helps to complicate their similarities as innovators of left-wing verse. Additionally, two generations separate these three poets; such a generational divide had a tremendous effect on each writer's politics.

An Irish-born immigrant anarchist, Lola Ridge became politicized by an urban radicalism developing inside the ethnic ghettos of New York City in the first two decades of the twentieth century. Not only do Ridge's poems record for posterity the everyday life of immigrant and working-class America; they also turn labor history into poetry. Ridge records the "legal" lynchings of Sacco and Vanzetti and Tom Mooney. She also records the "real" lynchings of Frank Little and Leo Frank. Her show of solidarity with other immigrant radicals connects her to an international rather than a homegrown socialism. She laments the deportations of Alexander Berkman and Irish Republican Army fugitive Jim Larkin, and subsequently the imprisonment and torture of the Dutch communist Van der Lubbe. These records suggest Ridge's deep beliefs in individual liberty; yet these beliefs also translated into a fierce independence from partisan organizations.

While never a party member, Genevieve Taggard had close ties with the Communist left and its affiliated groups throughout the 1930s and 1940s. She grew up in colonial Hawaii with missionary parents, which perhaps precipitated her early interest in Debsian Socialism as a college student. Yet the poems in *Calling Western Union,* which are discussed in some detail in chapter 3, suggest the poet's familiarity with the formulaic proletarian literary agenda that influenced many communist writers of the period. Taggard's activism in vanguard left organizations such as the New York Teachers Union and the League of American Writers shows an attraction to political orthodoxies rejected, for the most part, by the other two authors in this study. In fact, Taggard's politics appear to be the most rigidly marxist, and she was probably the widest read in marxist theory.

As an African American, Margaret Walker's radicalism developed out of a different social reality. In an interview in the *Mississippi Quarterly,* some time in the 1980s, Walker claimed that she was always very black nationalist.[18] She maintained a political consciousness in two significant periods—the radical thirties and the radical sixties—when black nationalist politics developed and grew. Walker's early years in Chicago provided her with a good marxist education, which included courses on dialectical materialism at the local worker's school. Yet the real influence on her political thinking probably came from the Methodist Church and her minister father. While the Communist Party had a significant impact upon certain black communities in the 1930s, according to black sociologist Horace Cayton, the party underestimated the black church's influence on the everyday lives of African Americans.[19] As evidenced in her verse, Walker's politics show a combination of black radicalism and Christian Socialism.

Not only do these poets' radicalisms need to be complicated, the degree to which these writers claim a feminist identity also needs to be addressed. While both Ridge and Taggard were active feminists in their verse and in their lives, Walker's feminist consciousness developed only in the late 1940s when she went to teach at an all-black college. With the specter of racism ostensibly absent, gender discrimination remained blatant.[20] While this particular study attempts to show each poet's attention to gender, it is necessary to point out that gender concerns are never exclusive tropes in the work of any of these writers. In fact what seems to separate Ridge, Taggard, and Walker from other modernist poets is their representation of and identification with men—most notably as acts of solidarity with male radicals, male workers, or other marginalized male figures. Ridge and Taggard acknowledged their feminism early in their careers. Ridge lectured on women and art and began, but later abandoned, a book on the same subject. Ironically many of Ridge's most compelling and overtly class-conscious poems are those paeans to male laborers and labor martyrs. It is with these poems that Ridge's feminism needs to be complicated. Her commitment to social change required her to privilege neither sex. Thus we often see feminist poems like "The Ghetto" in direct conflict with poems such as "Electrocution" and "Three Men Die." Taggard was an active feminist voice in Greenwich Village bohemia. She participated in the *Nation* magazine's survey of feminism in the 1920s, "These Modern Women." Her inclusion in this survey would ironically be contradicted by her later activism in a partisan left that tended to put gender issues on the back burner. While predominantly concerned with the collective needs of women and men, Taggard's poetry of the 1930s and 1940s also focuses on women's issues, albeit largely within the context of the communist left's discussion of the Woman Question.

Margaret Walker has maintained in a number of essays written after the 1930s that her identity as African American and female are inseparable parts of her consciousness. Yet in Walker's early work she refuses to separate the needs of black women and black men. She explores a shared history of oppression and acknowledges that the struggle to resist racism is one that has historically united both sexes. Feminism, of course, is a dynamic movement, and it spoke, in varying degrees, to a multitude of women artists and intellectuals in the modern period. Ridge, Taggard, and Walker thought differently as radicals; they also perceived women's position vis-à-vis a world that needed to be turned upside down from their respective experiences as women: Irish immigrant anarchist, WASP communist, and black Christian radical. None believed that a special women's language could bring about social change; neither did each believe that women's voices could be ignored altogether.

The lives of Lola Ridge, Genevieve Taggard, and Margaret Walker converge in the 1930s, arguably the most important decade for socially engaged verse in the West. Ridge, in her sixties, was finishing off a career filled with strong political passions and chronic ill health. Taggard was in "mid-career," to use a term designated by arts funders, in her forties and already possessed of a reputation. By the mid-1930s and still in her early twenties, Walker had begun her career having published her important poem "For My People" in *Poetry Magazine*. Though it is highly doubtful that Walker and Ridge would have met one another, Ridge is known to have been an influence on African American poets who came of age in the 1930s, as Robert Hayden testified in an interview many years after he had rejected literary radicalism.[21] Ridge and Taggard knew each other in the 1920s and early 1930s. In fact, Taggard tried to help promote Ridge's second book, *Sun-Up*, when she worked for Ridge's publisher, B. W. Huebsch, during her first years in New York. Additionally, in Taggard's papers is a postcard Ridge wrote her from Paris in 1931 suggesting they rendezvous. Ridge was on her way to Persia, and Taggard was in Majorca on a Guggenheim Fellowship. It is possible that Taggard was introduced to Margaret Walker at the League of American Writers conference in New York in 1939.[22]

The fact that these three women each come from different generations that converge in the 1930s is rather important. Most critical work done on radical culture centers on the 1930s. Lola Ridge's work, however, began to appear in the 1910s; her most prolific period was the 1920s. Genevieve Taggard became known as a literary radical when she edited *May Days* in 1925. Her most outspoken decade was the 1930s, but she continued to write important class-conscious, antifascist poetry up until her death in 1948. Margaret Walker comes of age as a poet during the red decade of the 1930s and publishes her first book in the early 1940s. Yet Walker did not publish a second book of poems until the 1960s, a decade also known for its radical art and culture. In fact, Walker creates a bridge from the old left to the New Left, and her radical black consciousness is recreated in the 1960s as a new audience and a new African American aesthetic began to appear.

The poetry of Lola Ridge, Genevieve Taggard, and Margaret Walker explores, expands, retains, and reinvents modernism's radical terrain. While *Women Poets on the Left* considers these three radical poets together, they are significant examples of a small, but unjustly neglected wave of American poetry activity during the first four decades of the twentieth century. These poets' individual contributions are highlighted in separate chapters. Each poet's poems are read as they comment upon and connect to social praxis, and although the poems are examined closely, they are not read as they function explicitly as poems, in the New Critical fashion.

Chapter 2 begins with a discussion of Lola Ridge's exploration of the bodily manifestations of violence: capital punishment, lynching, and labor exploitation in poems such as "Electrocution" and "Morning Ride" from her third book, *Red Flag*, and "Lullaby" from her first book *The Ghetto and Other Poems*. The chapter also probes her interest in representing labor martyrs, also as victimized bodies, in the poems "Frank Little at Calvary," also from *The Ghetto*, and "Stone Face" and "Three Men Die" from her last collection *Dance of Fire*. "Three Men Die," in addition to refiguring biblical and classical language to speak against political martyrdom, also explores Ridge's own participation in the protest against Sacco and Vanzetti's execution. In a separate section is a discussion of her important long poem "The Ghetto," from her first collection of the same name, published in 1918. "The Ghetto" characterizes Jewish immigrant life on New York's Lower East Side, and the poem is read through its metaphors of the female body.

Chapter 3 discusses the Depression-era poetry of Genevieve Taggard. It focuses on the proletarian collection *Calling Western Union* with an emphasis on poems that explore the Depression-era concerns of women. While poems such as "At Last the Women are Moving" and "Middle-Age, Middle Class Woman at Midnight" urge figures of bourgeois women to cross class lines in solidarity with their working-class sisters, "Mill Town" and "Everyday Alchemy" are written directly about the hardships of working-class women. The biographical essay that frames *Calling Western Union* permits a move backward to Taggard's earlier preoccupation with the metaphysical poetry tradition and the poetry of Emily Dickinson. The chapter ends with a look at how Taggard transports the classed articulations of *Calling Western Union* to the field of music and her interest in African American cultural practices.

Chapter 4 discusses Margaret Walker's award-winning first book, *For My People*. It explores how Walker's early years in Depression-era Chicago and her embrace of a Eurocentric male left tradition complicate the moving verse she composes about the rural black South. It examines Richard Wright's influence on her work as well as other radical associations on the W.P.A. as they helped to shape her militant perspectives about black labor, which she in turn shaped in her poems. Also examined are some of her own essays and reminiscences, which provide further insight into her development of a radical black consciousness.

Each poet would have described her writing through a different vocabulary; therefore it is necessary to briefly comment on terminology. A variety of terms are used to describe the subgenre discussed in this study: socially engaged verse, political poetry, revolutionary verse, class-conscious poetry, left-wing verse, committed writing. These terms are both satisfactory and unsatisfactory. The poets who are a part of this study are diverse in almost every way except that they all wrote poems that suggest the dynamic relationship that language has to social struggle. The vocabulary we use in literary studies to describe the works we encounter is often the product of fashion. To suggest the unfixity of terminology, a variety of descriptive terms appear throughout the book. I also want to write a readable criticism. This book and its subjects, and the desire to maintain a social and political dialogue within literary studies, bring its author outside current fashion. The complicated language of postmodernity, while creating a number of important new ways of describing literary practice, has also been used to shroud the very real social conditions about which a variety of writers wrote. In describing the political visions and personal as well as public desires of poets like Ridge, Taggard, and Walker, the importance of creating a political practice must not be sacrificed to linguistic play and artifice. Lola Ridge, Genevieve Taggard, and Margaret Walker appear to have been placed outside the modern American poetry canon because they wrote directly about political and social injustice. The political and social concerns these poets voiced in their work should become part of the continued conversation on modernism and modern poetry in the new millennium. To recall the painter Alice Neel, whose words began this chapter, we should reconsider those political signs that previous critics have either ignored or deemed "too obvious." And we should continue at the urging of poet Genevieve Taggard to search out "the fire & the ardency & the power & the depth" of women's radical lyrics in whatever form these may take. By suggesting the still relatively unmined tradition of left-wing women's poetry, *Women Poets on the Left* begins a discussion in which other scholars, students of literature, or progressive readers of poetry might wish to partake.

Writing the Radical Body of Modernism

Politics and Pain in Lola Ridge's Poetry

I'm beginning to realize I'm without dogma
except what I painfully construct for myself.
Lola Ridge in a letter to anarchist friend
Leonard Abbott

Lola Ridge was born in Dublin in 1873 and raised in New Zealand and Australia, where she studied painting. She came to the United States in 1907, settled in New York's Greenwich Village in 1908, and became active in the anarchist movement. She worked as an organizer for the Ferrer Association, established in New York by followers of Francisco Ferrer, a Catalan education reformer. Ferrer, whom the Spanish government executed in 1909 during a purge against anarchist activity in Catalonia, was an advocate of liberatory education and began a series of freedom schools in Spain. Ridge helped found the Ferrer Association's magazine *Modern School* and edited the first issue.[1]

Ridge's years with the Ferrer Association coincided with her development as a modernist poet. The private caveat with which this chapter begins suggests the complicated nature of any attempt to set down rules that would smoothly link radical political activity to the practice of poetry. One might infer from Ridge's remark that she is aware that dogma is not the stuff of which great art is made. It describes, as well, the poet's understanding of the conflict between aesthetic practice and the social life that shapes it.[2]

Ridge's negotiations between her political and poetic identities may have even affected her artistic output. Her literary career was comparatively brief. She published only five books, none of which are in print today. Her first book, *The Ghetto and Other Poems,* appeared in 1918, when she was forty-five. This collection, which championed the cause of labor and eloquently detailed the lives of immigrants, was a critical success, as was the collection *Sun-Up,* which followed it in 1920. Both texts were published by B. W. Huebsch, a risk-taking independent publisher who had put out books by Joyce and Lawrence. *Red Flag* appeared in 1927 and was followed in 1929 by *Firehead,* a book-length verse poem about Christ's crucifixion, presented as an allegory on the execution of Italian anarchists Nicola Sacco and Bartolomeo Vanzetti. Her last book, *Dance of Fire,* was published in 1935. Ridge died of tuberculosis in May 1941 at the age of sixty-seven, having spent the last few years of her life as an invalid.

Ridge had a number of significant admirers throughout her career, from Kenneth Rexroth, who as a young anarchist drew inspiration from hearing her read her poems at labor rallies, to William Carlos Williams and Marsden Hartley, who attended parties in her tiny Greenwich Village flat. Marianne Moore counted Ridge among her few intimates, and Jean Toomer was grateful to her for introducing him to the New York literati when he arrived from the Midwest in the early 1920s. Kay Boyle saw Ridge as a role model when she became her assistant on the avant-garde journal *Broom,* which Ridge edited for a short time. For years after her death on her birthday, Alfred Kreymborg sent gifts and cards to Ridge's husband, David Lawson. When Marianne Moore, Aaron Copeland, and Paul Strand attended Ridge's funeral to pay their last respects, none of these artists would have predicted that Ridge's work would be buried along with her.[3]

In reexamining Lola Ridge's work, it is necessary to direct attention to the poet's awareness of the difficulties of making art out of one's political convictions. This discussion of Ridge centers upon her connection of the pain of constructing and the pain of observing, as well as the pain experienced by a wide variety of victims of social injustice, whether it takes the form of psychological pain caused by racist laws and class oppression, or the physical pain associated with beatings, lynchings, industrial disasters, and executions.

In an early poem, "Submerged" from *The Ghetto and Other Poems,* Ridge confronts the paradoxical negotiation between the self and some set of rules for negotiating the social world inscribing it. She chides herself for knowing only "Safe, plumbed places," acknowledging that what she really desires is to "dive / Into the unexplored deeps of me—" and to "Delve and bring up and give / All that is submerged, encased, unfolded." The desire expressed in this thirteen-line poem, like the admission to Abbott, divulges a complicated set of requirements for the radical woman poet. The "safe, plumbed places" of the poet's "own shallows" need to be challenged in order for her to express her own subjectivity and agency. However, she must also ask herself whether that which is "submerged, encased, unfolded," in short, buried inside the unconscious—"the unexplored deeps of me"—is the only place where she, as a woman poet, can exist. Ridge seems to be suggesting that the personal expression "submerged" in the feminist poetics of her time is not completely satisfactory for her ultimate artistic ends. She wants to reach outward rather than delve inward to explore a complicated social world that impinges upon her own poetic spirit—her "deeps." Although one should not attribute a singular meaning to the poetic unconscious, Ridge's poetry is best understood within a social context. Lola Ridge might have very well agreed with Carolyn Forche's attempt to complicate the personal and the political, as Forche writes about social poetry at least three quarters of a century later:

> The distinction between the personal and the political gives the political realm too much scope and too little scope; at the same time, it renders the personal too important and not important enough. If we give up the dimension of the personal, we risk relinquishing one of the most powerful sites of resistance. The celebration of the personal, however, can indicate a myopia, an inability to see how larger structures of the economy and the state circumscribe, if not determine, the fragile realm of individuality.[4]

Very little of Ridge's work could be classified as personal, yet politically she was an advocate of individual liberty. She was an early proponent of women's rights, workers' rights, the rights of blacks, Jews, and other immigrant groups, as well as the rights of individuals to go against conventional standards to pursue sexual fulfillment. The scant critical work on Ridge informs us that she was a frail, sickly woman, but she had intense passion and revolutionary zeal. By reading her unjustly neglected writing we become aware of her political commitment and her desire to represent the oppressed and disenfranchised, the martyred and the misunderstood.

For Ridge, much of this painful construction of the political self appears to be in her negotiation, throughout her writing life, of her performance as both a feminist and radical, practicing her art within the now-contested terrain of modernism. As far as Ridge and the reception of her work is concerned, however, there is still a problem with collapsing the categories of personal and political poetries. As a political writer, whether she would agree or not, Ridge used her art as a weapon. Such can be seen in her exhortation to workers in the poem "Reveille": "out of the passion of the red frontiers / A great flower trembles and burns and glows / And each of its petals is a people."[5]

Yet by encoding political subjectivity into her work she places herself against the ruling dogma of modernist poetry, "no ideas but in things," which has largely influenced the way American poetry has been read, taught, and theorized.[6] With her aesthetic embrace of the social body and the exteriority implied through her representation of political subjectivity,

Ridge also sets herself against the female lyric tradition and its emphasis on the private life and the private couple, and what Genevieve Taggard refers to as the "decorative impulse."[7]

It is important to engage this painful construction of the political self as it relates to Ridge as a feminist and radical poet. In her own time period, and certainly today, Lola Ridge is described, if she is mentioned at all, as a "minor" poet. This chapter explores the significance of Ridge's vision and suggests how her political subject matter, as it represented a resistance to the dehumanizing practices of early-twentieth-century life, placed the poet against the mainstream of canonical modernism. She was in fact so committed to struggles for liberation, both in America and abroad, that she was either bitterly disparaged or lavishly praised by her contemporaries for using poetry for public advocacy. Ridge also embodies her own subject positions with painful trepidation. The word *pain,* with its many contexts, most aptly describes Ridge's aesthetic practice. In addition to the emotional pain that a radical writer like Ridge experienced in her attempts to represent the social world around her, she also suffered much physical pain throughout her writing life. This combination of emotional and physical pain, as this poet understands it, is transformed into a poetic practice whose representations often engender poetic subjects as agents of social change and/or victims of systemic torture.

Writing about Ridge is also a means of rediscovering her work and reestablishing her importance to contemporary readers who might want to read poetry as a source of social/political inspiration and engagement, and not only for its aesthetic pleasures. Additionally, for those seeking antecedent traditions to, for example, Denise Levertov's postmodern expression against the war in Vietnam, or Carolyn Forche's poem-critiques of U.S. policy in El Salvador, or the numerous black poets lyrically attacking racism in America, the poetry of Lola Ridge offers such a link. This discussion is organized around how the dynamic of pain is manifested in Ridge's poetry, focusing on the trope of the body, and exploring a group of poems, quite different in style, that address physical manifestations of violence: lynching, imprisonment, execution, and labor exploitation. These more overtly political poems, discussed within their historical contexts, will be followed in the second half of this chapter by an analysis of "The Ghetto," perhaps Ridge's most significant contribution to American letters. This long poem explores community as well as gender and cultural difference, and will be introduced through some of Ridge's observations on feminism and art.

One important consideration in addressing this politics of pain is the dichotomy of the public versus private body, which is evident in such women writers on the left as Meridel LeSueur and Tillie Olsen as well as Lola Ridge. The public is always complicated by the private and vice versa. Yet there is a problem of reducing the political in Ridge's poetry through the metaphor of the corporeal body. It must be acknowledged that Ridge, once described by an admirer as "more spirit than body," does not apply any specific Cartesian practice—separating the mind, or spirit, from the body. As previously noted, the painful construction of the political self in her work merges body and spirit; when she is writing about the body, as it is exploited in labor, lynched by racists, imprisoned by politicians, she is writing about the whole person. Physical chains are also spiritual chains.

Pain itself, as a phenomenological construct, must also be complicated. In the area of literary studies, though the text itself is not a critique of traditional literary texts, Elaine Scarry's *The Body in Pain* has succeeded in theorizing the complexities of physical pain (especially politically motivated torture) and its representations. Scarry engages ontological questions about one's ability to understand another's physical pain: "pain comes unsharably into our midst as at once that which cannot be denied and that which cannot be confirmed" (4). She further complicates this assertion by maintaining that physical pain "resists objectification in language" (5), obliging us to encounter the difficulty of using language to represent a phenomenon that resists it. She suggests that "the human attempt to reverse the de-objectifying work of pain by forcing pain itself into avenues of objectification is a project laden with practical and ethical consequences" (6). Scarry, nonetheless, presents a political thesis in this text, and the most vital to this discussion of Lola Ridge, by exploring Amnesty International's reports of torture victims, and by acknowledging that "the poems and narratives of individual artists . . . record the passage of pain into speech" (9). In fact, Scarry might term what Ridge creates in her poetic articulations of physical pain as utilizing a language of "agency" (as she terms the language used by Amnesty workers). She maintains that Amnesty International's effectiveness in "bring[ing] about the cessation of torture" relies centrally upon its ability to describe as well as authenticate the horrors of physical pain and suffering to individuals who have never experienced such pain. In her interest in exploring "the way other persons become visible to us, or cease to be visible to us," Scarry's articulation of the body in pain indirectly acknowledges a poetic concern like Lola Ridge's determination to resist both linguistic fashion and language's intractability to "communicate the reality of physical (and emotional) pain to those who are not themselves in pain" (9), as well as to give voice to those who have been deliberately and inhumanely silenced.

By depicting the desecration of the human body, Ridge wants her readers to identify with those who suffer injustice. While it is perhaps an ironic commentary on the act of representation, this body must first become a spectacle. Yet the spectacular body in pain that Ridge depicts in her poems is never presented in isolation from the human being in whom it resides. For example, in the poem "Electrocution," from Ridge's 1927 collection *Red Flag,* the reader must view the pain in order to interpret, as did Supreme Court Justices William Brennan and Thurgood Marshall nearly fifty years later, that the death penalty is indeed "cruel and unusual punishment":[8]

> He shudders . . . feeling on the shaven spot
> The probing wind, that stabs him to a thought
> Of storm-drenched fields in a white foam of light,
> And roads of his hill-town that leap to sight
> Like threads of tortured silver . . . while the guards—
> Monstrous deft dolls that move as on a string,
> In wonted haste to finish with this thing,
> Turn faces blanker than asphalted yards.
>
> They heard the shriek that tore out of its sheath
> But as a feeble moan . . . yet dared not breathe,
> Who stared there at him, arching—like a tree
> When the winds wrench it and the earth holds tight—
> Whose soul, expanding in white agony,
> Had fused in flaming circuit with the night.

This sonnet dramatizes both the "white agony" of the subject and the indifference, or perhaps shame, of the workers who stand by and watch, their "faces blanker than asphalted yards." The reader can be said to witness both the subject's death by electrocution and the guards "who stared there at him" and have become "deft dolls." Ridge adroitly constructs the image of puppets on strings to assert that capital punishment facilitates injustice by sanctioning the worker's complicity in the state's executions of other workers. Indeed, though the poem describes the subject's body "arching— like a tree / When the winds wrench it," Ridge is careful to connect a soul to it. "He shudders" as the electrodes are placed upon his head. "The probing wind that stabs him to a thought" suggests the subject's conscious confrontation with the "flaming circuit." He is aware of his imminent death and that it will be painful.

Ridge's representation of death by electrocution as the torturous and unjust spectacle that it was (and in a number of places still is) is important to contemplate in connection to historical accounts of the development of electrocution as a process of legal punishment. Philosopher Hugo Bedau, who has written extensively on the death penalty, describes the first electrocution. New York State installed its first electric chair in 1880. The theory behind the implementation of the electrocution process was that "executing a condemned man by electrocution was superior to executing him by hanging" (Bedau 17). In 1893, after his lawyer had unsuccessfully argued the Eighth Amendment protected his client's rights, William Kemmler became the first person put to death by electricity. Bedau's description of the Kemmler execution deserves mention:

Although the execution was little short of torture for Kemmler (the apparatus was makeshift and the executioner clumsy), the fad had started. Authorities on electricity . . . continued to debate whether electrocution was so horrible that it never should have been invented. The late Robert G. Elliot, the electrocutioner of 387 men and women, assured the public in his memoirs (1940) that the condemned man loses consciousness immediately with the first jolt of current. The matter remains controversial to this day. Despite the record of bungled executions, the unavoidable absence of first-hand testimony, and the invariable odor of burning flesh that accompanies every electrocution, most official observers favor the electric chair. (17–18)

Michel Foucault's discussion of the body as discourse, in particular his notion of the "condemned" and "carceral" body, is also worth noting, for it suggests important links to Ridge's evocation of the death penalty and in general her interest in representing the *condemned* and *carceral* body in so many of her poems. In historicizing the process by which the condemned body approaches its fate, Foucault maintains it is with the age of the Enlightenment that "the gloomy festival of punishment" began to die out. Torture as a public spectacle, long a practice in Western culture, disappeared and was replaced with a legal system that took over the management of disciplinary and penal affairs. Yet torture as a private spectacle, as hidden agenda, developed into its own discursive (and real) practice (Foucault 7–12).[9]

This masked character that transformed the penal system into "punishment as a political tactic" (23) is the very justification for bodily torture and exploitation against which Ridge writes. She explores themes of lynching (the hidden ceremony), execution (state sanctioned murder pitting working men against each other), race rebellions, and imprisonment. For example, two poems discussed later in this chapter examine the toleration of intolerance. These are "Lullaby" (1918) about two white women who throw a black infant into a burning house during East St. Louis's 1917 race riots, and "Stone Face" (1928) about the erroneous conviction and imprisonment of labor agitator Tom Mooney. As a political activist, Ridge no doubt felt she had to write about torture, imprisonment, and the exploitation of labor in order to "enlighten" her readers about political conditions and how they engender both physical as well as psychological pain. Such a strategy gives noticeable power to her poems.

"Electrocution" establishes the site for Ridge's intersection of poetry, politics, and pain. It presents the condemned body in terms of the spectacle to suggest to her readers the physical and mental cruelty that defines the condemned's space. His shuddering, wrenching, and expanding, as well as his shrieking and moaning, give the reader considerable pause. The poem's lyrical sensations hardly promote a passive response. The linguistic bolts and flashes of white light and lightning dramatically illuminate the scene, compelling the reader to look, participate, and feel the pain. Ridge also begs the question of how closely, or whether at all, a reader should embrace the horror detailed inside such verses. Yet at the same time, the poem incites dialogue on what was then—in the 1920s when the poem was written—as it is today, a crucial issue of human rights campaigns.

The terrible pain and destruction of the human body that is Ridge's message in "Electrocution" is also metaphorically represented through another image that she employs in a number of these political poems. She uses a symbol of absolute aesthetic familiarity, however secularly represented, in Christ's crucifixion. Ridge, in fact, wrote a book-length verse poem about the Crucifixion, *Firehead* (1929), written at Yaddo in six weeks. Inspired by the deaths of Sacco and Vanzetti in the electric chair, *Firehead*, as it evokes biblical verse, refigures Christ as our most famous victim of institutionalized murder. The line "roads of his hill-town that leap to sight" intimates Golgotha, the hill on which the Crucifixion took place. Of course if one wants to discuss the body in pain as it is fetishized and made a spectacle, Christ's crucified corpse needs no further introduction. Though allusions such as "storm-drenched fields in a white foam of light" equate execution with conflagration, Ridge is not concerned with Christ's body as it is embraced and contemplated in Christian ritual. She is interested in refiguring the martyred body through its symbolic subjectivity as another politicized body in pain.

The "hill-town" as it is articulated in "Electrocution" also appears in one of Ridge's earlier poems, "Frank Little at Calvary" (1918). In this three-part poem, Ridge describes Little's lynching by hired killers of the Anaconda Copper Company. Little, who was part Native American, was a much admired organizer for the Industrial Workers of the World, an organization founded in Chicago in 1905, which sought to recruit workers previously excluded from the skilled craft unions that made up the American Federation of Labor. Dubbed the Wobblies, the IWW wanted "one big union" and enlisted unskilled and migrant workers, exploited immigrants, nonwhites, and women. Little had come to Anaconda, Montana, to aid a group of striking copper miners. As suggested by the title, the poem describes Little's life as he is about to become a martyr, his body crucified upon a "Hill." According to Ralph Chaplin, poet-laureate of the IWW, and historian Melvin Dubofsky, Little symbolized the working-class body in pain as he traveled from town to town, strike to strike, beaten and left for dead in many places he went. As Dubofsky maintains in *We Shall Be All*, his definitive study of the IWW, by the time Little got to Butte, Montana, "he was an ailing rheumatic, bearing the vestiges of too many beatings and too many jailings, and hobbling about on crutches as the result of a recently broken leg" (186).

Ridge begins "Frank Little at Calvary" by placing Little under the watchful eye of mine owners whom she later terms "the Lords of the Hill": "He walked under the shadow of the Hill / Where men are fed into the fires / And walled apart . . . / Unarmed and alone." The hill she refers to is Anaconda Hill, where on June 8, 1917, about 200 miners working at the Butte Speculator Mine burned to death "2,400 feet below the surface of the earth" (Flynn 230); the company had ignored proper safety regulations. Ralph Chaplin describes the physical violence caused by the mine disaster: "Men trapped on the lower levels clawed at concrete bulkheads with bloody fingers for steel manholes that weren't there as specified by law. Almost half of the bodies were so charred that even their families could not identify them" (210).

The poem's ominous tones allow the reader to imagine Anaconda Hill as Golgotha or Calvary and Little another Christlike labor activist and war resister. In fact, the representation of Christ as a symbol of resistance was a popular trope used by artists and writers in the early decades of the twentieth century. For instance, a number of drawings appearing in the *Masses* during its years of publication (1911–1917) used the image of Christ's body to satirize World War I hypocrisy. George Bellows's "This man subjected himself to imprisonment . . ." (July 9, 1917) depicts Christ in prison stripes, with a crown of thorns on his head and a ball and chain around his ankles. Boardman Robinson's "The Deserter" (July 8, 1916) shows the long-haired, white-robed Christ before a firing squad consisting of officers from the various warring nations.[10] In a literary example, the pacifist and poet, Sarah Cleghorn, author of the much-anthologized poem of protest against child labor, "The Golf Links," wrote an antiwar poem called "The Poltroon" in which she refigures Christ as a draft resister.

Short phrases such as "walled apart" and, to a lesser extent, "Unarmed and alone," stand out in "Frank Little at Calvary." They signify the laboring body as it is entombed in a mine, separated from the collective social body that is also America. Little, as he boldly challenges the "Lords of the Hill" by walking beneath its "shadow," becomes liberator and Christlike martyr.

Note that Ridge endows Little with almost mystical abilities. He can cause "the silence of wheels," thus signifying his efforts in making the mountains, which have been unnaturally moved by the backbreaking work of laborers, stand still (literally, of course, through his strike tactics). The poem becomes an allegory for the martyrdom of workers as well as a protest against a burgeoning war industry. Ridge maintains the word *Hill* as a salient trope throughout this poem.[11] The *H* always capitalized, "Hill" represents two contrasting linguistic signs: "Hill" as the site of a lynching, a crucifixion, a martyrdom, and "Hill" as the place where capital designs its harsh and devious practices against labor. Class differences are also subtly inscribed by the juxtaposition of the mine-owning "Lords" high above the ground and the workers who labor beneath it.

What Foucault has characterized as the modern means of punishment, in which the execution as public spectacle was transformed into a private, "legally" administered practice, is suggested as Ridge conveys how the mineowners do away with Little in secret. His condemned body becomes the target of a hired lynch mob. Descriptions of the hidden ceremony that is lynching ("Who may know of that wild ride? / Only the bleak Hill") penetrate five tensely wrought stanzas. She informs us that "[t]hey covered up their faces / And crept upon him as he slept." Little's abduction, gruesome by so many accounts, is alluded to through extended metaphor, images of darkness: "a black bridge poised," "the black mask of night," "blind folded street." While Ridge alludes to the torture awaiting Little, Stewart Bird, et al., in *Solidarity Forever: An Oral History of the I.W.W.* records the event:

> On the morning of August 1, 1917, after Little had returned to the Finn Hotel following a speech at a rally held at the local baseball park, he was awakened by six masked men. The vigilantes beat him, then dragged his bound body behind their car on a rope. They drove to a railroad trestle, where he was castrated and hanged by the neck. On his chest was pinned a note reading: "First and Last Warning—3–7–77. D-D-C-S-S-W." The numbers referred to the Montana specifications for a grave: 3 feet wide, 7 feet long, and 77 inches deep. The capital letters stood for the names of other strike leaders. One of the Ds seemed to be a direct warning to Bill Dunne, militant editor of the *Butte Bulletin,* and the C was directed

toward local miner Tom Campbell, a radical opponent of the conservative WFM leadership. (128)

Hidden also are the bodies of more than a hundred dead miners. Though
the poem never mentions them, these laboring bodies become intertwined
with Little's condemned body, arguably the central articulation of this
poem. In fact, just as Ridge constructs "Electrocution" from the point of
view of the condemned man, she refigures Little through the condemned's
gaze. She imagines him confronting a painful, inevitable end that is realized
in his torture and lynching:

> I know he looked once at America
> Quiescent, with her great flanks on the globe
> And once at the skies whirling above him. . . .
> Then all that he had spoken against
> And struck against and thrust against
> Over the frail barricade of his life
> Rushed between him and the stars.

Ridge's description of America "with her great flanks on the globe," though
an allusion to the nation's shape as a continent, is more provocatively a
metaphor for the imperialist war in which the United States had entered in
full glory, while workers and radical intellectuals like Ridge protested vehe-
mently against it.[12]

Little himself had commented upon what he expected from America's
entry into World War I: "War . . . will mean the end of free speech, free
press, free assembly—everything we ever fought for. I'll take a firing squad
first" (Chaplin 196). While Little takes a rope instead, fellow Wobbly Elizabeth Gurley Flynn indeed proves how prescient he was in his articulation of
wartime paranoia:

> After war was declared a mounting wave of hysteria and mob violence
> swept the country. It was *not* shared by the vast majority of American
> people who became increasingly intimidated. Printed signs were tacked
> up in public places: "Obey the law and keep your mouth shut!" signed by
> Attorney General Gregory. The victims of mob violence were varied—
> Christian ministers, Negro and white, advocates of peace on religious,

moral or political grounds: Socialists, IWWs, members of the Non-Partisan League, which was strong among farmers in the Middle West; friends of Irish freedom, and others. Some individuals, both men and women, who made chance remarks on war, conscription or sale of bonds, were tarred and feathered, beaten sometimes to insensibility, forced to kiss the flag, driven out of town, forced to buy bonds, threatened with lynching. (229)

Ultimately for Ridge, the silencing of Little and the "frail barricade" formed by his body signify the silencing of all radicals—poets too—and thus directing the "quiescent" gaze of the masses upon the world powers as they attempt to reshape "the globe." Ridge's prolabor, antiwar sentiments are reproduced in her tribute to Little as she encodes her text with metallic images that suggest the all-too-menacing presence of armaments: "copper, insensate," "clogged windows of arsenals," "long sentient fingers in the copper / chips . . . / Gleaming metallic and cold." The poem, both literally and figuratively, reflects the war industry, especially as it is challenged by Little's activism and by the IWW's work stoppage campaigns. As Flynn reminds us, it was the effectiveness of the IWW ("some 50,000 lumber workers in the Northwest and 40,000 copper miners in Montana, Arizona and New Mexico were on strike at one time during 1917") that made the organization the target of mob violence as well as governmental censure from which it never quite recovered (230). Ridge ends her poem with sarcasm in the face of war's triumph and labor's ultimate defeat:

Wheels turn;
The laden cars
Go rumbling to the mill,
And Labor walks beside the mules. . . .
All's Well with the Hill!

In addition to announcing the poet's anticapitalist sentiments, the rather ironic tone of these final lines suggests the poet's recognition that this defeat is a familiar aspect of social struggle. The "wheels" silenced under Little's power are no match for the giant machinations of the Hill, and so must once again "turn."

The bloody summer of 1917, as it came to be known, not only tore apart mining towns but also visited industrial communities as well. Ridge's homage to Frank Little as a form of social protest is equaled if not surpassed by the powerful "Lullaby." A month before Little's murder there was a savage massacre of another sort in East St. Louis, Illinois. Like the deaths at the Butte Speculator Mine, the riots in East St. Louis were related to wartime labor disputes coupled with wartime hysteria. The deaths in this case had a racial dimension: white workers maimed and killed black workers. Predatory mobs laid siege to the black inhabitants of East St. Louis. Some of the town's black citizens had lived there for many years, while many others were newcomers—job-seekers migrating from southern towns where men earned eighty cents a day and women fifty cents a week. The three dollars a day the men could make in the slaughterhouses of East St. Louis and St. Louis—its twin across the river—and the dollar and a half per week the women could make in the service sector seemed like inconceivable fortunes by southern standards. "Lullaby," though written as an angry response to the massacre as a whole, voices rather a smaller, but no less horrific, episode of the riots. A parenthetical note at the end of the poem informs us: "(An incident of the East St. Louis Race Riots, when some white women flung a living colored baby into the heart of a blazing fire)."

Just as Ridge is a poet neglected by most literary historical records and this powerful poem accompanies her in her neglect, the East St. Louis massacre is a buried moment in American history. Even by today's standards of violence, in which nothing appears so disconcerting, where the most gruesome torture or brutal act can be either shrugged off with indifference and/ or fetishized to the point that we become oblivious or inured to it, the events of the East St. Louis riots still seem shocking.

It is not known whether Ridge followed accounts of the riot in the black press, but her poetic articulation emulates the outrage of writers and social critics like W.E.B. DuBois. Writing on the East St. Louis riots in the NAACP journal the *Crisis* (September 1917), DuBois and journalist Martha Gruening attest to the pervasiveness of racial hatred in wartime America. At the same time, they allow us to witness the complexities of working-class relations through depictions of the pernicious behavior of white men, women, and children against their black neighbors.[13]

There is not the space here to discuss the complicated relationship between white and black workers during World War I or the general period of
labor radicalism that interested Ridge as a poet. However, DuBois and
Gruening provide some background on the labor disputes that gave rise to
the riots. Unskilled white labor disappeared during wartime, as scores of
foreign-born white laborers were deported; cities like East St. Louis experienced labor shortages. With black migration north in search of higher
wages amid strikes in the meat-packing industry, there was a continuous
supply of black labor ready for work that was once performed exclusively by
white workers (220). In fact, as DuBois would argue later in the 1920 collection *Darkwater,* disparities in the American economy would ultimately result in dividing workers along color lines:

> How may we justly distribute the world's goods to satisfy the necessary
> wants of the mass of men[?] If the white workingmen of East St. Louis
> felt sure that Negro workers would not and could not take the bread and
> cake from their mouths, their race hatred would never have been trans-
> lated into murder. If the black working men of the South could earn a
> decent living under decent circumstances at home, they would not be
> compelled to underbid their white fellows. ("Of Work and Wealth" 99)

DuBois and Gruening begin their investigation of the riots beneath a photograph of the body in pain. A dazed black man attempts to lift himself
from the ground near streetcar tracks. As viewers would discover later in the
text, he has probably been forcibly removed from the streetcar by a white
mob and beaten until unconscious. DuBois and Gruening introduce us to
"The Massacre of East St. Louis":

> On the 2nd of July, 1917, the city of East St. Louis in Illinois added a foul
> and revolting page to the history of all the massacres of the world. On
> that day a mob of white men, women and children burned and destroyed
> at least $400,000 worth of property belonging to both whites and Ne-
> groes; drove 6,000 Negroes out of their homes; and deliberately mur-
> dered, by shooting, burning and hanging, between one and two hundred
> human beings who were black. (219)

Using regional press coverage, a letter from the secretary of a local labor
union, interviews, as well as the personal testimonies of observers and vic-

tims, DuBois and Gruening create a fervid excoriation of the twenty-four-hour ordeal. Indeed the accounts of beatings, shootings, and hangings are too numerous to record. The random violence culminated in arson, while police and the state militia that had been called in refused to intervene. In some instances, police and militia actively participated in the violence and destruction.

Ridge's poetic response to this tragedy, "Lullaby," singles out the terrible acts of white women, further complicating the presence of the body, pain, and politics in her poetry. Her focus on white women's complicity in racist wartime hysteria is of course grounded in her decision to construct a lullaby.[14] The poem employs traditional aspects of prosody in both structure and tone. Eight quatrains with an *abab* rhyme scheme rock the reader to the lullaby's classical rhythms. But then, in an ironic and ambiguous turn, Ridge subverts the anticipated mother's song into a racist's chant. The nurturing lullaby becomes a death dirge:

Rock-a-by baby, woolly and brown. . . .
(There's a shout at the door an' a big red light. . . .)
Lil' coon baby, mammy is down. . . .
Han's that hold yuh are steady an' white.

Here Ridge complicates the idealized vision of motherhood inscribed in the lullaby with the silenced black woman's voice; the woman's murderers speak in her place, appropriating her dialect, as they throw her child into a fire they have set with the aid of their husbands and children. The real shock is that the white women rock the baby and sing to it before they kill it.

"Lullaby" also renders the body in pain through the trope of the innocent black child victimized at the hands of enraged white women. In addition to being the poem's speakers, these white women inhabit the corrupt space that Ridge associates with white men and the white male gaze of the "Lords of the Hill" in "Frank Little at Calvary." In fact, Ridge indirectly reminds us of the familiar exploited black female body—the caretaker of white children—as she removes all nurturing qualities from the white women who are here represented as the slayers of the black child. Other persecuted bodies, the child's parents for example, are also described: "Daddy's run away"; "mammy's in a heap / By her own fron' door in the blazin' heat." The evisceration of the East St. Louis black community is also symbolically represented through the image of charred, innocent bodies. Yet the body in pain is most explicitly recognized in the tortured infant. Through this representation Ridge suggests that this child's body, as it is thrown into the fire, becomes an important signifier—a call for resistance to racist oppression.

By voicing in playful tones the vicious acts of individuals whose hatred has festered as if it were itself a diseased body, Ridge allows us to see intolerance as a game without end. The language of games is repeated throughout the poem in lines such as "the singin' flame an' the gleeful crowd," or "Han's that are wonderful, steady an' white! / To toss up a lil' babe, blinkin an' brown." Thus the poem's architecture, or more appropriately "playground," subverts the innocence of games associated with the nursery rhyme and reminds readers that the mob violence inciting the poem's production is itself articulated as a form of play. Note, for example, descriptions of the sportlike mood that DuBois and Gruening appropriate in their *Crisis* essay. They locate a riot report from the *St. Louis Globe-Democrat* that details the atmosphere of amusement surrounding the white mobs as they set fire to the black homes:

> They pursued the women who were driven out of the burning homes, with the idea, not of extinguishing their burning clothing, but of inflicting added pain, if possible. They stood around in groups, laughing and jeering, while they witnessed the final writhings of the terror and pain wracked wretches who crawled to the streets to die after their flesh had been cooked in their own homes. (224)

It is interesting to contrast Ridge's indirect response to the atrocity with the graphic intensity that DuBois and Gruening attempt in their journalism. Ridge's commentary on white racism is secured by her focus on one particularly horrific episode that could have the greatest impact upon her audience, in this case the murder of an innocent child by mothers of other children. As with any grisly story produced in a daily newspaper, there is a sensational cast to the above description. DuBois, no doubt, intensified his prose with language that could embellish the aspects of pain in his article in order to excite as well as incite his audience. Whereas DuBois and Gruening depict the magnitude of wartime hysteria and the racist and/or nationalist sentiments produced in its wake, Ridge's poem localizes the experience by complicating the familiar body of mother/child with the collective body of rage and intolerance produced in times of reaction. Yet as Ridge stirs up readers' emotions by depicting the enraged actions of women against an innocent child, she also mocks the sentimentality associated with the nursery rhyme. Readers are asked to equate rage with innocence and motherhood with intolerance. She shocks us into accepting women's complicity in maintaining the race hatred and discrimination seen then (and today) in American life. To engage Lola Ridge's power as a political poet and her immense passion and skill, it is important to read a poem like "Lullaby" intertextually with the impassioned prose of political writers such as DuBois. DuBois provides the social and historical background that enriches and expands our knowledge of what it must have been like for poets such as Lola Ridge to remake a "Lullaby" to speak for the cruelty and injustice of the age in which she lived and wrote.

The lynched body that Ridge tropes in "Frank Little at Calvary" appears again in "Morning Ride," which was written in 1923 and collected along with "Electrocution" in a section of *Red Flag* entitled ". . . under the sun." This poem curiously resembles no other poems that Ridge published, yet its representation of the tortured and slain human corpse is strikingly familiar. In "Morning Ride" Ridge experiments with form while she remains committed to expressing a political perspective.

Yet the poem is not a direct portrait of a lynching and might be more aptly subtitled "Cityscape with Lynching," as it puts a southern lynching in dialogue with the everyday life of the urban working class.

    HEADLINES chanting—
y o u t h
l y n c h e d   t e n   y e a r s   a g o
                      c l e a r e d—
Skyscrapers
seeming still
whirling on their concrete
bases,
windows
fanged—
l e o   f r a n k

l y n c h e d   t e n
    s a y   i t   w i t h   f l o w e r s
w r i g l e y's   s p e a r m i n t   g u m
    c a r t e r's   l i t t l e   l i v e r—
lean
to the soft blarney of the wind
fooling with your hair,
look
milk-clouds oozing over the blue
        Step Lively Please
        Let 'Em Out First Let 'Em Out
did he too feel it on his forehead,
the gentle raillery of the wind,
as the rope pulled taut over the tree
in the cool dawn?

"Morning Ride" contains two pronounced images that offer competing and distracting commentary on modernity. The skyscrapers along the New York City skyline embrace commuters on their way to work, while the newspapers they read, to occupy themselves during their morning ritual, recap a ten-year-old racially motivated murder, the lynching of Leo Frank. Frank was a young Jewish factory manager in Atlanta who, in 1913, was falsely accused of raping and murdering a fourteen-year-old white female employee. In 1915, while serving a life sentence for the crime he denied committing, Frank was abducted by local Ku Klux Klan members, strung from a tree, and executed. Although Ridge refers to the clearing of Frank's name, which occurred when a janitor confessed to the murder, the state of Georgia did not officially pardon him until 1986—seventy-three years later.

"Morning Ride" places Ridge in a contradictory critical position, for it embraces as well as critiques modernist aesthetic engagement with the machine age. The poet's typographic experimentation, her appropriation of advertisement as well as the mass transit conductor's voice, give the poem an aspect of collage. The juxtaposition of advertising slogans, the bus/metro locale, and the skyscraper backdrop suggest the influence of cubism, futurism, and vorticism—movements that attempted, by means of abstraction, to represent motion. Ridge complicates the New York skyscraper by representing it along with the body of the Jewish victim of injustice. Symbols of both modernity and industrial capitalism, skyscrapers "seeming still," whirl "on their concrete bases." They emanate a grotesque, distorted quality with their "windows / fanged—." Ridge redirects the modernist tropes she appropriates in the poem's narrative movement. Though Frank "lynched ten years ago" is but a headline in the pages passengers turn automatically, she resituates his slain corpse into the active body of her text, juxtaposing the "soft blarney of the wind," which mingles with commuters and their daily rituals, with the "gentle raillery of the wind," which the speaker imagines as Leo Frank's final sensation. Ridge reminds her readers that the lively, crowded metropolis celebrated in the modernist fascination with the eternally new (as characterized by Jurgen Habermas) and represented in the poem's vocabulary by the variety of verbs ending in "ing," must find itself engaged with Frank's silent corpse. Leo Frank's lynched body ultimately forces itself onto the consciousness of subway riders. It signifies the social and political realities that lurk behind the headlines, skyscrapers, and advertising that bind and blind the urban working class in its daily rituals.

Ridge's juxtaposition of whirling skyscrapers with Frank's swaying corpse suggests modernist montage and collage, but it also shows her insistence on politicizing the body in pain in her poetry. Ridge herself once remarked, "The machine age of America should by all means be represented, but *interpreted* not reported" (emphasis mine).[15] Frank's corpse hence becomes hermeneutically situated as an object that complicates modernist aesthetic representation, which merely describes. There is here a history of injustice and intolerance behind the landscape, or languagescape, rearticulated through the existing tropes of modernist aesthetics.

It is important to note that "Morning Ride" was composed soon after Ridge resigned as the American editor of *Broom*. One of the century's earliest and most innovative journals of art and literature, *Broom* was published in Rome and later in Berlin by Harold Loeb, a wealthy young American expatriate. Ridge's tenure at *Broom* was brief. She supported the development of a uniquely American aesthetic, whereas Loeb and his European associates favored the experimental art they encountered in Europe. Ridge was far from sanguine about continental, particularly French, influence on

American art. As she wrote Loeb, pointing to France as the leader of "the world's fashion," "what real growth shall we foster if we squeeze the feet of this giant child into a French shoe?"[16]

In fact, two books, published years later, tell the story of Ridge's *Broom* period with a kind of pernicious hindsight. As Loeb describes Ridge in his hubristically titled memoir *The Way It Was,* "she was . . . among the moaners whom the machines were tearing apart" (102).[17] Matthew Josephson, who became *Broom*'s European editor at the time of Ridge's resignation, writes the following: "[she] declared herself opposed to . . . giving reflection to the Machine-Age culture of our time, holding that artists would survive only by fighting against the machine and capitalism" (231).

Yet neither Loeb nor Josephson seem to have considered the modernist contradictions found within Ridge's own poetry. Elsewhere she has written about blast furnaces and Broadway, in which the body as laboring machine attempts to transform the objects it produces. Iron smelted by workers becomes "flaming petals" and "fiery blossoms" ("Song of Iron"). The electric light of "Broadway" is celebrated through imagery that also questions its tremendous power: "Light that jingles like anklet chains," "trillions of porcelain / Vases shattering," "captive light," "a huge serpent . . . / Over the night prostrate," equates Broadway with a seducing, ensnaring authority associated with a rising consumer capitalism. Yet in Ridge's work, the human body does frequently appear in thrall to modernist machinery, and the lone corpse of a Frank Little or a Leo Frank becomes more than a symbol and serves as a trope of resistance.

Throughout her career, Lola Ridge's own body played an important part in her poetics of resistance. In the mid 1920s she was active, along with tens of thousands of individuals the world over, in the defense of Nicola Sacco and Bartolomeo Vanzetti, the Italian anarchists, who were by most accounts erroneously charged, tried, and executed for a payroll robbery in South Braintree, Massachusetts, in which a paymaster and his guard were shot and killed. Hundreds of pieces of literature were produced internationally in response to the two men's imprisonment, trial, and execution, which took place in an atmosphere of postwar conservatism and xenophobia. Ridge contributed a powerful poem, "Two in the Death House," to *American Arraigned,* an anthology edited by radicals Lucia Trent and Ralph Cheney and composed exclusively of poems about the Sacco and Vanzetti case. Yet many of the works and reminiscences of this particular moment, such as Maxwell Anderson's *Winterset*, tend to sentimentalize the two immigrants. From her own anarchist stance, Ridge would have found such use of sentiment ironic. Noted historian of anarchism Paul Avrich writes in his book *Sacco and Vanzetti: The Anarchist Background* that both men were "ultramilitants, believers in armed retaliation" (159–60). Both carried guns and were involved to some degree in the plot to kill Attorney General A. Mitchell Palmer, the man responsible for the 1919–1920 deportation of hundreds of foreign-born radicals, including Emma Goldman and Alexander Berkman.

Ridge was never a pacifist, but probably did not support acts of violence, in most cases, though her later poems show an interest in understanding the historical uses of violence. In a 1923 letter, written when she was at Yaddo, to husband David Lawson, a Glasgow-born anarchist and engineer, she expresses some of her thoughts on political culture at the time of Mussolini's rise to power:

> I'm not a pacifist and am an individualist and I know individuals will always rule, no matter what the society . . . even in a democracy. . . . Just now I think the communists are more fit to rule than any other group, but I tremble to think of the result once the greater part of the world has become communist. When Ibsen said "The majority is always wrong" it stood for then, today and a hundred years hence.[18]

The Sacco and Vanzetti trial and execution as a vicious miscarriage of justice, as well as one of the most famous legal cases of the twentieth century, has been examined, from a number of perspectives, by writers, critics, and historians.[19] Edmund Morgan, a Harvard law professor, and Louis Joughin, a literary critic and professor of English at the New School for Social Research, found it necessary to respond to "the case that wouldn't die" by examining both the trial records and the staggering number of literary records written both before and after the execution. While Morgan and Joughin's text, *The Legacy of Sacco and Vanzetti*, reconfirms the Sacco and Vanzetti case as perhaps the twentieth century's worst miscarriage of justice, it also offers an ironic suggestion about Lola Ridge's importance as a social poet. In 1948 when their book was first published, Ridge was on her way to join her fellow protesters and other literary radicals in history's dustbin.

Joughin, who wrote the chapters on the literature, describes Ridge as a poet whose "volumes of verse are not widely known to the general public, but it is difficult to believe that this relative obscurity can continue indefinitely" (389).[20]

On another ironic note, Joughin uses the same kind of narrow, literary criteria to praise her that the critical history responsible for burying Ridge has traditionally maintained. In order to sift through the 144 poems on the case that he was able to locate, he divides them into categories—"very good literature, the middle ground, and the hopelessly bad"—further adding that the "extreme polarity of the first and third classes should obviate too personal an evaluation" (376). Joughin narrows the poems down to twelve that are most noteworthy. Two of these poems are by Lola Ridge: "Two in the Death House" and "Three Men Die."[21]

Ridge's use of her own body to protest the injustice as well as her poetic representation of the physical and psychological torment the two men endured are particularly interesting. Sacco's and Vanzetti's small, short, immigrant, working-class bodies were emblems for Ridge of the seemingly pathological hatred of foreigners and "foreign" ideas expressed by the courts and the establishment at that particular moment (one not all that different in outlook from the moment of this writing). Ridge vigorously protested the imprisonment of these two martyrs of labor whose anarchist principles she, in many ways, shared. While Ridge's main medium of activism was her public poetry, Sacco and Vanzetti had been widely involved in strikes and other forms of political agitation, including extensive antiwar work. They had been previously under police suspicion, probably because they were supporters of the important anarchist newspaper *Cronaca Sovversiva,* edited by Luigi Galleani.[22]

Ridge thought the case important enough to put her body on the line. She was arrested by Boston police at the protest and vigil held for the two men at the Charlestown prison on the evening of their execution, August 22, 1927. She had joined the rather sizable defense committee set up on their behalf along with diverse intellectuals such as Malcolm Cowley, John Dos Passos, Mike Gold, Edna St. Vincent Millay, Scott Nearing, Dorothy Parker, Katherine Anne Porter, and Mary Heaton Vorse. Indeed Ridge's actual presence at this sizable protest was still vivid fifty years later to co-participant Katherine Anne Porter. Porter's 1977 memoir, *The Never Ending*

Wrong, while excessive in its Cold War liberal apologia for 1930s' literary radicalism, points to Ridge's defiant body as police on horseback attempted to disperse the crowd of assemblers:

> Most of the people moved back passively before the police, almost as if they ignored their presence; yet there were faces fixed in agonized disbelief, their eyes followed the rushing horses as if this was not a sight they had expected to see in their lives. One tall, thin figure of a woman stepped out alone, a good distance into the empty square, and when the police came down at her and the horse's hoofs beat over her head, she did not move, but stood with her shoulders slightly bowed, entirely still. The charge was repeated again and again, but she was not to be driven away. A man near me said in horror, suddenly recognizing her, "That's Lola Ridge." (43–44)[23]

It is this image of Ridge and her protester's body that is evoked by another of the poems she created in response to this complicated historical moment. "Three Men Die," a long poem in five sections, appeared in her last book, *Dance of Fire* (1935). Rather than rendering a narrative of events, the poem, as Harriet Monroe said of Ridge's fourth book, *Firehead,* is a "meditation," and more specifically, a meditation on the body in pain.[24] It is a difficult poem. Ridge constructs her memorial to Sacco and Vanzetti as victims of an entrenched, intolerant political establishment through a heteroglossic languagescape that encodes angry protest, police violence, and legal corruption. She recreates the sense of fear, anger, helplessness, and a myriad of other physical and emotional sensations endured by the crowd of defenders, herself included. The poem's unusual, irregular rhyme scheme embraces the contemporary drama centering upon the seven-year-long trial as it suggests the formal tropes of biblical and classical verse. The poem refigures Sacco and Vanzetti within a historical continuum from ancient to modern, in which their carceral bodies become texts of social and political persecution, identifying them with the great martyrs of the past.

Indeed the poem's title as well as its opening stanza suggest yet another likeness to Christ's crucifixion, while also evoking the closing statement of Marx's *Communist Manifesto:*

> The workers of all lands that day
> Looked toward the death house where the two
> Lay with a thief between
>   (old myth
> Renews its tenure of the blood
> Recurrently; in a new way
> Reforms about an ancient pith
> With all the old accessories).

The "thief" refers to a Portuguese gang member who had been involved in a number of previous crimes. Nicola Sacco, in a letter to his son Dante, presents this man as conjoined in his and Vanzetti's fate, though this prisoner was not a fellow anarchist:

> [T]here is another young man by the name of Celestino Medeiros [who] is to be electrocuted at the same time with us. He has been twice before in that horrible death-house, that should be destroyed with the hammers of real progress—that horrible house that will shame forever the future of the citizens of Massachusetts. (Frankfurter and Jackson 74)

In 1925 Celestino Medeiros confessed to being involved in the South Braintree robbery and declared that Sacco and Vanzetti had had nothing to do with it. According to Medeiros's sworn affidavit, a group of Providence criminals known as the Morelli gang were responsible for the holdup and murder. The defense presented this new evidence to Judge Webster Thayer hoping that it would secure Sacco and Vanzetti a new trial. However, Thayer was steadfast in his determination to send "those anarchist bastards," as he was reported to have referred to them at a Dartmouth football game, to the electric chair.

The poem's title is symbolically resonant of the body in pain and recalls Ridge's previous interest in the Crucifixion. It seems a bizarre coincidence that allows Ridge to remind her readers of a significant "historical" moment (or as she suggests, an "old myth") in which "three men die." Christ is crucified with a thief (like Medeiros) and another common criminal—"one of each hand."[25] Just as one might interpret crucifying Christ along with two criminals as a means of denying the significance of his revolutionary

activities, one might argue that electrocuting Medeiros along with Sacco and Vanzetti allowed Judge Thayer to send the message that these men were criminals also, and nothing more.

Ridge creates a tribute to Sacco by using "death house" as the condemned man does in his letter to his son. She also indirectly reminds us, as do Sacco's words, of the physical and emotional damage that prisons cause to those incarcerated in them. In fact, the idleness of prison life seemed an ironic blow to Sacco and Vanzetti—men whose identities were formed through the fact of their labor.[26] Not only were these men physically and emotionally damaged by their incarceration in the "death house" but their beliefs in freedom were mocked by their appearance the day of their trial. When Sacco and Vanzetti appeared in the courtroom, they were forced to sit handcuffed inside a prisoner's dock—a wrought-iron cage that exposed only their heads. A famous photograph of the trial shows them inside this "cage," looking tired and well beyond their thirty-odd years. The artist Ben Shahn was so moved by this newspaper photo that he painted a gouache of it, *Sacco and Vanzetti: In the Courtroom Cage,* as part of a series that he made of the trial and execution.

In addition to the spiritual evocation of martyrdom, the opening lines of "Three Men Die" also suggest engagement with the genres of memoir and reportage produced during the case. Journalistic observation is evoked as Ridge recalls how the gaze of "the workers of all lands that day / looked toward the death house." Ridge sets a tone, both angry and decisive, that informs her readers of the case's magnitude, insisting that somehow the bodies of all working people, all individuals who desired social justice, were merged into the same giant tableau, moving as one dynamic force.

The Sacco and Vanzetti case became famous around the world. Radicals, working people, and immigrants expressed their solidarity by instigating forms of public agitation in great cities such as London, Paris, Leningrad, Mexico City, and Buenos Aires; even important Italian senators and diplomats tried to intervene on the men's behalf. The international scope of the protests eventually persuaded Massachusetts governor Alvan T. Fuller to consider giving the two executive clemency.[27] Radical journalist Mary Heaton Vorse, in her memoir of her years spent covering the labor movement, recalls the intensity and sense of solidarity the trial took on in faraway France:

The night they suffered their death I was in Paris. All working-class Paris paraded in protest. The city was tense as though it were something that was happening within the borders of France. There had been small riots and arrests in the demonstrations held in front of the American Embassy. We sat around in groups feeling the hour of doom approaching, feeling the horrible anguish mounting up within us as though a wave of grief had swept over us, the same wave that at the same moment was causing the massing of emotion in Union Square and the assembly of great crowds in Boston. (339)

Vorse's reminiscence suggests that as the volts that shocked the bodies of Sacco and Vanzetti were also felt by the French working class as a collective body, similarly transcontinental waves of emotion consolidated groups of outraged protesters from Rome to Paterson. In fact, the process of reading "Three Men Die" (at least for this reader) might be described as tension wrought, the sense of "anguish mounting up" as one moves carefully through the text. Probably Ridge hoped that "a wave of grief" would wash over her readers as they struggled through this long, intense poem.

Ridge was physically present at protests on behalf of Sacco and Vanzetti, up to and including the Charlestown prison on the night of their execution. In the third section of "Three Men Die," Ridge rather tacitly describes her own participation as "one who had been there." Yet her characterization of herself in the fight to reverse the two men's death sentences seems insignificant in contrast to the way she is romanticized by Katherine Anne Porter in *The Never Ending Wrong*. Porter presents Ridge as a "spectacle"—the lone figure who stands unflinchingly against the threat of police brutality—whereas Ridge's depiction implies that she was one of many protesters. The self-effacing poet is more interested in the fate of Sacco and Vanzetti than she is in celebrating her own act of resistance. In this passage, which evokes Walt Whitman's Civil War poem "Drum-Taps," Ridge pairs her own fragile protester's body with the horse's body in its task at riot control. It is the animal's body that dominates:

Drumbeats of the hooves . . . so close, so close . . . that
   one who had been there (and for some quite
Unbalanced reason did not run . . . but stood there in the
   hooves' path) had noted

(Knowing horses) the lead head, straight nose, clean flank,
Line of the onrushing shoulder, brought to this . . . and
    feeling the wet foam on his mouth, glimpsed spread
nostrils and the white
Fire of the eye, rolling as in agony; one might have seen
(All in the one beetling moment, there awaiting the falling
Cataract of the hooves) the great body-rear-swerve and
plunge sideways
And the lightning
                    strike from the stone.

The close attention to the animal's form brings to mind its uses as "war horse," "work horse," "beast of burden," even the horse attached to Vanzetti's fish cart as he peddled Christmas eels to shoppers—his alibi at the time the robbery and murder took place. In fact, Ridge symbolically refigures the class divisions in the Sacco and Vanzetti case by representing these animals through several distinct semiotic performances: work horse, police horse, and tournament horse.

Louis Joughin suggests that this necessary "long metaphoric digression" allows Ridge to contrast primitive man's early subduing of the horse in order to "use him proudly" with the animal's physical abuse by mounted police in the service of crowd control (391). The horse is presented as a contorted body with its "spread nostrils," the "white / Fire of the eye, rolling as in agony," and the "falling / Cataract of the hooves," and both senses of cataract are implied here—blindness and waterfall. The animal is of great body, making a "rear-swerve" and a "plunge sideways," and Ridge constructs a clash of performing bodies as she, in the act of protesting, encounters the horse or horses used in corrupt political performance: "O prancers, of your brave / Cavorting and your tournaments—to ride down brittle / bodies that shall bleat / Once—if the shot feet strike / out unseen / lightnings." The tacit suggestion made by the movement of the horse's body as a mocking gesture to the stillness imposed upon Sacco and Vanzetti in their prison cells is yet another striking reminder of the carceral body, the body of the prisoner, as it appears in this poem.

Toward the poem's close, Ridge reconstructs the execution site to which the three men are led and here provides perhaps the most concrete represen-

tation in the entire poem of the body in pain: "They led the thief out first" ("trembling"); then Sacco "came on with his usual tread." He came on "Intrepidly, / Beneath the arc that on him shed / A light as white as agony."[28] Vanzetti is brought out last and "fell / A silence on them." History, news stories, and memoirs about the case all repeat in some way, shape, or form Vanzetti's final words before being strapped to the electric chair. "I am an innocent man," they report. Ridge, however, chooses to write and celebrate Vanzetti's working-class body:

> He stood there, isolate, a man
> Fleshed heavily, of massive bone,
> With a warm, brooding eye, head thrown
> A little forward in the stoop
> That labor leaves upon its own
> Whose shoulders have held up the world.

With this construction of Vanzetti, the last of the "martyrs" to meet his death in "white agony," Ridge leaves her readers seeing Sacco and Vanzetti as flesh-and-bone men, "warm" but "isolate." The poem also works out a set of contradictions in terms of how the textual bodies of Sacco and Vanzetti may ultimately be read—and remembered. She has placed classical and biblical tropes throughout the poem, which are used as well in her closing assessments of the two working-class martyrs. Vanzetti, for example, is ordinary, but he is also Atlas, the mythical strong man, "Whose shoulders" hold up the world. She describes both men as unaware of "the sacrament, / Their little nimble hands had poured." Yet she also identifies them "Beneath their armed impertinence, / The mighty rhythms they had stirred." For Lola Ridge, Sacco and Vanzetti remain men of principle whose beliefs stood trial alongside them.

While Louis Joughin was certainly correct in naming Lola Ridge as one of the "chief" Sacco and Vanzetti poets, she also lent her name and poetic expression to another legal lynching. The trial and conviction of radical labor leader Tom Mooney was an important rallying cry for both workers and left intellectuals between the two wars. Mooney was (dubiously) linked to a 1916 bombing at a San Francisco Preparedness Day rally at which eight people were killed. Mooney and a younger associate, Warren K. Billings, represented to the West Coast legal and business establishment what Sacco

and Vanzetti and their anarchist comrades represented on the East Coast: militant labor as an active component of American economic life. Thus a conspiracy against them—complete with Pinkerton agents and a long list of paid perjurers and informants—began and the Mooney-Billings case continued for twenty-three years.

At the end of his 500-page study, *The Mooney Case,* Richard H. Frost sums up by making a rather curious remark: "The Mooney case never inspired novelists or poets," he writes. "The verses of his admirers are best left to oblivion along with Upton Sinclair's *100 Percent* and a play called *Precedent* by Isadore J. Golden, a St. Louis lawyer" (488–89). Yet Frost appears either ignorant of or unjustly dismissive of Lola Ridge's very public artistic contribution to the Mooney defense. Frost's text, published by Stanford University Press in 1968, is the most exhaustive study of the case to date. Frost's perspective is no doubt informed by a Cold War–era point of view that has dismissed all political poetry as propaganda and a conventional view that only "able writers who cared about the case" such as Sinclair Lewis, Drieser, or Zola could have helped secure Mooney his freedom (489). He is disappointed because as he claims, "Mooney often called for a Zola, but no Zola ever came" (489).[29] "Stone Face," included in Ridge's 1935 collection *Dance of Fire,* was probably written for the Mooney cause in the late 1920s, after Mooney's death sentence had been commuted to life imprisonment.[30] Before the poem was formally published in the *Nation,* it had a radical life on the left-hand side of a large broadside, on the right side of which appeared a photo of Mooney, in stripes, complete with prisoner ID number and face showing signs of deteriorating health. This poster traveled across America as a popular form of public protest, affixed onto facades of buildings and steel girders of bridges. It decorated union halls and night school classrooms, all in hopes of raising money on Mooney's behalf.[31]

Tom Mooney's imprisoned body is another of Ridge's brilliant rearticulations of the politics of pain. In contrast to Ridge's political performance in "Three Men Die," in "Stone Face" the poem rather than the poet does the performing. The poem's inclusion on this broadside, used to benefit the Tom Mooney Molders' Defense Committee of San Francisco, brings it into the multifaceted spaces of public engagement with a mass of readers.

A sizable defense movement grew around Mooney's imprisonment. Mooney, an already popular left-wing trade unionist, was able to gain support on both national and international fronts. A diverse selection of individuals donated time, space, and money on behalf of Mooney and Billings. Anarchist and *Blast* editor Alexander Berkman and cartoonist Robert Minor, who was later to become a Communist Party functionary, were two of his earliest active supporters.[32] Mooney had, in fact, contributed an article to *Blast* condemning military preparedness. Berkman donated much space of *Blast's* short life to exposing the gritty intricacies of the Mooney frameup, particularly to the contradictory testimony given by paid informants. Minor's hilarious cover drawing for the issue dated February 17, 1917, shows a prostitute being evicted from her lodgings by a big burly policeman. A caption below it announces, "The Vice Clean-Up," followed by accompanying dialogue. "But what other work can I get to do?" the woman asks the cop. "Well, I hear they need new witnesses against Mooney," he replies. Early on, Margaret Anderson, publisher of the *Little Review*, provided Minor with a column in one issue to announce the prisoner's plight to readers of poems by Carl Sandburg and Ezra Pound (Frost 148). Another early contributor was the wealthy benefactress Aline Barnsdall.

Two other interesting later propaganda performances show the Mooney defense committee's determination and creativity. After the committee failed to obtain a boycott of the 1932 Olympic Games in Los Angeles, at the end of one day's event, six members of the Young Communist League ran into the stadium in track and field outfits with "Free Tom Mooney" signs pinned to their chests and backsides; they ran around the track shouting "Free Tom Mooney." In the other stunt, a group of West Coast Socialists got a hearse, equipped with coffin, and plastered a banner across it reading "Justice is Dead in California." The driver, a well-spoken Mooney devotee, drove statewide handing out pamphlets and speaking on Mooney's behalf wherever he could find an audience. The tour was so successful that Mooney directed a second hearse to Washington, D.C. In fervent gloom it paraded past the Capitol building and the White House.[33]

Yet Mooney himself was his chief defender. He became responsible for molding his own image from his jail cell at San Quentin.[34] Throughout the long period of his imprisonment, Mooney oversaw a series of propaganda campaigns that insisted upon his innocence; these campaigns may be seen as successful in that he did not meet the same fate as Sacco and Vanzetti. Pamphlets, film, and photographs appear to have been Mooney's favored manner of approach, and sources suggest that Mooney was particularly intent on showing the proper photographic representation of the physical strain and toll that incarceration had taken on his body. Estolv Ethan Ward writes that Mooney "showed great concern for the facial angles and expression photographers should try to catch: No. 31921 (his prisoner number) should be made to look determined but not grim; he must show suffering without revealing weakness"(162). In fact Mooney gave directives on the very fine nuances of how the public should "see" him. Photos were not to be too dark, lest he should appear fierce; his prisoner number had to appear clearly on every picture—photos were often retouched if it did not; full body shots demanded handcuffs; his hair sometimes appeared grayer and sparser, his face more gaunt.

Lola Ridge's poem "Stone Face" acts as both homage to Mooney, complete with metaphors of rock and stone to emphasize the labor and body of the incarcerated, and as a call to action, affixed on a broadside collectively part of an organized solidarity campaign. The poem works as a dedication to the labor martyr by constructing, through poetic device, an image of physical and spiritual torment. Consider the poem's first stanza:

> They have carved you into a stone face, Tom Mooney,
>   You, there lifted high in California
> Over the salt wash of the Pacific,
>   With your eyes . . . crying in many tongues,
> Goading, innumerable
>   Eyes of the multitudes,
> Holding in them all hopes, fears, persecutions . . .
> Forever straining one way.

Ridge's Mooney is carved and chiseled like the rocks worked by San Quentin prisoners. As a stone breaker, he is linked with all imprisoned bodies. He is also exalted and symbolic—the "persecutions" of "multitudes" are reflected through his gaze. Ridge reveals Mooney's "stone face" through multiple suggestions: he turns literally "gray"—stone color—while he rots in jail; "stone face" also recalls the characteristic stare found in mug shots; and, finally, faces of stone belong to those "great men" to whom statues are erected. The poem also shows a tacit awareness of Mooney as exploited and exploiter, for he is presented as both erased and faced. On the one hand he is celebrated as ordinary worker, "a rough man, / Rude-nurtured, casually shouldering / Through a May-day crowd." Yet, on the other hand, he is also one who has been "raised with torsion to identity," victimized by a corrupt legal system that has also written into history "Sacco and the fish-monger."

"Stone Face" *molds* Mooney's body in pain; it describes his features as they have been abused and exhausted by prison life. Ridge's critics no doubt read the poem as propaganda. Yet perhaps the poem's greatest cultural intervention is its ability to work not only as propaganda (if it could help save Mooney's life, why not?) but also as social text and aesthetic object. It challenges the place of poetry in the literary magazine and its limited audience. "Stone Face" appeared in three disparate reading venues: a Tom Mooney Molders' Defense Committee poster; the *Nation*, a left-of-center magazine of opinions; and Ridge's last book, *Dance of Fire*, published by Smith and Haas, a small literary publishing company that later merged with Random House.

As the poem informs us, Ridge has imagined Mooney from a photo "in the Sunday papers." Ridge's Mooney, with his face "tight-bitten like a pierced fist" and eyes that "have a transfixed gleam," brings readers into a visual engagement with her subject's injurious predicament. Ridge's desire to construct her vision of Mooney, through an already manipulated image whose creation he directed from his prison cell, complicates the process of reading poems for their aesthetic value only, distanced from the problematic social communities in which they are produced. As Ridge constructs the poem to sustain the image of the suffering, deteriorating Mooney and lends it to the Molders' Defense Committee to advertise the cause, she raises some questions about traditional assumptions about where poetry belongs. What are we to make of Ridge's composition as we understand that Mooney's carceral body has been manipulated, retouched, its appearance completely negotiated? Rather than answer this question, it would make more sense to suggest that our need to ask it reflects the way we have been taught to look at modern poetry. As seen through a disinterested lens, poems belong to a historically unlocated solitary readership, disassociated from movements or other popular and communal discourses that can only turn the poem in question into propaganda. Lola Ridge and the Tom Mooney Molder's Defense Committee by rendering Mooney symbolic in fact poeticize as well as politicize the Mooney case. After all, poetic language is a manipulation of the word, and the poem as it becomes part of the "free Mooney" broadside also becomes linked to the defense committee's manipulation of the Mooney image.

For Ridge, this literary portrait of Mooney rotting in jail extends beyond the local desire to free one particular individual or to shed light on one singular aspect of legal corruption. The prison system itself, a place metaphorically linked to bodily pain and domination, becomes symbolic; as Foucault writes: "its very materiality . . . [is] an instrument and vector of power" (30). Lola Ridge is once again prescient in her understanding of the political location of the imprisoned body. In the final stanza of "Stone Face" the prison itself becomes a body. She imagines Mooney, symbol of labor's perseverance, set free (hence the poem and broadside announce their own efficacy in freeing Mooney), his face "clenched" like a fist "under the long / [g]aze of the generations," who will be, as Ridge hopes, witnesses to San Quentin's own demise, its walls "caved in and its steel ribs / [f]ood for the ant-rust." Ridge ends the poem by rendering "Governor Rolph," who refused to pardon Mooney, "[a] fleck of dust among the archives." While Ridge was accurate in predicting Rolph's fate, Mooney's trial and her poetic contribution to its cause have too been forgotten. By reassessing Ridge's poems, particularly those that were written in response to specific historical moments that are arguably still socially relevant, I hope to stir up some of the necessary "dust among the archives," the creative vestiges of a lost radical past that inspired early-twentieth-century social poetry.

The poetry examined in this chapter tends to emphasize the male body in pain over its female counterparts. The image of the charred and maimed bodies of African American women and children in "Lullaby" was an important exception; the Mooney Case, Ridge's activism at the trial and execution of Sacco and Vanzetti, her outrage at the lynchings of Frank Little and Leo Frank suggest that the poet has ignored the bodily pain experienced by her own sex. Yet Ridge, as an ardent feminist, was no less concerned with the female carceral body. It is the male body, however, which has always been in the public eye; its participation in social struggle and war, characteristically a subject of debate and (de)liberation, has played a major role in how it became a subject of interest to radical writers such as Lola Ridge.[35] The next section will examine "The Ghetto," a long narrative poem that

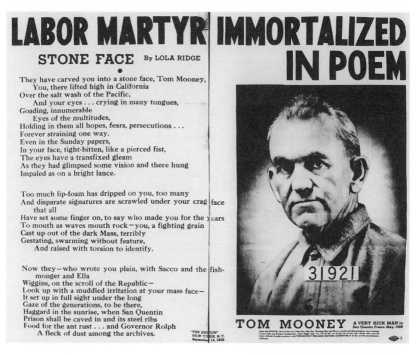

Labor Martyr Immortalized in Poem. Poster. Courtesy: Beinecke Rare Book and Manuscript Library, Yale University. Photo reproduction: Gerald Cyrus.

draws upon the female body as it experiences both pain and pleasure—a work that is perhaps Ridge's finest poetic contribution.

Murillo's Mulatto: A Feminist in the Ghetto

In 1919 Lola Ridge gave a lecture on feminism and art in which she discussed why there are no great women artists. She asks her audience to imagine a particular historical scenario by drawing upon the legend surrounding the seventeenth century Spanish painter Bartolomeo Murillo. The painter was reported to have discovered his slave putting finishing touches on the head of one of his paintings of the virgin. Murillo was so impressed with his work that he encouraged the slave to paint. As Ridge observes, adding a gendered twist: "If Murillo's mulatto had been a girl instead of a boy slave, his master would not have given him his liberty and helped him to develop into an artist. A girl slave who had the temerity to dream of painting a white Virgin would probably have been raped and left to forget her dreams in straining lips at her breast" (15).

Ridge's lecture, with its Nietzschean title "Woman and the Creative Will," explores women's artistic expression from Sappho up through Sweden's 1909 Nobel Laureate, Selma Lagerlof.[36] She insists upon the bisexual nature of "genius" and informs us that there are no "great women artists" because women have not been allowed to express themselves to their fullest capacity, and through the widest depths of experience, as have men. Ridge is in fact prescient in her assessment of the social and political roadblocks that historically have stalled women's intellectual and artistic growth. Her materialist position anticipates subsequent discussions on the social construction of gender encountered in diverse feminist theorists such as Juliet Mitchell, Michele Barrett, and Judith Newton. "Woman is not and never has been man's *natural* inferior," Ridge maintains (emphasis mine). "She has been and still is suffering from arrested development; and considering the mental and spiritual strait jacket within which she has had to grow, she has not made such a bad showing" (18).

The imaginative trope of Murillo's mulatto as a defeated and assaulted female artist interestingly connects Ridge to one of the century's most important feminists, Virginia Woolf. Yet Ridge's retelling of the legend of Murillo's mulatto appears ten years before Woolf introduced her readers to "Shakespeare's sister" in her classic discussion of feminism and art, *A Room of One's Own*, published in 1929. Woolf imagines Judith Shakespeare, who "had the quickest fancy, a gift like her brother's for the tune of words" (49). She runs away to London to seek training in the theater, but she could get no such training, let alone "seek her dinner in a tavern or roam the streets at midnight." Instead she becomes an object of pity of actor-manager Nick Greene. "She found herself with child by that gentleman and so—who shall measure the heat and violence of the poet's heart when caught and tangled in a woman's body?—killed herself one winter's night and lies buried at some crossroads where the omnibuses now stop outside the Elephant and Castle" (50).

While it is necessary to connect the forgotten feminist poet Lola Ridge with the canonical feminist Virginia Woolf, it is also necessary to point out that Ridge takes the "mental and spiritual strait jacket," which she and Woolf argue have bound women, a step further. Her reimagining the legend of Murillo's mulatto in gendered terms emphasizes the ethnic as well as class differences that have also restricted women's intellectual growth.

Class and ethnic differences as they affect women's lives are a significant feature in one of Ridge's most important poetic contributions. "The Ghetto" was published in 1918, and portions of it appeared in the *New Republic*.[37] It is a narrative poem of more than twenty pages that details immigrant Jewish life on New York's Lower East Side. Although the poem includes portraits of a number of ghetto inhabitants and provides glimpses at the activities of both sexes, as well as at the young and the old, the "green-horns" and those who have been "Americanized," the poet's interest in women permeates the very structure of the work. It is constructed through a divisional frame of nine sections that mirror the stages of maternal gestation, and it relies heavily upon the female body to explore its related themes of immigration, ghettoization, cultural difference, and assimilation. In addition, Ridge metaphorically represents the ghetto as a "cramped ova," replete with images of the mother "waddling in and out."

It is also a collage of Jewish working-class social, political, and cultural life, where in each of the poem's nine sections a different aspect of immigrant Jewish structures of feeling comes into view. Ridge introduces readers to Sadie Sodos and her family, to the Jewish new women Sarah and Anna, and as an important part of Ridge's agenda as a modern social poet, describes Jewish labor, the sweatshop, and the conflicts of religious conviction and social action. The poem's nine sections are imagist snapshots that show fragments of immigrant Jewish urban experience: history, family life, childhood, mercantilism, ritual, old-world attitudes, new-world activism, evening's passions, and the celebration of life.

"The Ghetto" introduces the immigrant experience into the language of modern poetry. Through Ridge's poetic evocation, Jewish immigrant life becomes a new language: modern, urban, and walled-in. With this poem Ridge made one of the first attempts to articulate urban immigrant experience in the form of a narrative poem. In the verse cadences of modernism, with its heightened sense of image and free-form lines, are gritty descriptions of destitute, Yiddish-speaking Jews. Ridge frames her ghetto as a place of communal desire with all its complexities: its squalor, overcrowding, ceaseless physical and mental activity, and its discussion and dissent. Moreover, Ridge presented a new America through these culturally isolated immigrants whose religious and linguistic rituals displayed their "otherness" against the more "familiar" American middle- and working-class traditions. Ridge embraces the "different" cultural body, the political body, and the women's "laboring and desiring" bodies that would become a focus of much proletarian literature produced by women later in the 1930s.[38] Yet Ridge has few peers in the first decade of the new century who can embrace both current experimental trends in modern poetry and a concern for the burgeoning social communities that would come to redefine the American landscape and languagescape. Her incorporation of modernist trends and her community concerns are maintained in the poem's narrative voice. Yet unlike the majority of modernist poems, Ridge's narrative voice wholly embraces rather than distances itself from its subject; she positions herself as a keen and admiring observer. In the poem's second, fifth, and ninth sections, the poet inserts herself into the narrative, describing what she experiences of the ghetto from a "bare" room she rents from a Jewish family. She also records her admiration for this community through use of the present continuous tense, describing Jewish ghetto life as a work in progress, a community in continual formation, perpetually making and remaking itself.

The poem begins in a manner similar to a director opening a film, establishing location through panning shots of buildings, roads, more buildings, focusing on particular colors and textures until he comes to the people— whose lives are about to be revealed. Ridge's ghetto inhabitants are at first offered to us not as specific individuals with descriptive features, but rather as bodies, massive flesh, "ponderous bulk." They "dangle from the fire escapes / [o]r sprawl over the stoops." Eventually they become faces that "glimmer pallidly" and are "herring-yellow" or "dank white." The colors of these faces are also important distinctions, for they create a contrast to "whiteness." The "litter of the East," as Ridge describes the ghetto dwellers in a later section, signifies the ethnic diversity that is transforming the landscape and languagescape of urban America and producing new and different cultural and political bodies.

The salient image of the opening section is the oppressive heat of the ghetto. "Inaccessible air / Is floating in velvety blackness shot with steel-blue / lights," she informs us. Ridge further characterizes the heat on Hester Street as "nosing in the body's overflow . . . [c]overing all avenues of air," and "[h]eaped like a dray / [w]ith the garbage of the world." The discomfort and decay she presents through heat and exposed flesh as the prevalent linguistic signs show Ridge's ability to identify with the social oppression of her subjects as well as invent a language to describe them. More to Ridge's credit is her apparent solidarity with her subject. She locates the Jewish ghetto's struggle in its particular historical context:

> The street crawls undulant,
> Like a river addled
> With its hot tide of flesh
> That ever thickens. . . .
>
> Flesh of this abiding
> Brood of those ancient mothers who saw the dawn
>   break over Egypt. . . .
> And turned their cakes upon the dry hot stones
> And went on.

The poet's attention to "those ancient mothers," their daily rituals, "their enduring flesh" (4), places women at the center of this context. Not only does Ridge emphasize the importance of reading ghetto Jewry through its biblical experience in slavery, she also specifies that the gradual arrival of the people among whom she lives must be recognized through the singular accomplishments of its "enslaved" women. Though Ridge clearly admires these people as a community, a communal body suffering in both literal and metaphorical flesh-enveloping heat, she sees the women and their labor (and here the pun must be acknowledged) as central to her poetic articulation.

Ridge establishes women's participation in Jewish ghetto life through their bartering and laboring. She also depicts their familial and religious devotion as well as their cultural and social breaches. Yet she finds metaphors of the female body and its biological capabilities particularly suitable for representing women's involvement in ghetto life. When in the poem's eighth section (and toward the final gestational stage) Ridge expresses that "Life in the cramped ova [is] tearing and rending asunder its living cells," she equates the painful (and joyous) process of birth, as well as the discomforts of pregnancy, with the creation and dissent of a community in various stages of transition. The ghetto may be dark and cramped, but it is also a positive site of cultural formation. This birth metaphor, while it articulates the labor pains associated with childbearing, also suggests the "pains of labor" in terms of the physically exhaustive labor performed by Jewish immigrants inside the sweatshops—a site of exploitation and activity to which she returns throughout the poem. Ridge's representation of the immigrant working-class female body in a modernist long poem situates her within the important discussions of gender and modernism. In her introduction to the anthology *The Gender of Modernism,* Bonnie Kime Scott suggests how women writers redefined the white male focus of modern literary practice, making it "polyphonic, mobile, interactive, sexually charged," and giving it "wide appeal, constituting a historic shift in parameters" (4). She also contends that adding gender to the discourse of modernism, "layered with other revised conceptual categories such as race and class, challenges our former sense of the power structures of literary production." In the case of Lola Ridge, her reading of ghetto life through female activity and the female body complicates any aspect of modernist poetics articulated, as in the case of Ezra Pound or Wyndham Lewis, through the phallus. She also creates a site for a reading of modernism that embraces the entrance of female and immigrant working-class readers (and writers).

The previously quoted lines "Life in the cramped ova / tearing and rending asunder its living cells" may be obvious to contemporary readers who will make the connection between the "ghetto" as any "walled-in" community and "vaginal" walls, but what of Ridge's readers in 1918? By fusing metaphors of the female body with representations of immigrant social life, she challenges the modernist masculinist gaze, centered upon the male body (particularly the phallus) and its dominant presence outside these metaphorical walls. Ridge not only intervenes into phallocentric space but also into the phallogocentric metaphor inscribed within the dominant text of male modernism.

Another way in which Ridge intervenes into the spaces of male (and Protestant) modernism is by writing about immigrant Jews and establishing her identification with them. Though not Jewish, Ridge is a foreigner who has been a factory worker like the characters in her narrative poem. She also shares the radical political sensibilities of many of the ghetto's inhabitants and is thus familiar with the debates and discussions in the cafes and meeting halls. She recognizes Jewish history as one of exile. As an immigrant and radical intellectual and poet living on the margins, she identifies with Jews and finds consolation and a sense of solidarity in acknowledging their historical circumstances.

Although Jews are not the only disenfranchised group that Ridge represents in her work, they are obviously significant in both personal and symbolic ways. As a child Ridge's mother reportedly told her that, "Jews are good people. You must always be very nice to them" (Drake 193). Yet her comfort inside the immigrant Jewish world of her long poem "The Ghetto" has probably more to do with her identification of the Jewish people with the state of exile that she shared with them. Of course Ridge is not the only modernist writer and exile to express such a state. Ira Nadel in his book *Joyce and the Jews* points to Joyce's identification with and unwavering admiration of the Jews for his and their "parallel conditions of exile, education, and displacement" (1). As a homeless stranger in the Joycean sense, Ridge would certainly have been attracted to the special relationship the Jew has had with the modern world. She was born in Ireland, but raised in Australia; she was a woman and an artist; she was politically left in right-wing America; she was a marginalized modernist. Her existence overflowed with the kinds of contradictions that were characteristic of the Jewish diaspora. Indeed, the variety of Jewish experience that Ridge documents in "The Ghetto" reflects her recognition of the difficulty of exile and the sense of fragmentation and dislocation it creates in those who must live it. What Ridge knew about and witnessed in the Jewish struggle for survival in diaspora, in the ghettos of the world, in the ghettos of New York, are indeed reasons enough for her tribute. While marginality defines the modern condition, Ridge also identified with the struggles to maintain community that Jews created for themselves as exiles in the modern world. She appears to have also been attracted by the contradictions of ritual and protest that were also part of Jewish survival in exile, and are themes that we encounter again and again in her work.

One might also ask why Ridge singles out Jews, given the variety of immigrant communities establishing themselves in American cities. One specific response locates the poet in the following lines, inside the Jewish ghetto, identifying herself and her own experience there:

I room at Sodos'—in the little green room
That was Bennie's—
With Sadie
And her old father and her mother,
Who is not so old and wears her own hair.

As the poet establishes herself as a boarder (and an outsider), she places herself in the middle of one of the poem's central conflicts—the changes brought to traditional Jewish family and cultural life through the process of immigration and the discoveries of a new world. Sadie goes to work in a sweatshop, while her father has lost his old-world trade: he "no longer makes saddles. / He has forgotten how." Sadie's mother breaks tradition by removing her shedl, the wig that signifies a married woman's modesty and submission. Sadie and her mother together make a serious traditional breach by abandoning the practice of lighting Sabbath candles. Yet while Ridge places herself as a boarder and witness to the changes that immigrant ghetto life produces, she also introduces an important aspect of immigrant Jewish economic life that was largely controlled by women. A 1911 Immigration Commission study observed that 56 percent of all Russian Jewish households in New York added to their monthly earnings by taking in boarders.[39] These tenants, many single immigrant girls whose bodies are also defining tropes within Ridge's ghetto, can be placed within both an old- and new-world practice in which Jewish women, though limited by their role as keepers of the domestic sphere, still managed to exercise economic control. Although Ridge never argues against the patriarchal codes of Judaism, choosing rather to show them in flux, women's participation in the economy of the ghetto needs to be understood through its historical significance. The majority of Jewish women had large economic roles because their handling of monetary affairs freed their husbands, as was required by religious law, to pray and study Torah.

Yet as we read the poet's "I" in this poem, we must acknowledge her difference from the community she describes. She is not a Jew nor does she speak Yiddish, the language of the ghetto.[40] This choice of "the Jew" and the construction of "Jewishness" present special problems for a modernist poet, especially in terms of Ridge's canonical reception. Eliot Weinberger perceptively outlines this point. He argues that the mixing, the collage, the fragmentation—essential components of modernist aesthetics—are in direct conflict with a number of aspects within Judaic tradition. "In the Judaism of Mosaic laws the human yearning for wholeness manifests itself . . . in a loathing for that which is incomplete, mixed, other" (170). He does maintain that Judaism's decree against mixing is not the direct basis for the anti-Semitism of American modernists such as Ezra Pound and William Carlos Williams, but Ridge's modernist embrace of Jewish life would no doubt be rejected by these poets as well. Her poem is an outright collage in its expression of Jewish cultural mixing, which she complicates as a painful, blasphemous, inevitable, and even desirable outcome of the diasporic condition and of modernity. Despite Ridge's own differences, her attempt to represent immigrant Jewish structures of feeling informs her position, as her friend Alfred Kreymborg suggested, "as another Babushka released from exile to a place of leadership among her contemporaries" (337).

Ridge's use of modernist collage to describe the richness and variety of everyday life in the urban, working-class Jewish ghetto brings to mind Bakhtin's concept of heteroglossia. Heteroglossia, or multivoiced discourse—the many speaking voices and social landscapes of a literary text—is certainly present in "The Ghetto." Though Bakhtin maintains that poetic genres "in the narrow sense" are primarily monologic, void of the extrinsic linguistic possibilities that foster heteroglossia, "The Ghetto" does not speak through the singular voice of the poet, but through a variety of voices—narrative passages, registers, images—which suggest the richly complex social material of the poem. "The social and historical voices populating language" noted by Bakhtin (300) are reflected through the ghetto's "majestic discordances," "multi-colored dreams," "world-voices / [c]hanting grand arias," and "words / [p]attering like hail" that suggest the disagreements and individual and communal passions that populate this poem and reveal Ridge's interest in conveying the multivoiced, cacophonic atmosphere of immigrant Jewish space. The poem's fourth section, in particular, is marked with an assortment of words and phrases representing the heteroglossic atmosphere of a bazaar. Grand Street is "Crowded like a float, [b]ulging like a crazy quilt / [s]tretched on a line." Ridge further admires "This litter of the East" through its "dissolute array" of goods displayed for sale throughout the market stalls. In fact she appears to find the dissonance and dissidence of the individual ghetto voices equaled in "the glitter and the jumbled finery . . . strangely juxtaposed."

Yet while the market atmosphere Ridge describes is heteroglossic, so are sections of the poem that explore the various ways in which women dominate immigrant Jewish space. In "The Ghetto," a variety of female figures populate the poem and contribute to the poem's polyphony, yet there is one particular location in which the cacophony of women's speech is most pronounced. The sweatshop as the "voice" of female labor is introduced in the poem's second section. It is where Sadie works, dressed all "in black." In fact Ridge's fondness for images of heat and the capacious bodies that fill the ghetto are interesting metaphors for the sweatshop, which she represents as a site of both exploitation and political action. Additionally, the sweatshop as the voice of female labor offers a glimpse of the complexities surrounding immigrant Jewish women as they participate in the social, economic, and political entanglements of ghetto life. For Sadie, necessity forces her to work outside the home, yet the workplace with its stifling heat, deafening din, and flesh-eating air is also responsible for her developing awareness of female exploitation and her resultant resistance.

All day the power machines
Drone in her ears. . . .
All day the fine dust flies
Till throats are parched and itch
And the heat—like a kept corpse—
Fouls to the last corner.

Ridge's depiction of Sadie's sweatshop-exploited body reflects her interest in the activist stance that working-class Jewish women took in response to their foul working conditions. Yet what is interesting are the phallic metaphors she uses to describe Sadie at her sewing machine. "Sadie quivers like a rod . . . / [a] thin black piston flying, / [o]ne with her machine." As Ridge represents the oppressive world of work as masculine, she follows these potent descriptions by showing an empowered Sadie who warns her fellow workers in one of the poem's few examples of dialogue: "Slow down—You'll have him cutting us again!" Ridge's language is also appropriately connected to the exploitive labor of garment factory work. The speed with which the women are forced to work makes them resemble "thin black piston[s] flying," yet the speedy "cutting" of garments also signifies the speedy "cutting" of workers. In fact, Ridge's feel for the stress and involvement of Jewish female garment workers can be related to the experience of an actual glove-maker and union activist, Agnes Nestor: "When I started in the trade and saw the girls working at that dreadful pace every minute, I wondered how they could keep up the speed. But it is not until you become one of them that you can understand" (138).[41] Sadie's fatigue and determination are also reminiscent of another garment worker and activist. In a 1912 editorial in *Life and Labor*, Anna Rudnitzky laments the absence of romance, music, theater, and opera, as well as the opportunities offered by a high school and university education, because her working life allows for no leisure:

> In the busy time I work so hard; try to make the machine run faster, and faster because then I can earn some money and I need it, and then night comes and I am tired out and I go home and I am too weary for anything but supper and bed. Sometimes union meetings, yes, because I must go. But I have no mind and nothing left in me. The busy time means to earn enough money not only to cover the slack time, and then when the slack time comes I am not so tired, I have more time, but I have no money; and time is passing and everything is missed.

While Anna Rudnitzky's remarks reflect the fears and anxieties of Jewish women as they grow dependent upon their factory work, Ridge somewhat sanguinely attempts to show other possibilities for ghetto girls and women. In addition to Sadie, Ridge introduces Sarah and Anna, who "live on the floor above." Sarah "reads without bias" and Anna "has the appeal of a folksong." Their differences from each other are celebrated, as they are depicted as complementary beings: "Sarah is swarthy and ill-dressed" and Anna, whose clothes may be "cheap," seems dressed "always in rhythm." Through her intimate portraits of Sadie, her quick sketches of Anna and Sarah, as well as nameless female bodies whose desires are evoked throughout the poem, Ridge suggests the transformative power of the new land, life outside the insular ghetto, and its influence on young women. Ridge creates in Sadie a complicated immigrant new woman who must make her way in a setting shaped both by traditions in which she no longer believes and a history that she acknowledges has prepared her for the struggles of the new world. As Susan A. Glenn observes in *Daughters of the Shtetl,* many immigrant Jewish women had been influenced by the Jewish Labor Bund movement in the Russian pale. Socialist in nature, the bundists embraced the radical philosophies circulating in late-nineteenth-century Russia: "Women derived from the socialist movement a sense of personal dignity and importance available nowhere else in Jewish society. With their commitment to the principle of social equality, Jewish socialists moved tentatively toward the idea of gender equality. . . . Women and men would together make the revolution as comrades in struggle" (38).

Sadie embodies desire, self-knowledge, perseverance. Ridge's powerful lines weave this character from laborer, "She—fiery static atom," to student of the latest philosophical trends: "Nights, she reads / [th]ose books that have most unset thought, / [n]ew-poured and malleable." She establishes the ambiguous position of the "static" female worker and the "malleable" mind of the immigrant woman in search of the new ideas. As Sadie embraces feminism and anarchism, like her creator, she further articulates ghetto activism, its internal and external influences, its embrace of the old world and absorption into the new. Sadie, in fact, personifies the very contradictions of ghetto life as they are scripted. Her "fire," whether in her exhausting sweatshop work, her intellectual pursuits, her sexual life, or her activism, like the candles lit by female members of the family on the Sabbath eve, is never extinguished. Sadie's voice, suggested by her "lit eyes kindling the mob . . . [that] dances madly at a festival" is reminiscent of a statement attributed to Emma Goldman that twenty-five years ago appeared on many T-shirts: "If I can't dance, I don't want to be in your revolution."[42] That pleasure must be conjoined with struggle is one of Ridge's important observations in "The Ghetto." Give us bread, but give us roses too, Ridge implicitly suggests, connecting the desires and dilemmas of young ghetto women like Sadie, Anna, and Sarah to earlier labor struggles such as the 1912 textile mill strike in Lawrence, Massachusetts.[43]

In fact, Sadie's voice is also reminiscent of the young immigrant Jewish women who created themselves intellectually and politically as strike leaders in New York City's rapidly expanding garment industry. Annelise Orleck's recent study of working-class women's politics in the United States, *Common Sense and a Little Fire,* outlines the contributions of four immigrant Jewish women who began their political activism on the Lower East Side: Fannia Cohn, Clara Lemlich, Pauline Newman, and Rose Schneiderman. These women, like Sadie, were born "into a world swept by a firestorm of new ideas, where the contrasting but equally messianic visions of orthodox Judaism and revolutionary Socialism competed for young minds" (17). Orleck defines the aspirations of these four women whose lives mirror the ascent of working-class women's political activism: "These marginally educated immigrant women wanted to be more than shop-floor drudges. They wanted lives filled with beauty—with friendships, books, art, music, dance, fresh air and clean water" (16). To further emphasize the importance of getting both "bread and roses," the trope most often associated with immigrant working-class women, Orleck quotes Pauline Newman, later to become an important figure in both the International Ladies Garment Workers Union and the Socialist Party: "a working girl is a human being . . . with a heart, with desires, with aspirations, with ideas and ideals." For radical outsiders like Ridge at that moment in U.S. history, immigrant Jewish female desire appeared to represent the energy as well as the social and aesthetic possibilities of a young land. And in this young land there was room for transgression. Perhaps Sadie's boldest act is taking a "Gentile lover." Sadie, secularized and sexualized, complicates paternal orthodoxy by mixing with goyim (and thus represents modernist mixing as well). Though her brother Bennie has himself a "Christian woman," Sadie's mother realizes that her daughter's "breach" will do less harm to traditional family integrity: "A man is not so like, / If they should fight, / To call her Jew."

Ridge seems particularly fascinated by such transgressions as they represent the inevitable clash of old-world traditions and new-world ideas. She focuses upon both the stifling grip of tradition and the communal spirit that is part of the Jewish legacy. The ghetto walls, oppressive in their enclosure of a "cramped . . . shut flesh," also act as nurturer, for the ghetto is the site of Jewish life and culture. Indeed it prompts "wars, arts, discoveries, rebellions, travails, immolations, / cataclysms, hates." The traditions and transgressions as they clash inside "The Ghetto" are perhaps best articulated through the poem's shifting focus from work to leisure. Evening is used distinctly as a bridge between the brutality of work, particularly in the sweatshop, and the erotic encounters between young working women and men after hours. As dusk descends upon the ghetto it is presented as a protective curtain shrouded in maternal imagery: "The old mammy night" with "wide-opening crooked and comforting arms," and "a voluminous skirt."

In the poem's penultimate section, Ridge juxtaposes the closing of the work day with sexual awakening:

Lights go out
And the stark trunks of the factories
Melt into the drawn darkness,
Sheathing like a seamless garment.

The factories, as they shut, "melt" away; the above lines also hint at the removal of clothing—the oppressive material of the workday. The "seamless garment" suggests the naked body, and the darkness that cloaks it will ultimately be its liberator. Ensuing descriptions of the moon "blond and burning, creeping to their cots" further intimate the laboring body released into the erotics of nightfall. Ridge endows this moon with sexual symbolism as it watches over the nighttime ghetto "like a skull":

Nude glory of the moon!
That leaps like an athlete on the bosoms of the young girls
     stripped of their linens;
Stroking their breasts that are smooth and cool
     as mother-of-pearl
Till the nipples tingle and burn as though little lips
     plucked at them.
They shudder and grow faint.
And their ears are filled as with a delirious rhapsody,
That Life, like a drunken player,
Strikes out of their clear white bodies
As out of ivory keys.

This passage is striking considering its location in a poem in which, as I previously discussed, cultural alienation and labor exploitation are so adroitly represented. Important to note, the moon invades this passage to suggest, as does the metaphor of the "cramped ova," that the ghetto is also a sexual and erotic space. The "Life" that has been drained from the young Jewish workers as they perform their sweatshop labor, "strikes out of their clear white bodies" as evening descends and enters their erotic bodies. While the image of life striking out of "clear white bodies" also suggests sexual climax, the poet hopes to connect the erotic possibilities of the crowded ghetto with "life" as a cause for celebration, a defining trope of Jewish communal existence that continues to sustain itself through centuries of exile.

While Ridge represents the Jewish ghetto from a feminist perspective—often depicting it as a feminized space—this discussion of the poem would be incomplete without pointing to her construction of men's experience of ghetto life. Ridge's interest in the "material" aspects of ghetto life highlights the social as well as economic contributions of its male inhabitants, and her exploration of the material has a double meaning here. There is literal material sold by peddlers, rewoven by ragpickers, and there is the material of life—cultural material. The figures that populate this text make and remake themselves; they find themselves "[f]lung / [l]ike an ancient tapestry of motley weave / [u]pon the open wall of this new land."

This juxtaposition of "ancient" and "new" is, as previously noted, another central motif of Ridge's ghetto. American newness, its open wall, is contrasted with a people whose history is as ancient as their American experience is new. The ghetto as a new, feminized space is also home to a patriarchal past, though one usurped by European (and hence American) exile, emancipation, and subsequent assimilation. For every "young trader" peddling "the notions of the hour,"[44] there is "an old grey scholar," or "one who holds / [t]he wisdom of the Talmud stored away / [i]n his mind's lavender." And there are men like Old Sodos who have lost their trades through emigration, not to mention other reminders that one is amidst "that old race that has been thrust / [f]rom off the curbstones of the world." Yet, Ridge best articulates this distinction of old and new when she presents, in the sixth section, a "dingy cafe" where "the old men sit muffled in woolens."

Here "young life and young thought are alike barred." The radicalism imported from Europe that is advocated in the sweatshop and outside the ghetto walls is prohibited lest it should enter "trampling with sacrilegious feet!" Ridge is acutely conscious of the "ancient things" that the old men strive steadfastly to preserve: their Judaic traditions, the talmudic teachings that faced contamination through incessant exiles and emigrations.[45]

Ridge also sees the influences these traditions and teachings have had on the developing revolutionary movements of her day. The young men engage in a clash of "Egos yet in the primer." Whereas the desire for change appears rather harmoniously when focused on women, Ridge seems to find the men's "majestic discordances" endearingly comic; thus she informs us that there is dissension even among the dissenters:

One, red-bearded, rearing
A welter of maimed face bashed in from some old wound,
Garbles Max Stirner.
His words knock each other like little wooden blocks.
No one heeds him,
And a lank boy with hair over his eyes
Pounds upon the table.
—He is chairman.[46]

If these lines suggest the poet's intimate knowledge of radical organizing, consider the following comment Ridge makes to Harold Loeb upon contacting him about her position as American editor of *Broom*. Probably to sell herself as one efficient in handling chaos, she describes her experiences as an organizer for the Ferrer Association: "Every new measure had to be put to the vote, and I had to fight hostile forces inside that mob of three hundred—mostly foreigners and all wild unkempt spirits, haling from one another by its hair that new, wonderful doll, Liberty" (Avrich, *Modern School Movement* 92). In fact, elsewhere in the poem's sixth section, Ridge gives a veteran organizer's attention to that "doll": "Liberty, / [t]railing her dissolving glory over each hard-won / barricade—/ [o]nly to fade anew." Ridge creates on the page a confrontational space in which to argue the difficulties of articulating and executing a program for social change. She reminds us that the battles of the poor, the disenfranchised, of women, and people of color are frequently losing ones. Acknowledging that "glory" dissolves, perhaps referencing her own political burnout in the Ferrer Association, which she left in 1912, and that "barricades" fade, Ridge is also suggesting that the realist elements she has presented in this poem are often overshadowed by the splendor and spectacle of the image.

"That Life," which emanates from the working-class Jewish bodies—both female and male—that Ridge describes in this important poem, is also part of her closing commentary on community. Ridge describes life as an electric current, intellectually charged, sustaining a "race" of people for thousands of years: renewing it, remaking it, creating in it a modern, urban core. As part of the poem's denouement, "Life" is at first capitalized and rounded with an exclamation point. It is "Startling, vigorous." It is also "Articulate, shrill, / [s]creaming in provocative assertion":

> Electric currents of life,
> Throwing off thoughts like sparks,
> Glittering, disappearing,
> Making unknown circuits,
> Or out of spent particles stirring
> Feeble contortions in old faiths
> Passing before the new.

Life is the movement of the communal body of the ghetto in the city: "Life / [p]ent / overflowing / stoops and facades / jostling, / pushing, / contriving / [s]eething as in a great vat." The body is in constant motion, perpetual activity, discussion, disagreement: "Bartering, changing, extorting / [d]reaming, debating, aspiring / [a]stounding, indestructible." Not only does this metropolitan communal body celebrate life by heeding its struggles and its "majestic discordances," but the language by which it defines itself as a communal body is spoken almost entirely in the present continuous. This grammar is perhaps Ridge's strongest suggestion—and hence the powerful impression she leaves us with: that this is a community in continuous formation. Thus Ridge's articulation of the working-class Jewish community inside "the ghetto" is one always producing potential, always a community of men and women making themselves in the world. "The Ghetto" sings the body electric of America's urban masses.

Lola Ridge published only five books of poetry in her life. Her productivity was continually interrupted by chronic illness. Critical assessment of her work was mixed throughout her relatively brief career, probably because Ridge was not interested in being fashionable. Yet her work was always topical. A fitting, largely unknown fact about Ridge is that she won the Shelley Memorial Prize two years in a row, in 1934 and 1935. After her death in May 1941, Samuel A. DeWitt established the Lola Ridge Memorial Award, which was discontinued in 1950. The Cold War had begun in earnest, and the recognition of American poets on the left began to disappear. In postwar poetry anthologies, histories of modern American poetry, and literary biographies, Ridge seemed never to have existed, despite the statement in her *New York Times* obituary that she was one of America's "leading contemporary poets."

The women's movement of the 1970s briefly brought Ridge back after her memory had been silenced for nearly thirty years. Her work appeared in two influential anthologies that came out during that important decade of "second wave" feminism: *The Women Poets in English* (1972), edited by Ann Stanford, and *The World Split Open* (1974), edited by Louise Bernikow. It would make sense that a new feminist movement would reclaim her. She had been, after all, a feminist and an anarchist. She had lived in a common-law union with a man twelve years her junior for close to a decade before they married legally. She had known Margaret Sanger, had done political work with Emma Goldman, had read Edward Carpenter and believed in "homosexual" rights. Although she had lived in poverty most of her writing life, she gave her last $100 to the young Kay Boyle for an abortion. Yet, unlike other rebel girls, second-wave feminism did not make Lola Ridge's name a household word.

Ridge's later works—from her book-length poem, *Firehead* to her sonnet cycle "Via Ignis," published in her final book *Dance of Fire*—as well as her travels to the Near East and Mexico, reveal an interest in mysticism. At the time of her death she was at work on "Lightwheel," a five-book project with an ambitious historical focus. It is also significant that in 1935, in the middle of the Depression, as national socialism threatened Europe, Ridge, in writing of past and current dark history, would remark that we "may come for a period, into a time of light" (Sproat 475). What would Lola Ridge have thought about the social and cultural revolutions of the West in the 1960s? It is unlikely that she would have characterized the West today as having entered into such "a time of light."

Calling Western Union

Party Lines and Private Lines in Genevieve Taggard's Poetry

She speaks from all these faces
and from the center of a system of lives
who speak the desire of worlds moving unmade.
Muriel Rukeyser, "Anne Burlak"

To "speak to the desire of worlds moving unmade" might be the best way to categorize the aims of radical women poets writing during the Depression. The above lines, written in praise of the efforts of a female communist organizer, also suggest the ways in which words themselves create the possibility for action. For women to recognize their "lives" at "the center of a system" not only evokes the transformative power of dialogue but also the necessary participation of women in any program for social change. Genevieve Taggard (1894–1948), an active left voice from the 1920s through the 1940s, whose work remains out of print and whose name has disappeared from our cultural memory, hoped to speak both to and for women.[1] She also hoped to find a way to understand the clash between private and public worlds within which women poets would make their identities in the interwar period. Taggard's activist voice particularly during the 1930s, which no doubt helped to bury her reputation as an important American poet in the highly conservative postwar literary climate, provides us with vital commentary, not only about the social crises of the decade but also of the participation of women writers and intellectuals in shaping its dialogue.

Genevieve Taggard was born in Waitsburg, Washington, in 1894. She spent her girlhood in Hawaii, where her Christian missionary parents had gone to open a public school. She attended the University of California at Berkeley, where her mother ran a boardinghouse to help pay for the education of her three children. Taggard published poems while at Berkeley, and she published her first book in 1922 after moving east to New York. Already a socialist since her college days, once in New York Taggard took part in radical and feminist Greenwich Village bohemian culture.

While a key component of this chapter is the poetry Taggard wrote and published in the 1930s, her writing and activities of the 1920s helped to shape the mature militancy in her later work. It is also important to consider Taggard's early work as part of an enormously prolific period for feminist poetry. Taggard also began to take on an activist role, an important step that challenges the claim that the woman activist role disappeared after 1920 with the ratification of the Nineteenth Amendment, granting suffrage to adult women. Lola Ridge's antideath penalty, antilynching, proworker lyrics of the 1920s suggest that women still actively engaged in public discourses. Similarly, by 1925 Taggard had become an active participant in left cultural debates about transforming society in the wake of widespread feeling that capitalism had failed. She edited *May Days,* an anthology of poetry from the *Masses* and the *Liberator,* left magazines with which she was associated. When the *New Masses* was founded in 1926 she became a contributing editor along with Lola Ridge and a long list of other left-oriented writers. In fact, *New Masses* founders Mike Gold and Joseph Freeman had been admirers of Taggard's early work.

Taggard published seven books in the 1920s. She wrote or edited a total of eighteen books in a relatively brief life: she was only fifty-two when she died in 1948. Though Taggard published her significant volumes of poetry with an important publisher (Harper Brothers) and frequently read her work "over the air" on radio stations WQXR and WNYC, she is best known by scholars for her biography of Emily Dickinson, which was published in 1930. When asked to describe her reception as a poet in *Twentieth Century Authors* (1942), she remarked: "When I face the fact my poetry is not very much read in my own country I console myself by the fact that my work has been translated into many foreign languages" (Kunitz 1381).

Taggard was also an internationalist. She desired to see herself as part of the "excellence of world literature," while acknowledging that the American literary culture of her time was stuffy, elitist, and removed from "the life and talents of the American people." Curiously, Taggard's description of herself as "unread" contradicts the very active connection that Cary Nelson notes left poets had with their audiences during the Depression: "For a brief moment in American literary history writing poetry became a credible form of revolutionary action. Reading poetry, in turn, became a way of positioning one's self in relation to the possibility of basic social change" ("Poetry Chorus" 32).

Though it is hard to imagine now, there was a lively culture of class-centered writing and reading in the 1930s in the United States and internationally. Taggard no doubt saw herself marginalized within a modernist tradition that devalued the kind of work the Depression consistently asked her to produce. Yet, regardless of whether Taggard was able to see herself from outside the canonical modernist and masculinist gaze, she nonetheless participated in an aesthetic campaign that was "paradoxically, one of the triumphs of a time of widespread suffering" ("Poetry Chorus" 34). Though

Taggard may have been neglected by the conventional canons of American modernism, she was embraced and appreciated by many women, other radicals like herself, those she taught, and those otherwise marginalized who recognized themselves and their struggles in her poetic articulations.

This chapter focuses on the work Taggard did as a poet-activist within the context of the Depression and its accompanying left-wing mass movements. Through this focus, the neglected territory of women's activist poetry of the 1930s is navigated. These women's commitment to representing themselves and the struggles that mattered to them is suggested here in Taggard's importance as a Depression-era feminist poet, represented through her insistence upon merging the poetic line with the picket line. Two works that reflect on her earlier concerns—her Hawaiian childhood and her interest in the metaphysical poetry tradition respectively—are examined. This chapter is foregrounded with Taggard's representative Depression-era text *Calling Western Union*. It is an important text because it not only reflects Taggard's interest in reading the Depression through both poetic and gendered lenses but also shows, through memoir and the inclusion of a poem previously published in the 1920s, a revision of her radical self to meet the demands of the increasingly radicalized environment of the 1930s. While connecting Taggard's interest in women's participation in social struggle with her attempt to map out a female tradition, this chapter also considers her cultural work as it reaches beyond gender and politics. Her interest in African American cultural practice as an inspiration to her own creation of a socially conscious aesthetic connects race to her classed and gendered work. The chapter closes with a series of poems Taggard wrote "to the Negro People," which appeared in *Long View* (1942).

Taggard's 1936 work *Calling Western Union* created a space in which women's activities, both domestic and political, could be represented. Rebecca Pitts described *Calling Western Union* in her review in the *New Masses:* "The poems range from little satirical portraits of decay, through simple and moving records of poverty and sorrow, and militant chants of the masses, brave and unbeaten, to songs of the future which somehow clothe with emotional reality our dreams of collective living" (22). Pitts, who, like Taggard, wrote philosophical pieces on communism for the *New Masses* (including some on women in the communist movement), names a central concern of Taggard's 1930s' verse as images that "clothe . . . our dreams of collective living." Images of men and women moving together, through labor and through protest, dominate the text.

The collection's title evokes the urgency and emergency of desperate times to which Taggard, with a large number of writers and artists, bore witness. Poems became emergency messages sent via Western Union. In the age in which telecommunication was just beginning, poems chanting headlines like telegrams were a novel response. During the Depression, Taggard decided that lines of poetry would be created "along the lines of" a social narrative. She would confront the aesthetic world of poetry and its "lines" with the materiality of everyday life. Poetry could no longer be written or thought of as merely "lines" of verse or as a series of "lines" that extol an idea or "thing," as William Carlos Williams had insisted. Reading modern poetry in the middle of the Depression began to evoke other lines. The poetry in *Calling Western Union* exposes us to bread lines, picket lines, and party lines (meaning the dogmatic strictures of certain left-wing discourses) inextricably linked to lines of poetry.

Taggard also saw how the domestic and social spaces inhabited by women were tied to these lines. Women were confounded daily by material lack, and women poets like herself were confounded daily by the need to address the private and public spaces contained inside editors' and readers' lines of expectations about what poetry should and should not do. What is more, the protest or picket line, a significant symbol of Depression culture, was a site where women could be found chanting their demands like lines of verse. Taggard's interest in working-class politics expands the role of women and their lines. If working-class women were not writing their own verses, they were at least supporting or standing on picket lines. Taggard uses the poetic line to articulate the protest or picket line, and creates political subjectivity for women in her poems.

Throughout *Calling Western Union,* Taggard engages her readers through a desire to stretch the lines of her poems out to the protest line, to merge "word" with "deed," as she tells us in "Life of the Mind, 1934." Her desire is to transform the isolated line of poetry into a script for collective chants. By making poetic lines themselves metaphors for social engagement, Taggard insists that protest lines and political lines, as they develop an alternative to the bread line and employment line, become the next "line" for poetry. Similarly by urging a new line for poetry, Taggard is also calling for a "new product." Given her interest in women, one might equate this new "product line" for poetry, as if it were the latest lipstick color.

In "To My Daughter," with its epigraph "On Refusing to Take Out Life Insurance," Taggard attempts to complicate the conflation of poetic and protest line. By constructing a poem in which men, women, and children move together in protest, she asks poetry, now wedded to social action, to offer a "different insurance," as well as to rewrite the bread lines endemic to Depression life. Taggard's lines of poetry as they become merged with, conflated by, and extremely entangled within the social theater of want and lack begin to form their own discourse.

Not only does Taggard problematize both poetic and picket line, she crosses class lines. In the poem "At Last the Women Are Moving," she celebrates middle-class women who have finally come out in protest, finally emerging from their seemingly disconnected lives to join the struggles of their working-class sisters. Taggard is herself a middle-class writer crossing class lines in solidarity, taking the private middle-class expression found in the poetic line and recharging it with the public energy found in working-class protest. For example, in the poem "A Middle-Aged, Middle-Class Woman at Midnight," she describes a woman, much like herself, who can't sleep because she is thinking about the misery of striking marble workers. Taggard revises her stance as distanced observer, as modernist poet, by crossing into the territory of the popular, leaving behind the Eliotian figure of white male modernism as he cries "metaphor, metaphor why hast thou forsaken me" ("Funeral in May"). With this challenge to modernism's traditional canon, Taggard engages in uniting both private and public lines. She hopes to see those poetry lines traditionally associated with the domain of the individual, isolated poet reach out to embrace public desire. She literally takes her writing *out on the line.*

Taggard constructs these politicized lines of poetry in a radical literary atmosphere in which the party line was debated by communist and other left-wing poets in terms of how to represent working-class subjectivity in their verses. By the time *Calling Western Union* appeared, two distinct left literary lines had developed. The *New Masses,* closely associated with the

Communist Party U.S.A., weakened its stance toward proletarian realism, abetted by the party's rightward shift to accommodate a Popular Front. On the other hand, radicals disillusioned with the magazine's sectarianism started the *Partisan Review.* Their goal was a magazine that "would be free of any political ties and would be devoted to the most advanced literature, adopting the style of earlier magazines of aesthetic revolt" (Gilbert 159). Neither tendency, as both Constance Coiner and Paula Rabinowitz have argued, was able to *see* gender issues. On the rare occasions when such issues were acknowledged, they were dismissed as unimportant.

"At Last the Women Are Moving" epitomizes the linguistic ambiguity of poetic line and picket line. It not only gives voice to women's activism in Depression-era America but also challenges both modernist and male-left lyrics by politicizing the poetic line and gendering the picket line. The poem appears early within the pages of *Calling Western Union* and assumes the inevitability of women's participation in social struggle. In "At Last the Women Are Moving," Taggard acknowledges and constructs the importance as well as complications of (to use Sheila Rowbotham's dichotomous phrase) "women in movement." Movement is an important trope. It signifies the progress these women make, while they participate in the "progressive." Their moving will make a movement.

The poem engenders female empowerment by presenting women in two stages—uncertainty followed by commitment. Its flow is direct, like the procession it describes—a protest march and women's enlisting in acts of resistance. Yet the poem does convey an ironic tone as it asks where have the women been—why have they been still? Taggard, in effect, wants her readers to consider the significance of these first steps, even if they are done with trepidation: "Last, walking with stiff legs." She also conveys the silence blocking women's entrance to public actions, which further emphasizes the importance of the women's neophyte steps because "Such women looked odd, marching on American / asphalt." Thus Taggard's vocabulary stresses the awkwardness of movement: this last group in a procession of marchers, these "mothers, housewives, old women." Their clothes are "bunched," their steps "stiff" and "anxious." They "hobble," compared to the more experienced marchers (read men) who erectly bear "wide banners." Curiously, these "sexualized" bodies of men are clichéd, so the entrance of these awkward women creates an anarchic twist to the smooth, masculine line of the procession.

Taggard juxtaposes what the women normally "know"—"kitchens . . . sinks, suds . . . pennies"—as well as "Dull hurry and worry, clatter . . . back-ache" with the fact that they now have achieved a kind of parity of militancy with the men. Yet it is the newness of their participation, the oddity that they seem to represent, that makes their action—their presence—that much more powerful. These women, generally identified through the private body of the domestic sphere, become part of the larger public space; thus they are resituated as militant workers and refigure women's work as work. Important to note, one of the underlying (and culminating) articulations of this poem is the absolute preparedness of all women for the task of taking militant measures. Taggard rhetorically asks: "How did these timid, the slaves of breakfast and supper / Get out in the line, drop for once dishrag and broom? / Here they are as work-worn as stitchers and fitters," that is, their sisters and brothers who are wage laborers. She thus suggests that women belong here; their domestic responsibilities have paved their way to the line: "These, whose business is keeping the body alive, / These are ready, if you talk their language, to strike." The poet ultimately wants her readers to see this private "language" of domestic life as converging with all the other languages of labor.[2]

Taggard's attention to the movement of women's bodies is an important representation of where a number of women poets placed themselves in the 1930s. As stated in this book's introduction, a wide spectrum of left newspapers and journals from the Communist Party paper the *Daily Worker* to the NAACP journal the *Crisis* published radical lyrics by women poets in which they reminded readers that gender (and race) were as much a part of the Depression landscape as were bread lines, picket lines, and employment lines. In fact these women's verses, written in a variety of styles, reflected the quotidian concerns of 1930s readers. For example, Muriel Rukeyser's work refashions the fragmented modernist lyric into a brand of documentary reportage, which in the case of one particular poem cycle, records the spread of silicosis in a West Virginia mining town: the voices of the victims, their wives, and mothers speak through her pen. Lucia Trent's poetry, written in traditional forms such as the sonnet and ballad stanza, satirizes ruling class indifference toward mass hunger and unemployment. "Breed, Women, Breed" represents women trapped in their reproductive role, breeding "for the owners of mills and the owners of mines" (Nekola and Rabinowitz 168). African American poets like Margaret Walker and Gladys Casely Hayford sought to give voice to their working-class sisters by exploring the harsh conditions of black female labor while also depicting the women's fortitude.[3] Martha Millet, whose poems and articles appeared in Communist Party publications such as *Working Woman* and the women's pages of the *Daily Worker,* produced poetry to help encourage women's participation in mass actions.

As I also maintain in this book's introduction, as much as these women wrote, and however loudly their poems screamed issues of central importance to Depression-era women, their writing was overshadowed by male voices. Proletarian realism, as advocated by the communist movement's chief literary arbiter, Mike Gold, assumed a male body—the muscular, toiling sensibility of the male worker.[4] In Gold's view, proletarian writing should be "masculine." Bourgeois writing was, for Gold, by definition "feminine"; it was self-reflexive and explored the nuances of language rather than examining and detailing the experience of labor.[5] In "Go Left Young Writers!" Gold exalted the young workers writing in "jets of exasperated feeling" (but with "no time to polish") (51). Yet women's proletarian poetry about "feeding the children," joining the pickets, selling their wares (and their bodies), and fighting for a new world alongside their men was for the most part ignored by both the radical literary circles under Gold's persuasive gaze and the "bourgeois" tradition he detested.

The Depression in the United States brought devastating changes to the lives of ordinary women and men. Writers like Taggard, sensitive to the social demolitions they saw exponentially increasing, altered their aesthetic practice to reflect the bleak realities they witnessed daily. The Communist Party, with its many organizing campaigns, its cultural groups like the John Reed Clubs, and its little magazines, began to inspire and create a sense of identity for those writers concerned about the culture of deprivation the Depression had created. Women's issues, concerns central to both Taggard and to this discussion, are decidedly absent from the party's particularly androcentric agenda. Though it would be shortsighted to maintain that

Calling Western Union is written mainly with Taggard's feminist interests in mind, the poems from this collection center upon those that engage, not to mention merge, gender and class concerns, as in the poem, "At Last the Women Are Moving." Taggard's verse from the 1930s never advocates a feminism separate from her interest in communism, yet her insistence in writing women into the spaces of radical literature is evident in poems like "Feeding the Children," which complicates women's inscription within the domestic sphere. This is a way that Taggard begins to challenge the party line, even as she remained a committed communist, though not a party member.

The focus on Taggard's merging of labor and domestic politics within the pages of *Calling Western Union* highlights what Paula Rabinowitz rightly maintains to be the important documentary tendency of 1930s radical intellectuals: "By creating a rapport between the direct experiences of those who suffered and struggled and the writers who came into contact with them, reportage served to link the bread lines to the headlines." Rabinowitz contends that the various genres of fiction, drama, and poetry "sought to re-create the immediacy and power offered by the direct testimony of reportage" (2). Rabinowitz examines Taggard's own "intellectual" metaphor for documenting action, "word-in-deed," from her poem "Life of the Mind, 1934" (see below).[6] Rabinowitz complicates the netherworld of the woman intellectual with the androcentric male left's inability to reconcile the contributions of intellectuals in general with its predilection for masculine images of direct action. She maintains:

> For women writers, as for all leftist intellectuals, the Depression functioned as the political ground onto which the figure of personal aesthetic response was etched. This response dwelled in contradictions—between personal experience (the body) and political doctrine (the text), and between personal witness inscribed in the (narrative) urge to act. (41)

Women intellectuals like Genevieve Taggard "who wrote about their working class sisters" embodied this dichotomy between "word" and "deed" (the personal and the political), as part of the "substance of their writings" (42). Taggard's 1930s verses—indeed the poems in *Calling Western Union* examined here—often chant like headlines, while inscribing the theater of social deprivation evidenced in the bread line. They describe women empowered by strikes and mass actions and link poetic language to the social viability of reportage. In fact, Taggard as a committed marxist and signer of the call for an American Writers Congress (to combat "the new wave of race hatred, the organized anti-Communist campaign and the growth of Fascism") (Aaron 313) seems to have developed, through her radical affiliations, a desire to work with the aesthetic agenda endorsed by certain communist literati. A few poems utilize a formula: in effect, a translation of proletarian narratives into the cadences of modernist verse. Yet Taggard, unlike most party writers, sees it necessary to include women within this formula, which (roughly) presents them, in the first half of "At Last the Women Are Moving," as timorous or even hostile to the idea of strikes and other forms of social activism. As the poem progresses, through their own experience with shortages, hunger, or even emotional fatigue, the women realize their social victimization and join those already enlightened men and women in action.

What is significant about Taggard's attention to this particular narrative of progressive enlightenment is that she generally does not construct the poems so that this propagandistic agenda is its most obvious aspect. Nor does she adhere merely to an agenda that is completely realist. Familiar modernist tropes such as ambiguity and irony, fragmented speech and fractured lines invade her representations of class struggle. In fact, one critic, reviewing *Calling Western Union* for the *New Republic,* described the poems as "so truncated and subtle that only a poet like the one [Taggard] gleefully buries in 'Funeral in May' would be capable of the discriminating response which their refractory method seems to presuppose" (324).

"Funeral in May," the poem to which the reviewer refers, though hardly representative of the social and popular aims of *Calling Western Union,* is Taggard's critique of the modernist poet's assertions of individuality as well as displacement. Taggard, in fact, attempts to take modernist music along with her on the picket line. The ironic tones and sense of estrangement represented by the solitary, apolitical figure characterized in "Funeral in May" is also evidenced in poems like "Adding Up America—You Try," and "Sing Lullaby," which castigate those who exist ignorantly and unfeelingly between bread lines and protest lines. With these more subtle critiques, she hopes to dispel the myth that the modern lyric needs to be objective—and the poetic line distanced from the protest line.

Whereas "At Last the Women Are Moving" presents the protest line as a new place for women in the public sphere, "Feeding the Children," in an attempt to represent the complicated spaces between the private and the public, both justifies and condemns women's reticence to engage in social action. "Women are conservative," she begins. "They want life to go on. . . . Groceries / Are important, and milk delivered each morning." Yet Taggard's emphasis on "conservative" has little to do with any political orthodoxies or theories; she uses conservative in the sense that women's obligation to their families places them in a precarious position of mediation: "I must feed my children. Keep the peace." Yet as the radical's outlook on conservatism maintains, traditions can stand in the way of action, of change. These women as they rightfully acknowledge responsibility also "frown at strikes" and "oppose / Sacrifice outside family." However, like the women in "At Last the Women Are Moving," these housewives too become witness to the trickle-down effects of the mean economy. The strike their husbands entertain ("risk your job for nothing, starve my babies! / . . . Tear up your card!") shortly becomes the very fight to "feed" the children and "Keep the peace." The word *feed* as it is juxtaposed with the word *peace* intimates the very clash that is at the center of these women's dilemma. Can there be peace when there is hunger? In a Depression-era setting of declining wages, rising prices, and massive shortages of necessary staples, Taggard inserts her economic critique as it specifically speaks to women:

> Now the egg-shell wall of home-sweet-home, holy and
>   humble,
> Cracks with the price of meat, the lack of milk.
> Out in the street they demonstrate her question.
> Food, clothes, beds . . . The picket-line is the
>   answer.

Ultimately privation consumes these "conservative" women, and they come around to the idea of social action. The poem's final stanza finds them transformed into fighting union wives: "We must feed the children. March today."

In "Feeding the Children," the end lines, from the penultimate and final stanzas—"The picket-line is the answer" and "Vote the strike!"—suggest sloganeering rather than the subtle textures and veiled meanings of canonical modernist verse. As is implied in the text's title, *Calling Western Union,* Taggard creates lines intended to carry urgent social messages. She resists modernist distancing as a way to offer direct engagement with her readers, in particular with those Depression mothers who are worrying about feeding the children.[7] The lines, instead, record the popular voice. They contain elements of the chant shouted by protest marchers since at least the early nineteenth century. For the poet who understands that she must "talk their language," lines that chant within the given social reality that they address enliven the poem and connect it to its readers. These chantlike verses, which may appear jarring to a reader taught to dissociate art from propaganda, enable the writer to subvert the complacent expectancy of both the domestic sphere she sees women attempting to transform and the stodgy literary codes that eschew both political and popular expression.[8]

Yet this propagandistic edge that the poet seemingly attaches to "Feeding the Children" is also connected to Taggard's search for an alternative discourse to the domestic sphere located within capitalism. Yet what Taggard sought was not as simply achieved as she desired. Shortly before the publication of *Calling Western Union,* the Communist Party shifted its focus "from the Third Period's emphasis on working-class revolution to the Popular Front's struggle against fascism," which saw a transformation from concern with "revolutionary girls" to "partisan mothers" (Rabinowitz 55). Since Taggard's poems combine the concerns of both periods in question, it is difficult to know whether as a nonparty radical she felt obligated to follow party prescriptions.

The radical woman artist's complicated task of negotiating the left's ideological terrain between revolutionary girls and partisan mothers might be better understood in a specific historical context. In 1936, Taggard visited Soviet Russia. In an interview with poet Martha Millet, printed in the *Daily Worker* shortly after her return, Taggard praised the gains Russian women had made, claiming that there was no "woman's problem" there. Women participated fully in all cultural endeavors with men and had equal access to traditional men's jobs such as flying planes, driving "trucks and street cars," "parachute" jumping, as well as editorial and technical work; she added that "of course" they were paid "the same as men for the same work" (13). Yet perhaps her highest praise was reserved for the treatment of mothers and their children: there were maternity and health insurance such as could not be hoped for in America "under any reform government," not to mention child care instead of child labor (13).

Taggard's uncritical remarks about the situation of women in the Soviet Union suggests how intellectual fellow-travelers, sporting their rose-colored glasses, embarked upon their tour of the revolutionary promised land. As Barbara Foley informs, the Communist Party made demands for services that would be beneficial to women and, during the Third Period, connected these demands to a critique of the capitalist nuclear family. Demands for maternity leave, day care, and birth control were also tied to a comparison between women's situations in the United States and the Soviet Union, quite like the comparison made by Taggard. Yet as Foley maintains, "[T]he praise of the presumed revolution in Soviet gender relations was at times embarrassingly uncritical" (226).[9] Constance Coiner finds similar prevarication that may have influenced the way Taggard and others viewed Soviet gender roles. "The CPUSA both misrepresented the status of women in the Soviet Union and exaggerated the advances women had made there, simplistically assuring its followers that, as one 1935 *Daily Worker* headline proclaimed, 'Legend of the Weaker Sex Effectively Smashed by the Position of Women in the Soviet Union: All Inequality Abolished by the October Revolution'" (41). Paula Rabinowitz, critiquing the CPUSA's glorification of motherhood, reminds us that by 1935 "Stalin had abolished many of the most progressive elements of the 1926 Family Code by making abortion and homosexuality illegal and by curtailing divorce" (7). Certainly Taggard's interests in women were not merely centered upon "feeding the children." Yet her overly sanguine reception of the changing gender system she noted in the Soviet Union as well as her uncritical response to the stepped-up repression of Soviet women's freedom suggests a contradiction that seems particular to socialist women of the 1930s. Taggard employs tropes to show mothers liberated through their willingness to take collective action; yet the voice that was once boisterous about women's personal freedom is quieter in *Calling Western Union.*

"Feeding the Children," as well as a few other poems explored below, must also be situated in an important national context. It appears to have been composed in direct response to the 1936 marble workers strike in Rutland, Vermont. Taggard became both active participant and poetic observer as a member of the United Committee to Aid Vermont Marble Workers. She had important connections to Vermont: she had taught at Bennington College from 1931 to 1935 and had bought a farm in East Jamaica. Though little scholarly attention has been paid to this strike, Taggard did help to write some of its history, not only through her poetry but also through her participation on the strike committee. The committee organized a hearing in which the workers and union officials could air their grievances. Though the marble bosses and government officials were invited to participate, none did. The hearing produced the "Verbatim Report of Public Hearing, Town Hall, West Rutland, Vermont, Feb. 29, 1936,"[10] a document that exemplified how the organizers, workers, wives, and committee members helped to write the strike's history. The initial dispute began, according to one West Rutland Union official, in early 1934 when the Vermont Marble Company refused to recognize the workers' right to organize and "tried to foist . . . a company union on [them]" (4):

On November 4, 1935, some 600 quarry and marble workers of the towns of Danby, Rutland, West Rutland, Center Rutland, Proctor and Florence, Vt. went on strike against the Vermont Marble Company, owned by the Proctor family. They were faced with unusual difficulties—tight company control of the marble industry and the political situation, lack of experience in industrial dispute, complete absence of governmental relief to the destitute, and an exceptionally severe winter. (N.p.)

Taggard's task as committee member was one of confrontation—though she had little success. She was asked to interview Mr. Proctor, the Vermont Marble Company president, as well as a Mr. Williams, the company treasurer. Mr. Proctor was "out of town." Mr. Williams "had no desire to be called to the phone," and another contact, a Mr. Frank Partridge, had nothing to say to a member of "this delegation," nor did he think would anyone else. It appears that Taggard's encounter with the company bosses fueled her desire to chant lines of hope and solidarity with those victimized by harsh economic conditions only exacerbated by one powerful family's greed.

A number of poems in *Calling Western Union,* for example, though not directly connected to labor struggles such as the Vermont strike, contain an air of sarcasm toward upper-class snobbery, middle-class indifference, and general social lethargy. Such verses, it seems, are there to remind readers of those, as was said in the 1960s, who were part of the problem, rather than the solution.

The strike was already into its third month at the time of the hearing. Discussions were particularly focused upon police brutality by drunken deputies that the company had hired essentially to provoke the strikers. A bloody battle ensued when the deputies set upon the men, slugging them "without any proclamation or orders to disperse." Five men were knocked unconscious and had to be "sewed up in the hospital" (5). A seventy-five-year-old rag-picker complained of being knocked down and bloodied by the deputies.

Wage discrepancies were also at issue. While the marble workers were unable to feed themselves and their families, the Vermont Marble Company incurred considerable profits. Ironically, while the workers and their wives and children starved, the company made hundreds of thousands of dollars supplying marble to the government so it could build new and refurbish old so-called halls of justice.

It is important to connect the Vermont strike and certain aspects of the strike in particular to Taggard's interest in representing the concerns of Depression women. No doubt the "women in the various communities involved in the strike" (22), whose testimony may have been brief, inspired Taggard in constructing women's complaints for a number of the poems in *Calling Western Union.* Rockwell Kent, a prominent left-wing artist and one of the organizers of the hearing, illustrated the front cover of the committee report, which was later published and distributed. The cover shows Kent's characteristic style of stark, streamlined figures. A statuesque woman carries an infant wrapped and crooked into her left arm; in her large right hand she clutches the tiny paw of a scrawny female child. Two other children, a boy and girl who appear mostly in shadow, flank her on each side. What Kent's cover illustration depicts is documented by the testimony therein of one

Mrs. Mereau.[11] Taking the stand with a baby in her arms, Mereau contended that the union had been responsible for supporting the strikers' families until they received relief from the state—the infamous relief that more often than not was not given to the needy who requested it. Mereau, testifying to the committee with statements about hunger and hopelessness ("We have enough potatoes for supper for the children tonight. None for tomorrow" [22]), exemplifies an important trope of Depression life generously used by writers and artists of the period.[12] Beyond describing generalized deprivation, she also depicts social attitudes toward working-class families harbored by the state institutions and industry-owning families to whom the destitute were in thrall. Mereau claims the right of working-class women to the essential dignity no doubt considered sacrosanct to families such as the Proctors.[13] Indeed it is documentary evidence of what Taggard stridently invents in "Feeding the Children":

> [I received] two quarts of milk a day, then they cut it down to one and said [the children] could drink water. I asked for underwear for the children. [They] said they could wear BVDs, they were good enough for them. We got one set of heavy underwear to go to school in; he told us to put the children to bed Saturday night, wash the clothes and dry them before they needed them for school. We asked for stockings and mittens and suits, and they didn't give them to us. (27)

Another of the striker's wives, a Mrs. Bujak, corroborated Mereau's testimony. She claimed she could no longer send her children to school because they had no warm clothes. Moreover, she told those present at the hearing that when she went to the Overseer of the Poor to request relief she was told that she was not eligible because she owned her own house.[14] (As Taggard reminds us in the preface to *Calling Western Union:* "In Rutland County the Overseer of the Poor is a Marble Company official" [xxxii].) Another woman, Mrs. Felyeo, discussed the difficulty of getting food. She requested relief from the authorities "three or four times" without success and informs the committee of her continued frustration:

> Last Thursday we went over to the Overseer of the Poor, Mr. Bromley, and we walked about seven miles to find him in the woods. He gave a

small order of a half-bushel of potatoes, one sack flour, two oleomarga-
rine, and two yeast cakes. He gave us the order to go down to the store
and get this stuff. When we got down there we could not lug the flour
home and also the potatoes. The storekeeper was supposed to bring it up
in the morning. When we got home when we could get the food, the
flour had not come. Only half the order turned up. (25)

The women's testimony provides only a fraction of evidence in the thirty-
plus page document that the committee produced, yet it provides an important look into the working-class domestic sphere within a Depression context. For Taggard, it seems that the laboring bodies of men in the quarries
and the activist bodies of men on the picket lines, as they are predictable
signs of Depression life, become complete representations only when they
are conjoined with the laboring bodies of women attempting to clothe and
"feed the children."

Another poem also inspired by the Vermont marble workers' strike, the
self-revelatory "A Middle-Aged, Middle-Class Woman at Midnight," suggests Taggard's attempt to work with and yet refigure the proletarian formula. The poem articulates Taggard's own position as a middle-class artist
while it explores her relationship to the dispossessed. In the poem Taggard
poignantly constructs her difference from the women moving en masse.
The fervent anticipation of "At Last the Women Are Moving" dissipates
into alienated longing. Instead a woman resigned to a "middle" ground,
where tranquilizers spell comfort, contemplates the coldness of her space:

> In the middle of winter, middle of night
> A woman took veronal in vain. How hard it is to
>   sleep
> If you once think of the cold, continent-wide
> Iron bitter. Ten below. Here in bed I stiffen.

With "continent-wide / Iron bitter," a metaphor for a Depression winter
that leaves a middle-class woman sleepless, Taggard then juxtaposes the
subjectivities of rich and poor against the realities of midwinter Vermont
where workers at the Vermont Marble Company have been on strike: "It
was a mink-coat Christmas said the papers. . . . / Heated taxis and orchids.

Stealthy cold, old terror / Of the poor, and especially the children." Still her desire to medicate stems from an anxious awareness: "In Vermont near the marble-quarries . . . I must / not think." In fact the speaker bears witness to starving men, women, and children, to "Hunger that has no haste."

Through this anxiety Taggard creates the speaker's somewhat ambiguous position. The poem splits in two (similar in formula to "Feeding the Children"). It begins with the speaker's desire to medicate herself as a form of removal, as if to announce that class difference isolates her from these striking workers. Nonetheless, her sympathies emerge. The reader, about to turn the page, discovers that the starving children become "our" children; the capitalist way of life, which has traditionally provided comfort to the middle classes, becomes the culprit: "In the Ford / towns / They shrivel. Their fathers accept tear gas and black-jacks." Thus Taggard draws a connection between hunger's "shrivelling" effects upon children and the police violence against the striking workers: "When they sleep, whimper. Bad sleep for us all." The poem in which a woman moans "O medicine / Give blank against that fact," assuming medication is the way to live through "the strike, the cold," approaches its denouement in teleological reflection. There is someone responsible for this misery—the hunger that "haunt[s] the houses of farmers, / destroyers / Of crops by plan." The folks in the city have been victimized too. And the voice of the "middle-aged, middle-class woman" floats through them: "Veronal / Costs money, too. Costs more than I can pay." The angry speaker, guilty by association, cannot afford another "night's long nightmare." The costs of poverty are too much. She sets her allegiances with the people exploited by those she holds responsible for the metaphoric poverty of her sleeplessness, which she connects with the more dire poverty of the strikers and their families: "Sheriffs, cops, / Boss of the town, union enemy, crooks and cousins." Moreover, she chants as finale a line so unpoetic it asks us—as do so many of the other poems from *Calling Western Union*—to reexamine how we have been using the concept *poetic:* "I hope the people win."

Taggard also explores the middle-class subject in the poem "Interior." Yet the self-castigation that floats through "A Middle-Aged, Middle-Class Woman at Midnight" is directed away from the author and projected upon an anonymous, apolitical "you." "A middle-class fortress in which to hide!"

she begins, exclaiming the isolation of middle-class life through its meta-phoric rampart, complete with a curtain that shrouds it "as if saying *No.*" "Noon" which is "ablaze, ablaze outside," is the important center of engage-ment where "outside people work and sweat." Yet Taggard's complicated contempt for middle-class isolation expresses itself most pointedly through images of a kind of feminine vanity and slothful emptiness:

> And after you doze brush out your hair
> And walk like a marmoset to and fro
> And look in the mirror at middle-age
> And sit and regard yourself and stare and stare
> And hate your life and your tiresome friends
> And last night's bridge where you went in debt;
> While all around you gathers the rage
> Of cheated people.

The repetition of "And" captures the mundane drone of the idle middle class that Taggard sets against those who are being "cheated." With these sentiments she echoes proletarian realist writers who often portrayed middle-class characters or referred to middle-class sensibility as impotent, ineffec-tual, noncommittal, and lethargic. These descriptions of weakness were then paired against portrayals of the working class as tough, resilient, and downtrodden.

Taggard, once again, ends her poem with the trope of mass action. The final reproach is both snide and absolute: "Will we hear your feet / In the rising noise of the streets? Oh no!" The streets become the dividing line for those willing to *blow the trumpet all the way,* to paraphrase Meridel LeSueur from her essay "The Fetish of Being Outside,"[15] and those who hide com-fortably behind their vanities inside their fortresses, mumbling to them-selves in low tones, "Oh no!"

The poem "Mill Town" returns us more directly to the site of labor struggle. It stands out from the majority of poems in *Calling Western Union* that speak particularly about women's Depression-era experience. Rather than presenting women in their middle-class security as in "A Middle-Aged, Middle-Class Woman at Midnight" and "Interior," or as they come to political consciousness as in "At Last the Women Are Moving" and "Feeding the Children," "Mill Town" presents the bleak realities of laboring women. Taggard introduces the poem with an epigraph from medical historian Paul de Kruif.[16] His book *Why Keep Them Alive* (1936), which appears to have inspired the poem's composition, details the public health crisis the Depression created, particularly the malnutrition and starvation of America's children. Taggard begins the poem as an accompaniment to de Kruif's dispiriting scenario, imagining the woman whose "womb is sick of its work with death."

> then fold up without pause
> The colored ginghams and the underclothes.
> And from the stale
> Depth of the dresser, smelling of medicine, take
> The first year's garments. And by this act prepare
> Your store of pain, your weariness, dull love,
> To bear another child with doubled fists
> And sucking face.

"Mill Town" provides a gendered vocabulary of working-class experience by suggesting the double meaning of the word *labor*. The woman of this "mill town" experiences the excessive strains of wage-labor and that of repeated childbirth. As the poem's opening lines explore domestic routine, the infant's tight rage is a reminder of the tenuous grasp the Depression-era mother has on the domestic milieu.

The poem's last seven lines show an ambiguous attitude toward the woman's poverty. What we might construe as a scolding tone stands out in these last lines. It is unlikely, however, that Taggard would intentionally reprimand the mill mother for her passivity. Her sympathetic eye for working-class conditions as they affect women and children would provide a more critically engaged treatment of her subject's circumstances. Since nowhere else in *Calling Western Union* does Taggard take the male left to task for its insensitivity to gender issues, it is unlikely that she means to appropriate its voice, chiding the woman for not politicizing her position. Instead it appears that the speaker's reproachful tone appropriates the voice of a hypocritical and judgmental social order, which rebukes working-class mothers who become pregnant repeatedly in an atmosphere of economic want.

Clearly it is best, mill mother,
Not to rebel or ask clear silly questions,
Saying womb is sick of its work with death,
Your body drugged with work and the repeated bitter
Gall of your morning vomit. Never try
Asking if we should blame you. Live in fear. And put
Soap on the yellowed blankets. Rub them pure.

In keeping with the poet's desire to portray the Depression-era woman who was not on the barricades, one must notice the poem's negative representation of the female body. Childbearing and mill work take serious tolls upon it. In childbirth it readies its "store of pain," "weariness," and "dull love"; negative too are the fruits of its labor. This "store of pain," one of Taggard's most disturbing images, exposes the womb as complicit in life as death; the "mill-mother" gives birth to children who then die of starvation. Thus the female body "drugged with work," incapacitated by morning sickness, and later the childbed of unanesthetized home birth, also represents the isolation of those women whose participation in the social struggle so important to the poet are eclipsed by domestic burdens; of course inequalities of class and gender officiate these burdens—a "womb sick of its work with death."

"Mill Town" presents perhaps the bleakest portrait of working-class life in *Calling Western Union*. It also complicates Taggard's desire to create a sense of hope in her readers and to keep with the objectives of the proletarian literature of the period to present the working class as progressive agents determined to usher in a new age and new culture. Taggard never claims, as did socialist and feminist writer Crystal Eastman in the early 1920s, that if and when capitalism fell, women would still be enslaved.[17] Yet her portrait of the captive mill-mother placed alongside a variety of poems whose themes are positive and optimistic, reveals the feminist poet's tensions between representing difficult social realities and imagining a future that could transcend them.

The poems directly or indirectly inspired by the Rutland marble workers' strike leads to another important signifier for Taggard's radical verse. Location played a major part in constructing the poet's identity. Taggard spent many years living and writing in New York City, yet Hawaii, Washington State, California, and Vermont also held territorial claims on her development as a radical and writer. Her geographic identity, which moves in a trajectory from West Coast to East Coast, calls into question any connection the poet might have to a fixed locus, preventing her from becoming a writer of one place, a New York poet, or, as Edmund Wilson, writing in the late 1920s, once referred to her, "a Poet of the Pacific." Vermont represents several distinct categories of "place" for Taggard. It is a part-time residence—a place, she maintains, to know as a "tourist"—as well as a site of her own continued radicalization. Although Taggard was born in Washington State, where her Puritan ancestors had gradually moved, first from Vermont, then from Missouri, she remained strongly identified with multicultural Hawaii, where she lived as a child. When she was two years old her parents, who were evangelical Disciples of Christ, took the family to these "colonized" islands, where they opened a missionary school. Taggard's descriptions of her seemingly unconventional Hawaiian childhood appear in the memoir "Hawaii, Washington, Vermont," first published in *Scribner's Magazine* in 1934, and then, in a revised form, as a preface to *Calling Western Union.* In addition to detailing the economic deprivation of her youth, the memoir is an early tribute to multiculturalism—though complicated by her parent's role as missionary "educators." Her fond reminiscence of Hawaii, evoking the child's perspicacity, explores racial and cultural difference and its effects upon her developing radical consciousness. Taggard reads her evangelical and Puritan roots by adopting Hawaii as her "garden of Eden; [her] newfound-land." Her saviors became the "Portuguese, the Filipinos, the Puerto Ricans, the Japanese, the Chinese, the Hawaiian-Chinese, and the hap-a-haoles" (xv). She came to identify herself as an islander, "as brown as natives and as happy-go-lucky," with her speech "full of Hawaiian expressions."[18]

The memoir is also an essential situating devise for Taggard's concerns as an American radical writer and political activist in the 1930s. Her early witnessing of colonial practice in Hawaii, as well as the social othering she experienced on her return to the mainland United States, enabled her to identify with, and skillfully interpret, the depth of suffering caused by racism at home, European fascism, the Depression, and the Civil War in Spain. The dust bowl, a familiar Depression-era symbol, appears with comparative familiarity in Taggard's reminiscences of eastern Washington State, where her family settled after leaving Hawaii when her father's health failed:

"Dust, ankle-deep, paved the main street" (xvi). "Dust storms blew over the wheat hills" (xvii). As Hawaii represented natural abundance available to even poor island dwellers, eastern Washington State represented only lack, mostly as a result of small-town prejudice and individual repression. "Outside there was stubble or dust, no grass. Children must not play in the orchards. If little girls were bored they could hem dish towels or swat flies" (xvi), and "[t]here were no ice cream cones, no cold lemonade, and no soda pop" (xviii).[19]

Taggard ends the memoir (as it was originally published in 1934) in contemporary Vermont where she owns a farm, where she has taught, and where "some of [her] people were buried more than a hundred years ago" (xxx). She expresses a fondness for Vermont, which reflects an attitude of detached interest. Though the poet has become "rooted" to Vermont through familial connections and through a desire for the beauty of its natural landscape, both connections engender, for Taggard, a falseness, when she begins to understand the state in terms of class relations. In her decision to resituate the memoir "Hawaii, Washington, Vermont," as a prefatory frame for *Calling Western Union,* she revises her conclusion. She attempts to distance herself from her earlier experiences seeing Vermont only through the eyes of "the summer visitor," the metropolitan intellectual who sees selectively, seeking out a space in which to rest and relax. In 1936, at the height of the Depression, Taggard begins to understand the actual, material and physical, "everyday" Vermont:

> I saw canned wood-chuck in the farmers' cellars. I saw slums in Brattleboro and Burlington. I knew children who picked ferns for a few cents a day. I knew a man who worked in a furniture factory for ten cents an hour! I saw his starved wife and children. . . . I saw five men who were sentenced to jail for their activity in the Vermont Marble Strike. I saw a voucher for two cents one worker got for a week's wages, all that was left after the company deducted for rent and light. . . . When they eat, the quarry workers eat potatoes and turnips. . . . In Rutland County the Overseer of the Poor is a Marble Company official. (xxxii)

Taggard rewrites "Vermont" from country retreat/weekend getaway to a site of working-class struggle and solidarity, using her own awakening to prepare readers for the militant lyrics of *Calling Western Union*. Many of the poems, written in response to the strike and the general state of Depression America, complicate the pastoral Vermont—vacationland of America. If she can learn to see the workers' struggle there and the horrors of rural poverty, so may the reader.

Yet before Taggard admits that she was "wrong about Vermont," she recalls a preoccupation of the 1920s modernist writer with the search for community and recalls that what led her back to Vermont was a sense of communal desire. In the 1930s much of this communal desire was taken up through involvement in the communist movement: organizations like the League of American Writers and its Writers' School in New York, the Teacher's Union, as well as communist-affiliated publications like the *New Masses*. Earlier, however, she had found her community in New York and Connecticut, where she lived after she was "married."[20] Yet Taggard writes of her Connecticut community with irritation rather than admiration:

> I saw . . . a writer or two who cheated our neighbors and wrote them up as country bumpkins. I knew when that happened that I did not agree with my group of fellow-writers that it was all right to outwit and exploit farmers who shared with them. But this was the doctrine of writers returned from Paris in *the dark ages, the 1920s*. (xxx; emphasis mine)

This mention of the 1920s as "the dark ages" and the confession of her developing alienation from "fellow-writers" are important to understanding Taggard's embrace of the idea of political subjectivity as she rearticulates her literary desires to the tune of 1930s proletarian culture. She describes 1920s culture as enforcing an elitist, individualist practice. Though Taggard was a politically committed leftist in the 1920s, her negative reading of the decade, constructed as "liberating" especially for women, is exemplified in rearticulations of work she produced during this time. She disengages two poems, "Life of the Mind, 1934" and "Everyday Alchemy," from their entanglement with "the dark ages" of the 1920s and its literary discourses. "Life of the Mind" invokes a biography of Emily Dickinson that Taggard worked on through much of the 1920s, and "Everyday Alchemy," originally published in 1921, represents Taggard's emphasis on the love lyric as well as her interest in the metaphysical poetry tradition. Their appearance in *Calling*

Western Union situates both poems within the discourse of literary radicalism, placing them and their author in dialogue with a changing readership inside a significantly altering social world.

"Life of the Mind, 1934," though not a poem about Emily Dickinson, tacitly reminds readers of Taggard's biography of the poet, *The Life and Mind of Emily Dickinson,* published in 1930 and reprinted in 1934.[21] The biography's title reflects Taggard's interest in giving "mind" to woman; in fact she wrote an "intellectual" biography of Dickinson, exploring how the dimensions of this nineteenth-century poet's idiosyncratic brand of verse reflected her peculiarly isolated existence.[22] Taggard's "life of the mind" meant one thing in the 1920s, while she worked in solitary on the very solitary literary figure, Emily Dickinson; by 1934, "life of the mind" became a call to action.[23] In "Life of the Mind, 1934" Taggard again merges poetic line with protest line, expressing the "will to endow" . . . "word-in-deed." The poem equates hunger with battle: "Necessity to eat, / Necessity to act," as well as equating writing with that very same battle: "And act aright renews / The mind's link with the arm." The poem's ultimate message is to align writing itself with struggle, "Now action like a sword. / Now to redeem the word." Finally, the linguistic byproduct of that battle must serve a particular end, as expressed in the poem's epigraph: "The words in the books are not true / If they never act in you."[24]

"Everyday Alchemy" has an interesting publishing history. It originally appeared in Taggard's first collection of poems, *For Eager Lovers* (1922). She then republished it in *Calling Western Union,* along with "Revolution" also from *For Eager Lovers.* In their early creation "Everyday Alchemy" and "Revolution" reflected the Greenwich Village bohemia's new social outlook of the 1910s and 1920s. Taggard joined important radical intellectuals such as John Reed, Max Eastman, and Floyd Dell in establishing an alternative literary and public culture. The Russian Revolution, experiments in nonconformist art and education, discussions about "alternative" forms of living, and a fascination with Freudian psychology, sexology, and sexual experimentation informed radical culture at this time, and no doubt influenced the writing of these two poems. Yet by republishing "Everyday Alchemy" and "Revolution" in the fervently political *Calling Western Union,* Taggard remakes these works. She emphasizes their social messages at a crucial point in her career as a writer and at a crisis point in American history.

In a 1938 interview in the *Daily Worker*, Taggard comments that during the period in which "Everyday Alchemy" and "Revolution" first appeared she had not yet developed her revolutionary potential as a poet. (The orthodox vocabulary that marxists such as Taggard adopted in the 1930s rejected, for the most part, the idea that one's personal politics—one's sexuality, one's expression of personal freedom—suggested any revolutionary potential.) As she claimed, "I really hadn't as yet found a way of writing. Most of the poems in my first few books were about love and marriage and having children." Taggard both acknowledges and distances herself from the postwar period and its experimental values: "There was a long period in the twenties, after the World War, when I was very discouraged. . . . We writers were still too involved in all the foolish ideas of our generation." Whether these ideas were foolish or not, Taggard's change in political outlook was the direct reason for republishing "Everyday Alchemy." The poem extols the private values that the poet's public consciousness would reject by the mid-1930s. Its republication complicates the poet's theme of the private body valorizing the private relationships of individuals over their social relationships as civil subjects:

> Men go to women mutely for their peace;
> And they, who lack it most, create it when
> They make, because they must, loving their men,
> A solace for sad bosom-bended heads. There
> Is all the meagre peace men get—no otherwhere;
> No mountain space, no tree with placid leaves,
> Or heavy gloom beneath a young girl's hair,
> No sound of valley bell on autumn air
> Or room made home with doves along the eaves,
> Ever holds peace, like this, poured by poor women
> Out of their heart's poverty, for worn men.

In form "Everyday Alchemy" is a truncated sonnet. It revises the love sonnet and reverses the relationship of strong man, weak woman. Rhythmically the poem holds a kind of simplicity; the repetition of the word *peace* suggests an overriding calm within the negative space constructed by the words and phrases (though used as tropes of comparison) connoting lack: "No mountain," "no tree with placid leaves," no sonorous "valley bell on autumn air." Thematically the poem makes social commentary about poverty, while it presents women as work-worn through their roles as nurturers to men. It also symbolically treats working-class women and men who possess nothing but each other. In fact it complicates the sonnet as a form traditionally associated with love. "Everyday Alchemy," when originally published in 1922, might have been read as a gesture toward the love lyric tradition of Edna St. Vincent Millay, Elinor Wylie, and Sara Teasdale.[25] Yet Millay's and Teasdale's lyrics evoked the poet as lover, as one generally oblivious to the social landscape in which the love is either lamented or celebrated. Taggard explores the private couple (or couples) as a distinct social unit: the poverty surrounding working-class women and men who can seek only each other. This distinction would seem awkward in Millay's complaint, "I let my candle burn at both ends," or Teasdale's question, "Why am I crying after love?" Taggard creates through these women and men a place to demystify the magic of love, made metaphor by the poem's title—the medieval practice of alchemy: making gold out of dross—wedded to the reality of material deprivation.

"Everyday Alchemy" is also a refiguration of the metaphysical tradition that Taggard, like other significant modern poets, had begun to embrace in the 1920s. The publication in 1921 of T. S. Eliot's essay "The Metaphysical Poets" helped rekindle an interest among modern poets in this sixteenth-century literary tradition.[26] One may read "Everyday Alchemy" with John Donne's "Love's Alchemie," in which the poet muses on the "hidden mysterie[s]" of love. Yet Taggard translates the "sexual chemistry" implied in Donne's poem into a kind of alchemical nurturing, the mothering of world-weary, destitute men.[27]

The meeting of "poor women" and "worn men" in "Everyday Alchemy" might have reflected a tendency of the youthful poets of the 1920s to romanticize poverty as if it were a key ingredient to some of the social experiments they endorsed. When Taggard reprinted the poem in *Calling Western Union*, at the height of the Depression, her readers would find verse that evoked the collective concerns of ordinary men and women in a time of crisis. We recognize these ordinary men and women through the poet's symbolic rendering of their bodies. The proletarian literary genre's prominent tropes represented working men through images of virility and resilience. Yet Taggard complicates the genre's essential metaphors by representing the male workers' bodies through weakness and by describing the female bodies in strength: the worker's long-suffering wives.[28] Though poverty silences the bodies Taggard describes in "Everyday Alchemy," she depicts the male bodies as more vulnerable; they are mute and bent. They provide nothing, but seek. The female bodies are active (of course because of love), making a "solace" for the male bodies as they seek "peace." Taggard informs us that nothing in the natural world can provide the solace that women provide; their hearts, which in more prosperous times would reflect love as an idealization, now "pour out" only poverty, to men who, far from being ideal lovers themselves, are "worn."

While "Everyday Alchemy" suggests the primacy of the couple whether times are good or bad, it also permits the reading of other tropes, nonsexual unions (such as nurses and patients in wartime, or mothers and sons). Whether or not Taggard had it in mind, we cannot overlook the poem's evocation of women, men, and war, especially if we are to read the poem in its social context and as an answer to the erotics of Donne's "Love's Alchemie." With the line "men go to women mutely for their peace," Taggard evokes the image of a pietà or a woman holding a wounded or dying soldier to her breast as in war memorials and antiwar posters.[29] Finally, by removing the poem from its association with both the love lyric and the metaphysical tradition, Taggard complicates the relationship of poetic form in general.

Taggard's resituation of "Everyday Alchemy" into the proletarian collection *Calling Western Union,* her efforts to put Emily Dickinson into the canon of American literature, as well as her rehistoricizing the poetic tradition of John Donne, show how firmly grounded she was as a "public intellectual." In fact Taggard's appearance in one of the pivotal works of postwar radical literary history, Daniel Aaron's *Writers on the Left,* helps maintain her significant, albeit marginalized, role as a left public intellectual. Both Paula Rabinowitz and Alan Wald have pointed to the exceptionally "even-keeled" discussions of the literary left that Daniel Aaron created in this important text, which also helped define a place for radical literary history. What is additionally surprising is that *Writers on the Left* was published in the early 1960s at the height of the Cold War.[30] Yet while the general absence of women in Aaron's text is not surprising, his attention to Genevieve Taggard suggests the importance and even the "tokenness" (after all she is one of the *few* women represented therein) of her work on the left. In addition, when we consider that Taggard has become one of the literary disappeared, her presence in Aaron's book—a presence cited through her participation in "public" left intellectual debates—reminds us of her significance to the intellectual community of writers on the left, which the conservative focus of literary and American studies has resolutely ignored.

In a chapter devoted to communist literary influence via writer and critic Mike Gold, and the *New Masses* as an important left venue in the late 1920s, through the Depression, and on into the 1940s, Aaron focuses upon a dialogue in its pages, "Are Artists People?" (January 1927), in which Genevieve Taggard was a key participant. Her comments in the *New Masses* of the late 1920s, as fitting as they are with the tenor of the times, as it were, offer significant insight into ideological changes that would occur among left intellectuals during the Depression. Taggard's interest in the proletarianization of culture, which is evident in certain poems in *Calling Western Union,* is hardly discernible in these earlier discussions. Fourteen writers responded to a variety of questions about their relationship to art and society. One of the questions had indirect gender consequences for "modern" women like Taggard and their roles both inside and outside the domestic sphere.[31] The posing of that question, whether the "advent of the machine meant the death of art and culture" or "the birth of a new culture," inspired Taggard to readdress the question in a separate essay, "The Ruskinian Boys See Red" in the July 1927 issue.[32] Focusing on "Are Artists People?" Aaron maintains that various responses were given in support of the machine age, and none of the artists agreed with Mike Gold "that a person was likely to become a better artist by accepting the Machine age and the proletarian cause" (166). Taggard seemed particularly piqued by Gold's adamancy. She did not want to see the writer accepting "proletarian stocks and bonds, glories and goodies." Interestingly, the class lines she urges middle-class women like herself to cross during the Depression are kept separate in this particular dialogue: "*The New Masses* is making a great mistake if it tries to convert bourgeois artists into proletarian ones." She preferred to see it help the artist "take hold of the spectacle of modern life by printing the work of those who have begun to make inroads upon it" (166).

Except for a brief mention of her participation in the communist-oriented League of American Writers, Aaron does not look at Taggard's Depression-era militancy and thus never gives an accurate description of the changes in her political outlook. He does, however, suggest her difference from the liberal writers who shared the intellectual dialogue with her. He suggests that, while remaining fiercely independent from any party programs, radical intellectuals like Taggard began to register "self-contempt" (168). "If I were in charge of a revolution," she writes,

I'd get rid of every single artist immediately; and trust to luck that the fecundity of the earth would produce another crop when I had got some of the hard work done. Being an artist, I have the sense that a small child has when its mother is in the middle of housework. I don't intend to get in the way, and I hope that there'll be an unmolested spot for me when things have quieted down. (168)[33]

While the above comment paves the way for Taggard's more militant Depression-era stance, as I have maintained, her public activity, from her accomplishments as an editor and biographer to her participation in the significant left dialogues of the period in the *New Masses,* to her work on behalf of striking marble workers in Vermont and her executive position in the League of American Writers, not only created Taggard's role as "public intellectual" but also suggests how deeply entwined were these activities with her life as a creative artist.

In 1942, Genevieve Taggard published *Long View.* Like *Calling Western Union,* this book contained poems of social urgency. Yet Taggard had also begun an interest in writing for music, and in undertaking this interest in musical forms, explored the social and public relevance of both poetry and song. At the end of *Long View* Taggard provides a brief essay, "Notes on Writing for Music." She informs readers that a disparate but largely popular tradition has influenced the poems she has drafted for musical settings:

My own experience, my learning process acknowledges Robert Burns and the Negroes, who have made up words for Spirituals and Blues, many of them nameless people. Leadbelly is a clear case of a person who knows [how to write for music] and does. Blitzstein. Gershwin. Shakespeare. Woodie Guthrie. Earl Robinson. Cole Porter. Certain hymn writers. The writers of songs you hear in the middle of the night on the air. This is my song book. (103)

In "Notes on Writing for Music" Taggard enjoins her readers to consider the communal possibilities of writing for music by including a list of suggestions for those interested in putting words to musical settings. These suggestions still bear the marks of the mid-Depression conviction of *Calling Western Union*: "Song is collective. (Poetry should be.)" (104).

Taggard perhaps best realizes her advice that poetry should engage in the "collective" in a series of poems from *Long View* that she wrote "To the Negro People." Through these particular poems Taggard reads African American cultural tropes, such as music, as examples of a people's struggle for "truth" and social justice. In the series "To the Negro People," Taggard's social vision, along with her interest in the collectivity of song, presents African Americans as cultural innovators whose voices have been denied and whose "collective" contributions have been buried.

Three of the four poems from this series, "Spirituals," "City of the Blues," and "Proud Day," explore the distinct voice of African American music. Taggard had great difficulty publishing these poems. She sent three to Richard Wright, asking if he could recommend a place for her to send them. In her communication with Wright, she put forth her idea to send the poems to black publications. She requested no pay in return for a community of readers that would find value in the poems. Thanks to Wright's efforts, two poems, "Spirituals" and "Proud Day," appeared in the October 1940 issue of the NAACP journal, the *Crisis*.

It is not surprising that established white literary journals rejected Taggard's tributes to African American culture when the musical legacy of black Americans was similarly rejected by the Eurocentric attitudes of classical music communities in the United States. In "Spirituals" Taggard reminds us of the unsung poet(s) of the South whose "bones / Sleep in the dust of song." While evoking the spiritual song form—"My way's cloudy, I cry out, / Cloudy Lord"—Taggard names the South as a "burying ground" for neglected African American spiritual art. "Spirituals," as it laments a collective past, a musical and aesthetic practice whose cultural importance has been overlooked, also implicates the poet's own sense of neglect. Just as much of the writing (including her own) of radicals of her generation has been forgotten or marginalized, the classical focus of a Eurocentric American musical canon has ignored the musical contributions of the black South. Most literary history written under the influence of the New Criticism has disregarded Taggard's contributions to American poetry in the twentieth century; it has buried her along with the popular traditions of working-class poetry and the African American lyric traditions.

Celebrating African American cultural tropes against the mainstream canon, Taggard hoped to subvert the mainstream art world's exclusive practices. "Proud Day" conflates both popular and high traditions as it honors a black artist whose work and person embraced both aesthetic spheres. "Proud Day" is an especially moving tribute to contralto Marian Anderson. Anderson, who was denied a voice in Jim Crow America in both the literal and figurative senses, became the toast of Europe where she sang to sold-out audiences. Constructed like a gospel hymn, "Proud Day" celebrates Anderson's famous 1939 performance on the steps of the Lincoln Memorial. Anderson had returned to the United States from Europe in 1935. She was by then an international star and sang her spiritual and classical repertoire to a sold-out crowd at New York's Town Hall. In the following year impresario Sol Hurok tried to secure a performance for Anderson at Washington D.C.'s Constitution Hall, which the Daughters of the American Revolution had founded. A clause in the hall's contracts, however, stated that no blacks could perform there. When Eleanor Roosevelt learned of this blatant act of discrimination, she resigned from the D.A.R. Finally, with a little help from his friends, Hurok secured the Lincoln Memorial:

Our sister sang on the Lincoln steps. Proud day.
We came to hear our sister sing. Proud day.
Voice out of depths, poise with memory.
What goodness, what splendor lay long under foot!
Our sister with a lasso of sorrow and triumph
Caught America, made it listen. Proud day.
The peaceful Lincoln sat so still. Proud day.
Never, never forget how the dark people rewarded us
Giving out of their want and their little freedom
This blazing star. This blazing star.
Something spoke in my patriot heart. Proud day.

The voice presented in "Proud Day" appears intentionally ambiguous. A black audience is represented as mesmerized with awe and pride as it experiences Anderson's moving performance; yet there is also the white audience of the poet and other progressive whites who support black artists and engage in antiracist activities. Yet the demarcation between a black audience, black performer, white poet, and white audience is blurred. The poet historicizes the conflict surrounding Anderson's appearance in Washington by deliberately integrating the audience within the poem. "Our sister," whom Taggard addresses in the opening lines, suggests her making a gift of the poem to a black audience that would value it. Yet there is also the gratitude of the white audience suggested by the lines, "never forget how the dark people rewarded us." It is "their want" and "their little freedom" that have produced and given this *gift.*

Taggard's emphasis is on the heroic; she juxtaposes the great black singer as she performs "Ave Maria" and "My Country 'Tis of Thee" with the stone face of Abraham Lincoln looking on. Though Lincoln was responsible for granting limited suffrage to black men and allowing "the Republic to be born again," Taggard wants readers to acknowledge the neglect and burial of African American voice as she symbolically renders it through Anderson's performance: "Voice out of depths, poise with memory / What goodness, what splendor lay long under foot!" The underlying theme of this poem's celebration is the fact that racism and legislative injustice have denied blacks creative integrity, as well as denied whites the possibility of ever knowing this integrity.

Taggard constructs the poem to suggest the Spiritual musical genre refigured by African Americans in the antebellum South. It shows Anderson's role as interpreter and keeper of tradition as well as reinterpreter of the European canon of Schubert and Mahler.[34] Taggard repeats the phrase "Proud day," like a gospel refrain, in six end lines of this twelve-line poem. Her final line shifts the attention from "our sister," spoken at the beginning of the poem, to "[s]omething spoke in my patriot heart." She reinforces the ambiguity of the voice and punctuates this final line with a final "Proud day." Taggard leaves us with a powerful image of Anderson and her diverse audience standing in front of the symbolic Lincoln. The image itself signifies the poet's renewed sense of patriotism.

Sometime in 1939 Taggard corresponded with Langston Hughes, sending him "City of the Blues," also from the "Negro" series. She had admired Hughes's work since the 1920s when she solicited poems from him for her journal the *Measure*. She admitted to Hughes that "City of the Blues" was her favorite of the series and lamented the fact that every magazine to which she sent it rejected the poem. Eventually, the journal the *Clipper* published it. The *Clipper* was a small Los Angeles literary review put out by the California chapter of the League of American Writers, a Popular Front organization in which Taggard was active.

In "City of the Blues," Taggard also explores the collectivity of song. Rather than representing pride and dignity, however, as "Proud Day" does, "City of the Blues" offers lamentations, following another rich African American innovation, blues music. Whereas "Proud Day" describes a musical tribute in the heroic sense, "City of the Blues" pays its tribute in the discordant strains of a "river-whistle turned harsh." Taggard takes St. Louis, a city romanticized because of its rich musical traditions, and presents it through the vantage point of an unemployed black worker, "[i]n the chicken yard, listlessly, beside the piles, waiting for / nothing." (One should note the homage to William Carlos Williams's "Red Wheel Barrow.") The heteroglossic landscape that Taggard creates of St. Louis, that city on the river, with its "river-side, piles rotted with river," suggests an ugly desolation, and thus a Depression-inspired mood that was all too familiar to her 1930s' audience. Taggard represents a socially and economically ravaged St. Louis through a staccato placement of words, which suggest several competing scenarios. A slaughterhouse "[w]ith its droppings and molted feathers[,] [f]ence, coop, mash-/ pans, wire," can also be interpreted as home, a shantytown of "slums and slime" with "frame houses, [d]ark, wet, cold." There is also a teasing possibility of industry, "[t]ug going by, puff puff," about to proceed to the "St. Louis dock / [s]tacked high" where there is "[c]oal smoke, winches, shovels,—crash of freight." St. Louis music is also a distant music that expresses itself through the "[y]'hoo's" of trains and boats. The black body that gets to comprehend "silence" is juxtaposed against this industrial movement. The silence "[b]lows clean through your bones."

Whatever is fiercest about St. Louis's riverbeds as they symbolize Depression poverty, Taggard reinforces the misery that variously visits African American communities. Those who know the place know that "(When they kill, they kill / Here, and dump the body here)." The ambiguity of these parenthetical lines evokes more than the mundane suggestions of a slaughtered animal's carcass. It intimates both the criminal nature of social and economic deprivation and the community continually victimized by the ubiquitous lynch mob. Taggard steeps her poem with bleak images of filth, stench, lethargy, and decay. She comments upon blues as a social condition born of these metaphors of lack and to blues as a musical cultural formation that can only develop out of such despair. The blues then is a metaphor for the literal rottenness of place, both social and economic; if the Depression aggravated the already unjust working and living conditions of African Americans, the cultural expressions they explored at this time were not only accurate responses but also necessary tropes with which to create resistance.

The last poem in the series, "Chant for the Great Negro Poet of America Not Yet Born" (1941), informs us that a rich, anonymous past will produce a talent "[b]orn, awake, with the urgent rising of his people," an unprecedented new talent from a future world finally ready for him. Like "Spirituals," "Chant for the Great Negro Poet of America Not Yet Born" acknowledges the modernist's transformation of the musical god Orpheus into a poet and refigures the African American experience with song into a poetic contribution. "Chant for the Great Negro Poet of America Not Yet Born" asserts that from this rich, unsung tradition will come, in the spirit of "Blake" and "Whitman," a great poet of his people. Taggard's "Negro poet" is both social poet and black Christ: "Kin—Blake, Whitman, and the honest preachers of his / people." "[H]e is heir," she also informs us, to "[t]he Hebrew poets." He will produce a new poetry born from the spaces where social oppression and art meet. She insists that he will understand not only just "the powerful mass of his people" but also he will share the radical poet's concerns. "He will be our poet when he comes, he will wear / Scars." These scars also reveal a hope, a "universal singing." Taggard's black poet of the future will keep his own cultural traditions. He will also continue the important tradition of political poetry created through mass social movements and other forms of resistance.

Genevieve Taggard had a surprisingly prolific career for a writer who has been so thoroughly neglected since her death in November 1948. Yet considering her dedication to left culture in the interwar period, it is not impossible to guess her fate in the horrific climate of red-baiting and anticommunist witch-hunts that plagued America's early postwar years.

After *Long View,* Taggard published three other books of poems, *A Part of Vermont* (1945), *Slow Music* (1946), and *Origin: Hawaii* (1947), her final book, which gives one last recollection of her childhood home. The revolutionary zeal found in *Calling Western Union* is quieted in these later volumes, albeit with memorable exceptions in *Slow Music,* and suggests the difficulty of publishing radical poems in a climate inhospitable to lyrics of social change. In the activist 1960s young American scholars became interested in reexamining left culture of the 1930s for its obvious kinship as another age of American social activism. However, the New Left, suspicious about the rigidity of Old Left political doctrines and their subsequent failures as well as the masculine biases of the new scholarship, showed little interest in Taggard's contributions to left culture. Yet, like her radical sister, Lola Ridge, Taggard found a new readership in two second-wave feminist poetry anthologies, Ann Stanford's *The Women Poets in English* and Louise Bernikow's *The World Split Open.* Taggard was a "premature socialist-feminist," as Alan Wald characterizes the 1930s generation of left-wing women who were concerned with women's issues. One would assume that Taggard's voice might appeal to those second-wave feminists who attempted to combine their gender politics with an interest in radicalism. After all, she wrote new woman poetry in the 1920s—poems about pregnancy and sexuality—suggesting that she understood then that the "personal is political." In the 1930s she was writing about women's participation in social and political struggles. It is difficult to say why Taggard's work—diverse in subject, spirit, and style—did not remain in the cultural vanguard of American literature once it began to be read by feminists and radicals in the 1970s. Probably the modern American poetry canon remained too rigid to welcome her. Perhaps it is testimony to the deep-rooted sexism and conservatism of modern American poetry studies, as well as class biases in feminist studies that have signaled her continued neglect.

In a culture where so few people read poetry (though we have no actual statistics), the narrowness of the canon and the political apathy of many of today's more mainstream poets continue Taggard's exclusion. She worked tirelessly for a more open society; the ultimate irony is how the art form she worked in for four decades would be so resistant to the changes she advocated throughout her career. Yet Taggard's work is still relevant today, even as the cultures of the left are fragmented—perhaps beyond repair. If only we would take her advice about poetry: "Swing the great stanza on the pavement,—use / The public street for publishing good news" ("Definition of Song" [1936]).

The Girl Who Went to Chicago

Political Culture and Migration in Margaret Walker's *For My People*

This is my century—
Black synthesis of time:
The freudian slip
The Marxian mind
Kierkegaardian Leap of Faith
and Du Bois prophecy: the color line.
These are the comrades of Einstein,
the dawning of another Age,
new symphony of Time.
Margaret Walker, "This Is My Century," 1983

Looking back over fifty years of writing poetry from the vantage point of a black woman, Margaret Walker paradoxically names her "black synthesis of time" through conflicting, totalizing ideologies of the white male thinkers: Freud, Marx, Kierkegaard, and Einstein. While crossing DuBois's prophetic "color line," Walker, a celebrated novelist, poet, essayist, and teacher, engages the discourses of class, psychology, religion, and science. Yet an important feature missing in her synthesis is gender. The gender consciousness that is absent from the twentieth-century equation that Walker sets up is more a problem of her Depression-era influences, to which the above names belong, than of her development as a black woman writer. How Walker uses these influences, and into what remaining spaces she places her gendered articulations, is the focus of this particular discussion.

Margaret Walker was twenty-seven years old when she published her first book of poems, *For My People*. It was the first by an African American writer to receive a national literary prize—the 1942 Yale Younger Poets Award.[1] To come of age as a black woman poet during the Depression required a peculiar sense of awareness of the social, political, and economic structures that shaped the artist's manner of seeing. Walker was born in Birmingham, Alabama, in 1915. She went north to attend Northwestern University and spent the decade of the 1930s working and writing in Chicago. In 1949 she became a professor of English at Jackson State University in Mississippi and later founded the black studies program there. Critical attention to Walker's work focuses almost exclusively on her evocations of southern life. She is perhaps best known for her important best-selling novel *Jubilee*, which she worked on for nearly thirty years, based upon her great-grandmother's experiences as a slave during the Civil War.[2] The critical work on *For My People* has tended to emphasize the text's geographical aspects, its connection to the landscape of the American South as well as its articulation of myth and ritual within the contexts of the African diaspora.[3] Though it would be inaccurate to de-emphasize the centrality of the tropes of the South in her work, Walker's participation in the northern migration—her early years in Chicago—had a significant impact on her construction of southern life in *For My People* and needs to be more thoroughly engaged.[4]

During her years in Chicago, Walker was exposed to the proletarian literary tradition through her close associations with Richard Wright, her participation in the South-Side Writers' Project (affiliated with the Federal Writers' Project of the Works Progress Administration), and her membership in the Chicago chapter of the League of American Writers. Reading *For My People* should be informed by both South and North, the journey and the arrival, the rural and the urban, Walker's Chicago years, the marxist influence upon her work, and her infusion of working-class politics into African American myth and ritual. The dual importance of the Great Migration and the Depression on Walker's movement from southern "petty bourgeois" black society into the social and cultural spaces of northern cities is also noted, including her discovery "that people who worked with their brains were also workers" (*How I Wrote* Jubilee 7). Walker's letters to Richard Wright, written in the late 1930s, offer a glimpse of the kind of activities that she immersed herself in at the time. She attended classes and lectures at the worker's school on dialectical materialism, Marxism-Leninism, art and society, the proletarian novel, and proletarian poetry.[5] She promoted and enlisted subscriptions for the black radical literary journal, *Challenge,* which Wright, Dorothy West, and others were editing on the East Coast. She wrote a novel, *Goose Island,* about the shattered hopes of a talented female musician from Bronzeville.[6] She was a poetry editor of and contributed fiction to Jack Conroy's refurbished *New Anvil,* which he put out with Nelson Algren. Walker organized meetings in support of loyalist Spain at a local black church and was active in the union chapter formed by members of the South-Side Writers' Project. Yet in her letters she complains to Wright that her writing remained her top priority and that her organizational commitments would have to be sacrificed in order for her to get her creative work done. More closely linked to her writing than attempts at activism, Walker occupied herself by reading the white male and largely European canon of socially conscious literature: Zola, Malraux, Gide, Gorky.

As a black woman, Walker's experience of the Depression was decidedly different from and often more difficult than the realities faced by her white contemporaries. The radical culture of the 1930s encouraged Walker to struggle to represent the contemporary concerns of *her people,* while providing a historical record of her reading of black structures of feeling. This chapter follows Margaret Walker's journey across the color line in literary forms. As Cary Nelson suggests, *For My People,* with its urban laments and odes of slavery and its trickster ballads and sonnets of protest, shows "how a plural textuality can articulate the fragmented, conflicted subcultures of the social formation" (*Repression and Recovery* 178).

A tacit feminist awareness can be found in several important poems in *For My People,* even if gender is not the predominant focus in the developmental stages of Walker's career as a social poet. She does interweave gendered articulations within the more central categories of race and class. In various places throughout *For My People,* Walker shows interest in the complicated movements of African American women. In fact, her own fascination with the stories her maternal grandmother told of her own mother's experiences in slavery gave her an early understanding of the significance of women's labor. Many of the poems in *For My People* depict the strength of working women and men in the face of adversity, with their muscular bodies, knowing only exploitation. Such representations of the strong, impassive, yet exploited working-class body invoke the Depression-era tropes found in the proletarian realist manifestos of Mike Gold as well as Walker's Chicago compatriot Jack Conroy. Important to note, however, Walker's characterizations of black female labor are subtle; she is cautious of feeding the stereotyped representation of the black female laborer's super-strength. Such a line is drawn in "Lineage," an ironic testimony of gender power created by unfree women and memorialized by a daughter of freedom:

My grandmothers were strong.
They followed plows and bent to toil.
They moved through fields sowing seed.
They touched earth and grain grew.
They were full of sturdiness and singing.
My grandmothers were strong.

My grandmothers are full of memories
Smelling of soap and onions and wet clay.
With veins rolling roughly over quick hands
They have many clean words to say.
My grandmothers were strong.
Why am I not as they?

The poem explores the writer's regret at the divide created between her life as a black female intellectual and the laboring history of her female ancestors: "Why am I not as they?" she asks. Although Walker composed the poem as she discovered that intellectual labor was also "labor," she projects an inferior status upon her manner of toil to the far superior physical work performed by her grandmothers who "moved through fields sowing seed." The grandmothers, with their "many clean words to say," reverse the idea of physical labor as *dirty;* mental labor in its distance from sweat and earth becomes *dirty;* it is, in a sense, ineffectual; it *yields* nothing. In fact Walker refigures a popular proletarian trope and writes black women into proletarian literature by subordinating intellectual desire and angst to the laboring black woman who "followed plows and bent to toil." Indeed, with "Why am I not as they?" Walker laments her own disconnection from the *real* work of her ancestors and asks: How is it that women with far fewer choices than the poem's speaker were able to create and maintain unimaginable worlds against unimaginable odds?

"Lineage" restores a history to black women and anticipates the early demands for inclusion that feminists of color advocated in the late 1970s and early 1980s as a result of liberal and cultural feminism's failure to see race as a central problem within the women's movement.[7] Walker does not entertain a separate struggle for black women in *For My People* as a whole. Yet in several of her poems, representations of black female experience as distinct from black community experience are clear examples of her awareness of gender difference, even if such differences remained untheorized in Depression-era black communities. Yet it is most likely that Walker hoped poems like "Lineage," which address issues unique to African American women's experience(s), and "For My People," which describes African Americans' historical and collective movements (and named through the masculine linguistic sign, "men," as was standard at that time), would be understood as representations of community rather than as explorations of gender identity. Additionally, as suggested in the beginning of this chapter, Walker also filters her representations of community and gender through dominant cultural tropes such as class, psychology, and religion, which seem to play an even larger role in her articulations of African American life.

For My People is very much a text of discovery, and Walker's realization "that people who worked with their brains were also workers" allowed her to place herself within the discourse of race and class consciousness as these began to infuse African American writing in the 1930s. Whereas the Harlem Renaissance of the 1920s exemplified race pride at the level of cultural trope, the radical lyrics that Walker and other African American poets began to produce in the 1930s called for a more militant expression, a demand for lyrical evocations of the need for social transformation: "Let a race of men now rise and take control" is how Walker closes "For My People." This poem depicts the immensely complicated and arduous movements African American men and women have made through immutably hostile terrain, while searching in these movements for the possibility of social change.

The volume *For My People* challenges the modernist poetics of the American male left by bringing to it a black, gendered vision. The book is divided into three parts, each exploring distinct African American cultural, social, and historical tropes. The first section contains stylistically varied, experimental poems about black social history, with emphasis on the southern landscape. The second section contains rearticulations of African American folklore, from the labor hero John Henry to the infamous trickster bad boy Stagolee. Walker's insistence on representing black female social and communal agency presents some feisty heroines who refigure the folklore genre's male-centered biases. The third and final section is comprised of sonnets. Though these sonnets were criticized by several of the book's reviewers, and, as Walker claims, her friends "the black male scholars and critics" (*This Is My Century* xvii) also maligned them, they resist and collapse the associations that the sonnet has had in traditional discussions of the form. Like the other two poets in this study, Lola Ridge and Genevieve Taggard, Walker wrote "political" sonnets. Perhaps to emphasize the formal interventions she hoped these poems would make, she gave them blunt titles such as "Whores" and "The Struggle Staggers Us." As Ridge desired with "Electrocution" and Taggard with "Silence in Majorca," Walker attempted to turn the form on its head. The tension and resolution found in the first and final sections of the sonnet form, conventionally concerned with love or honor, get quite a jolt as they convey the effects of the death penalty, of fascism, and of racism.[8]

The title poem that opens *For My People* is perhaps the best introduction to the book as a whole, particularly in a reading that emphasizes the cultural and historical material that informed its production.[9] As Walker would tell Alferdteen Harrison fifty years after the book's publication:

I wrote these poems . . . in the decade of the 1930s. It was a period of depression—black people suffered along with everyone else from lack of jobs, from lack of standard housing, from lack of appropriate schooling. We were literally outcast from the general society. But then there were poor white people too, and poor working people. It was a time when unions were struggling to have collective bargaining, to have a forty-hour week. (9)

"For My People" is a powerful, mantralike prose verse testimonial on the experiences of African Americans. It moves chronologically from the culture of slavery to the author's bitter present of "hypocrisy and misunderstanding" to, finally, a militant resolution in the closing stanza calling for "another world to be born" in which "martial songs" replace "dirges" and a "new earth" unfolds for a new generation of people fully shaped by a revolutionary black consciousness.[10] "For My People" captures an important American historical moment as the black South moves north; it is a text of migration and rural dislocation.

The poem's opening emphasis is on the cultural products of slavery— "dirges" and "ditties," "blues" and "jubilees"—it also explains Walker's more general attraction to folk ritual, which permeates the entire book. She presents the aesthetic practice of "slave songs," however, in contradictory fashion, creating a tension between musical settings: lamentations, devotionals, and popular balladry. Yet behind the powerful spiritual intensity created through song is the tacit reminder that such tropes are also products of domination, of a subduing of spirit and will. As the stanza closes, the songs are rounded out by "knees" bending "humbly" in prayer to an "unseen power." Walker fuses the attitudes of her Methodist upbringing with the marxism of Chicago radicals: if resistance is to be created it must be done through an understanding of one's surroundings. As the poem proceeds, it explores the variance and incongruities of developing and maintaining race, class, and gender consciousness, keeping alive folk traditions while yearning for all the forms culture can take.

The poem's momentum is best characterized by a vocabulary of activity, while each stanza replicates a stage in the life cycle from birth, to adulthood, and finally toward regeneration. Walker laments the "strength" of her people being spent "washing ironing cooking scrubbing sewing mending / hoeing plowing digging planting pruning patching / dragging along." The present continuous tense used in the second and seventh stanzas suggests the exhaustion of labor without any of the romanticization that certain types of proletarian poetry have used to mute the grim realities of working-class life. Walker spares us the commas; these tasks run one into the other. Endless and mindless, they describe a people "never gaining never reaping never knowing and never understanding." Again no commas: and even then, out-of-breath readers will not know the half of it. This straining toil, evoking southern labor on the land, is matched in the seventh stanza's evocations of displacement, probably to metaphorize the disorientation caused by the northern migration: "For my people walking blindly spreading joy, losing time being lazy, sleeping when hungry, shouting when burdened, / drinking when hopeless." In fact the poem's sixth stanza, which just precedes the above lines, speaks directly of dislocation, whether caused by the move north in which so many African Americans took part, or the equally disordering move from country to city:

For my people thronging 47th Street in Chicago and Lenox
Avenue in New York and Rampart Street in New
Orleans, lost disinherited dispossessed and happy
people filling the cabarets and taverns and other
people's pockets needing bread and shoes and milk and
land and money and something—something all our own.

The wants and needs and desires that are evoked by the use of the conjunction "and," always a grammar of continuation, characterize the sense of being "lost disinherited dispossessed." Yet Walker is careful to construct contradiction within the interstices of movement: "lost disinherited dispossessed and happy / people" fill "cabarets and taverns." There is desire even in dislocation, the search for something "all our own," a people who, in the penultimate stanza, try to "fashion a better way / from confusion"; they attempt to refashion themselves within their new surroundings.

Two million African Americans migrated from the South to the North between 1900 and 1930. Postbellum life for southern blacks continued to be limiting in every conceivable way—socially, politically, personally, and most evident, financially. Historian Jacqueline Jones provides a more concrete explanation for the migration:

> [There was] . . . the oppressive sharecropping system, disenfranchisement, Jim Crow laws, a plague of boll weevils working its way toward the Cotton Belt. When World War I opened up employment possibilities in the industrial Northeast and Midwest, mass migration began in earnest: the lure of high wages and a freer life proved irresistible to a people limited to agricultural and domestic service in the land of neoslavery. (153)

A prominent visual image that appeared during the period of the Great Migration was the newspaper photograph of African Americans—men, women, and children—boarding trains by the hundreds for the great northern cities: Chicago, New York, Detroit, Washington, Cleveland, Philadelphia. Chicago's preeminent black newspaper the *Defender* advertised jobs in hopes of luring young black men to the booming industrial city. These ads screamed opportunities that would have been inconceivable in the South. One such ad read: "Laborers wanted for foundry, warehouse and yard work. Excellent opportunity to learn trades, paying good money. Start $2.50–$2.75 per day. Extra for overtime" (quoted in Takaki 343). Although black men would benefit far more than black women in terms of job choice and financial reward, women were no less anxious to be part of the migration. In fact, men who migrated along with their wives looked forward to seeing them treated fairly—not only as workers but also as shoppers. Yet as Jacqueline Jones maintains, "[f]ew migrants, male or female, abandoned the South totally or irrevocably" (159). Individuals made frequent returns, relatives were sent for, money and goods flowed south, but southern goods were also sent north, along with the culture and lore people brought with them. One positive, irrevocable change that the northern migration affected was the cultural contact between the black South and the largely white North. As Henry Louis Gates Jr. writes of the important cultural significance of the migration: "Just as slavery inadvertently created a new

'African' culture—a New World Western, Pan-African culture and ethnicity—so, too, did the Great Migration create a new culture, one northern and urban yet thoroughly southern in its roots" (17).

Margaret Walker claimed her coming north in the early 1930s to attend Northwestern, her father's alma mater, was based on Langston Hughes's advice. Hughes, whom Walker had met while living in New Orleans as a teen, felt her writing talent could never be nurtured in the South.[11] Yet the North as a place of opportunity was not without its own incongruities. The discrimination she assumed would be reversed in the North, she soon discovered was an everyday reality for her northern sisters and brothers. In the essay "Growing Out of Shadow" first published in *Common Ground* in 1943, Walker notes her surprise that the expectations she had about northern opportunities and promises were proved wrong. She quickly understood that racism did not disappear once one crossed the Mason-Dixon line. "In the South," she writes,

> I had always thought that, naturally, white people had more money than colored people. Poor white trash signified for me the lazy scum of the marginal fringe of society with no excuse for poverty. Now I discovered there were poor white working people exploited by rich white people. I learned that all Jews were not rich. I discovered that all Negroes were not even in the same economic class. While there were no Negro multimillionaires, there were many wealthy Negroes who made money by exploiting the poor Negroes, who had some of the same attitudes toward them that rich whites had toward poor whites and that prejudiced whites have toward all Negroes.[12]

She also writes about being "refused service in restaurants in Evanston and Chicago time and time again" (6). Though this is but one of many instances of northern racist practice, it had a symbolic resonance for African Americans that would eventually give birth to actions such as the Student Nonviolent Coordinating Committee lunch-counter sit-ins during the nascent years of the Civil Rights movement.

The "people thronging 47th Street in Chicago," the image that begins the sixth stanza of "For My People," signifies the poet herself as witness to the migrating bodies creating a new community in the Midwestern metropolis. The need and desire, the sense of dislocation, and the urgency evoked by Walker's descriptions register a lament and longing for the South as home. However, there is also a sense of vibrancy; cities like Chicago still offered hope. "47th Street in Chicago" was a hub of African American community and must have surely given Walker a sense of identity, albeit complex and contradictory, even if she saw herself as a transplanted southerner. The contradictions Walker found in the crowded streets of Chicago's black belt might be better understood by considering an important study of the city, which examines both the resignation of Chicago's black community and its pride and fortitude. St. Clair Drake and Horace Cayton provide an exhaustive analysis of Chicago's black belt in their *Black Metropolis: A Study of Negro Life in a Northern City*. Richard Wright, who wrote the introduction to the first edition published in 1945, describes the book as an important "scientific report upon the state of unrest, longing, hope among urban Negroes" (xxv).[13] Drake and Cayton describe "Bronzeville," the name given to Chicago's South Side with 47th Street as its main thoroughfare, with a liveliness in sharp contrast to the white world surrounding and enclosing it. A "continuous eddy of faces—black, brown, olive, yellow, and white" (379) circulates through a neighborhood filled with its own newspapers, professionals, clerks, and policemen. Theaters and billboards announcing black art and entertainment, and a plethora of churches, steady streams of shoppers, agents, "irate tenants," job seekers, and picketers create a vital atmosphere of heterodox enterprise. Yet like Walker, Drake and Cayton are aware of the temptation to romanticize the ghetto and pointedly avoid doing so. The thronging bodies of 47th Street are casualties of a Jim Crow system, and their separation and their enforced poverty are ever present and reminders of a people "preyed on by a facile force of state and fad and novelty," as Walker tells us in "For My People." Richard Wright, in his introduction to Drake and Cayton's book, also expressed a sense of the city's contradictions. His dialectical response was no doubt something he was able to share with Walker during the years of their friendship in Chicago:

Chicago is the city from which the most incisive and radical Negro thought has come; there is an open and raw beauty about the city that seems either to kill or endow one with the spirit of life. I felt those extremes of possibility, death and hope, while I lived half hungry and afraid in a city to which I had fled with the dumb yearning to write, to tell my story. (xvii)

A sense of despair, of crampedness, of wonder and discovery, the contradictions and confusions that make up the bemused quest of a people cut off from their past and determined to fashion a future, set the pace for Walker's final message in "For My People." In her forecast looms "a bloody peace written in the sky," the birth of a "second generation full of courage," and a "beauty full of healing and [a] strength." But these requisites belong to a hope predicated upon a belief, shared by many radical writers of the 1930s, in social transformation: "let a new race of men now rise and take control."[14]

Walker's militancy in these last lines reflects her education as a black intellectual together with her Chicago 1930s' marxist education.[15] Yet it is interesting to see the dichotomy created in the radical desire of "For My People" when reading it with a later poem like "Today." This poem, written in a similar style as "For My People," with its enjambed, unpunctuated lines, calculates race intolerance in America with the "international" fight against racial oppression in fascist Europe. The black nation as it rises in America must gaze across the Atlantic to see a new "race" of men arising and taking control in Europe—the white "Aryan" race calling for the obliteration of the "other." "Today" was written just as war was commencing in Europe. Like "For My People," it transcends yet remains a creation of the Chicago years. Ideologically, Walker embraces a tacit left internationalism with an implicit prompt that racial oppression has fueled war in Europe. The poem juxtaposes "Middle America" with "Middle Europe," and a contradiction takes shape. Because the poem was written before the United States entered the war, instead of containing images of homefront pride, the poet creates a linguistic surface on which to convey indignation at the nation's apathy in the face of world problems.

"Today" is also a radical rewriting of Walt Whitman's "I Hear America Singing" and "I Sing the Body Electric." Yet it is closer to the pessimism and outrage expressed in the late Whitman of *Democratic Vistas*. Rather than celebrating the possibilities of America, Walker begins her song using Whitmanesque prose/verse form to cast a shadow of doubt on the future of humanity: "I sing of slum scabs on city / faces." Her lamentations, in fact, reach far beyond the ghettos she has walked through, to draw a line that will connect them to the cities of Europe as they anticipate and experience bombing: "scrawny children scarred by bombs and dying of / hunger." Then she reminds us again of the American landscape dotted with her people as "wretched human scarecrows strung against / lynching stakes." And of course workers, black and white, "dying of pellagra and silicosis." Their "houses" are "rotten" and "fall on slowly decaying humanity." Whereas Whitman "sings" his "body electric" as a praise of the human body in its social engagement with the luscious body of its rich, capacious land— America—Walker sings that body struggling against decay, overwork, and exhaustion, where praise must be mediated through unrelenting pain and sorrow:

> I sing of Man's struggle to be
> clean, to be useful, to be free; of need arising from our lives,
> of bitter living flowing in our laughter, of cankerous mutiny
> eating through the nipples of our breasts.
>
> I sing of our soon-to-be-dead,
> of last escape: drunkard raising flasks to his lips never
> tasting the solace, gambler casting his last die never
> knowing the win, lover seeking lips of the beloved never
> tasting fruit of his kiss, never knowing the languorous sleep.

Contradicting Whitman's texts of American abundance, the singing of "Today" represents American lack. "To be clean, to be useful," the body here is hardly replete; its "laughter" is the "bitter" gall of living. To be human in Walker's "Today" in the U.S.A. is to be half-living or "soon to be dead": to be drunk, but without consolation. It is wager without potential prize and romantic love without consummation. The American body which she sings has been exploited beyond pleasure. The Depression that encloses her words has paved its way to war. She ends the first section with a biblical foreboding: "I sing these fragments of living that you / may know by these presents that which we feared most has / come upon us."

While the specter haunting Europe in Walker's "Today" is fascism, it also haunts America, as indicated in the poem's second section. The poet discon-

tinues the Whitmanesque sorrow songs; she represents America "compla-
cently smug in a snug somnolescence" by suggesting its removal from
Europe's theater of bombs. She even points a finger: "You walking these
common / neighboring streets with no disturbing drone of bombing /
planes." Though it appears the sense of desperation described in the poem's
first section attempts to unite a common degraded humanity, the poem as
a whole suggests how distant are those Americans from the fact that they are
"fearing no severed baby arms nor naked / eyeballs hurtled in [their] hands."
Instead Americans have unappreciated advantages "riding trolley and jitney
/ daily, buying gas and light hourly." Moreover, they have the distracting
pleasures of popular culture (a theater without bombs): "Wild West Indian
and Shooting Sam," "Mama Loves Papa," and "Gone by the Breeze." The
fate of Europe's war victims might also be a tacit reminder about America's
denial of its own history of racial hatred and violence. Walker seems to
suggest, with her representations of complacency and her attack on a certain
"it can't happen here" mentality, that war in Europe stemmed from the very
race hatred that is also a pernicious American disease. Although Walker's
poetic critique chides complacent attitudes before the United States entered
the war, a comment by her friend Richard Wright written sometime after
is perhaps not far from Walker's own imaginings: Would America, when
"brought face to face with the problem of the Negro, collapse in a moral
spasm, as did Europe when confronted with the problem of the Jew" (xxxi)?

As Walker juxtaposes Europe's war-ravaged body with a "Middle
America / distantly removed," she upbraids the American body for busying
itself with "petty personals." She lists consumer goods unavailable to allied
women in Europe such as: "eyemaline," "henna rinse," "dental cream." She
reproves America for its privileges and records the guilt-filled inactivity of
the white middle class "washing your lives with pity, smoothing your ways
with vague apologies." The cleansing suggested by the list of personal care
products and the "washing" and the "smoothing" of "lives" and "ways"
tacitly represents America's isolation from the rise of fascism across the Atlantic, reflecting the apathy and denial that is placated by trivialities in a
time of crisis.

In the poem's final stanza, Walker alludes to the structures of belief that
appear to shelter individuals from a wider understanding of the social dis-

enfranchisement and dislocation she sees at the center of oppression, both on the national and international scale:

Pray the Men of Mars to
descend upon you. Pray Jehovah to send his prophets before
the avenging fire. Pray for second sight and inner ear. Pray
for bulwark against poaching patterns of dislocated days;
pray for buttressing iron against insidious termite and beetle
and locust and flies and lice and moth and rust and mold.

Here Walker seems to take on the role of preacher and prophet to curse the lukewarm. She both borrows from and challenges the religious language of black culture. She also equates the trope of Armageddon as it is preached in black churches with the bombs falling on Middle Europe. The "buttressing iron" hints at the manufacture of war; the biblical plagues of "locust and flies" ask the audience to acknowledge that war might be a wake-up call. To close "Today" with the language of religious foreboding links Walker's social consciousness to the consciousness of African Americans decidedly shaped by the Christian church.

It should be noted that religion played an important role in Margaret Walker's upbringing. She believed in religion, which sets her apart from a good many other writers on the left while it connected her to black people and many white Protestants. Both her parents were deeply religious, and her father was a biblical scholar as well as a Methodist minister. Yet two critiques of religion are prevalent in *For My People:* the palliative role that religion plays in communities where prayer replaces social action and political resistance, and the forcing of the white man's religion onto the slave communities in the new world. In "Since 1619," for example, Walker, referring to the year the first slave ship reached North America, laments: "How many years since 1619 have I been singing Spirituals? / How long have I been praising God and shouting hallelujahs?" The collective voice, the poem's construction as a series of self-defining questions, speaks of a weariness and anger that the "hallelujahs" in thrall to the "money-gods" cannot quite penetrate; these are, after all, epochs of misdirected voices. Thus she asks "[w]hen will I burst from my kennel an angry mongrel. / Lean and hungry and tired of my dry bones and years?" This questioning trope, the desire to see her people develop the necessary consciousness to take action, is an important feature echoed throughout the first section of *For My People*. Yet Walker is also concerned here with the complicated nature of the battle to free the self from superstition, from pie-in-the-sky platitudes, and from all forms of indoctrination connected to slavery's rhetoric—its institutionalization and its aftermath.[16]

Walker writes the complicated nature of belief and its contradictory role as a trope of resistance in the poem "We Have Been Believers." The poem also explores how Africans in America created a new cultural body by assimilating "the black gods of an old land" with "the white gods of a new land." With this conflation of old and new she renders belief as dichotomy: "we have been believers / believing in the mercy of our masters and the beauty of / our brothers." Each stanza of "We Have Been Believers" exposes the contradictions inherent in the integration of black belief into the white man's world, and it is important to see that this belief is both tenacious and transformative. For example, stanza three begins: "Neither the slave's whip nor the lynchers' rope nor the / bayonet could kill our black belief," and ends by evoking the book of Revelations (also a radical Puritan creed): "we have been believers in the new Jerusalem." Yet Walker is perhaps most concerned here with the relationship of faith and labor. As "silent and stolid and stubborn and / strong" as black belief has been, there is behind it the tacit question of whose new Jerusalem will be built. Black labor has certainly a tradition of building, but not a Jerusalem of its own. That the American economy could not have survived and grown as it did without the slave labor of African Americans is a fact that cannot be ignored.

> We have been believers yielding substance for the world.
> With our hands have we fed a people and out of our
> strength have they wrung the necessities of a nation.
> Our song has filled the twilight and our hope has
> heralded the dawn.

Walker became quite interested in the plight of contemporary black labor during her years in Chicago. Her interest in labor issues and worker militancy seems to have been shaped by her contact with radical writers in the WPA. In letters of the period that Walker wrote to Richard Wright after he had left Chicago for New York, she discusses union matters concerning the Federal Writers' Project. By becoming an "organized" intellectual worker she was able to feel empowered in ways the generations she speaks of in her poems were not. Though Walker's participation in the Writers Project in Chicago brought her in contact with various forms of radical practices, the Communist Party being the most prominent, Walker has claimed that it was the Congress of Industrial Organizations—the CIO—rather than the party that spoke to her and other members of Chicago's black community. As Drake and Cayton write of the CIO's influence on African Americans in Chicago: "Belief in racial equality was a component part of its ideology, and was kept constantly before the membership by a vigorous left-wing minority within the CIO. Formerly skeptical of the white man's union, both the Negro workers and the Negro community became pro-CIO" (313).[17] Black skepticism of unions had been traditionally maintained by companies using black laborers as strikebreakers. Employers also used race hatred and fear consistently to divide workers. As the CIO became identified with class solidarity, it also became one of the first arenas in which black workers could question and condemn racial inequality. The CIO's organizing tactics to attract African Americans were not only centered on fighting discrimination in the workplace but also in protesting segregation as well as campaigning for fair housing practices and overall improved living conditions. Of course the CIO could offer no absolute guarantee that discrimination would fade from the workplace, but as one worker admitted contemplating "the former role of [African Americans] as strikebreakers," "[r]ace prejudice will only be overcome through a sustained campaign of education. It will take years to do this. We need the universities, the radio, the press to help us" (339).

One strike of major importance in the annals of CIO militancy in the 1930s that included the participation of African Americans, was the Republic Steel Strike. In May of 1937, twenty thousand workers at the South Chicago–based plant walked off their jobs. They struck for "union recognition and a wage increase" (321). Margaret Walker's memory is closely connected to an incident of the strike that made national headlines, the Memorial Day Massacre. In fact she confessed to Richard Wright, in a letter written a month after the event, that her attempts to produce a poem on the subject did not prove "effective." As Drake and Cayton describe the massacre:

On Sunday, May 30, 1937, a crowd of some 5,000 people [white and black]—strikers, their wives and children, and union sympathizers—were assembled near the plant for purposes of mass picketing and demonstrations. During the afternoon a disturbance occurred and the police fired into the crowd. Ten workers were killed, and nine more persons were injured. The police were severely and widely denounced for unprovoked and excessive brutality. They claimed they were "attacked," but impartial evidence assembled at the time contained nothing to justify their conduct. (321)

Walker may have been unable to produce a poem that could satisfactorily represent the anger induced by the massacre. Her belief in industrial organizing that might successfully integrate blacks into American political and economic life suggests, however, a turn from a false set of hopes to acknowledging a new, albeit violent, struggle for freedom. One might read these beliefs into the strident ending of the poem "We Have Been Believers":

We have been believers believing in our burdens and our
demigods too long. Now the needy no longer weep and
pray; the long-suffering arise, and our fists bleed
against the bars with a strange insistency.

The bleeding fists transform a passive faith connected to "burdens" and "demigods" into an active body capable of moving forward. Like the "race of men" (and women) that will "rise and take control" in the finale of "For My People," belief becomes an insistent cry to resist both acquiescence and the oppression that has produced it.

Walker's representation of the culture of belief embedded in African American life reflects the strong spiritual influences of her southern background. It is not surprising that the South, and the conflicting set of images associated with it, permeate *For My People*. It is important to consider how, as a radical poet, she imagines and shapes the South's problematic history. The location of the writer is another important consideration. Walker's poems are products of the northern migration, and in their scripted distance they present a dichotomy in terms of representation. They reproduce the migration as a text, much the same way Jacob Lawrence's paintings did in his series "The Migration of the Negro." These aesthetic documents record the experience of many.[18] Moreover, they speak both longingly and angrily of the South. They also contain a sense of militancy familiar to Depression-era readers of poetry. As angry indictments of slavery and the continuation of racial exploitation in its aftermath, they concretize social and economic injustice. Walker often uses the angry linguistic codes of the labor chants from the radical literary circles in which she traveled while in Chicago, but she exchanges the northern industrial setting for the rural south. The North has always represented more relative freedom for African Americans, yet the South is kin. A kind of schizophrenia develops. The South is a place longed for, at the same time its need for transformation is acknowledged. Thus Walker finds herself creating from two places: the material realities that dictated the northern migration and the southern homeland that resides inside her heart.

The poem "Sorrow Home" exemplifies this sense of displacement. Its title alone suggests it could be an anthem for the two million African Americans who went north in the first three decades of the twentieth century. As she speaks for her people in this poem, Walker takes a glance backward. She confesses, "[m]y roots are deep in southern life. . . . I was sired and weaned / in a tropic world." She continues to remind readers of the lushness in stark contrast to "steel and wood and brick far from the sky" that is Chicago. "Warm skies and gulf blue streams are in my blood. I belong / with the smell of fresh pine, with the trail of coon, and / the spring growth of wild onion." In fact Walker identifies her distance from this familiar territory through a trope of organicism. "I am no hothouse bulb to be reared in steam-heated flats / with the music of El and subway in my ears." Geography for Walker is more than just the binarisms of rural and urban; it is the source of her conflict and alienation. The contradictory elements that name both the South and the North as problematic residences keep the poet above romanticizing either place. Yet as she faces homesickness for her Southland, she must always be conscious of the historical price tag sewn into the "cotton fields, tobacco and the cane."

Perhaps Walker's most penetrating look at the southern landscape is in the long poem "Delta." In "Delta," Walker imagines the homeland reclaimed by those who created both its economic and historical significance. She describes a people who move "beyond your reach O mighty winnowing flail! / infinite and free" through their ability to recognize themselves as historical agents. While "Sorrow Home" possesses a resigned terseness, a South constructed through a history of racial oppression, its "Klan of hate," its "hounds," and its "chain gangs," "Delta" reveals Walker's attempt to denaturalize the desire for the South as home through the left ideological perspectives she learned in Chicago. Yet, however important it is to reflect upon social being as mediated through material conditions, the acknowledgment of class conflict and class consciousness does not adequately explain the institutionalized racism endured by the people of the "Delta." The frustrations and desires of a people whose social being is so inextricably linked to both class and race antagonism require a more complicated analysis. The marxism that influenced Walker during her Chicago years, with its European industrial origins and blindness toward gender concerns, could hardly theorize the lot of most delta women, although some women benefited from the Share Croppers' Unions that the Communist Party helped organize in Alabama, Mississippi, and Louisiana in the early 1930s.[19] The question of race most certainly complicates an ideological framework structured to unite a working class consistently at odds with the contradictions of its own racial privileges in the case of white workers, or lack thereof, in the case of black workers. Moreover, the sexual division of labor that existed in northern working-class communities was radically different for black women of the delta; traditionally, women and men worked side by side in the fields—a phenomenon that few white workers would experience or understand. What is more, however, both black and white women shared the burden of the double shift: work in the fields or the factories, and work in the home.[20] Perhaps Walker did not foresee the complicated relationships black workers in the South encountered through the narrowly conceived marxist pedagogy at her disposal in Chicago; yet the poem "Delta" itself grounds such contradictions surprisingly well.

"Delta" conveys, through the lusciousness of its language and its rhythmic verse cadences, a sorrowful history that makes the poet's problematized territorial desire for the South all the more powerful. The poem lovingly renders the South as a fertile, voluptuous body, while also portraying it as a tormented and enslaved body that has cultivated itself in its own chains. "Delta" is not only a travelogue told by one of its homesick exiles but also a survey of the political economy told in verse by the offspring of its laborers.

The poem constructs its South through the trajectory of birth, labor, and rising consciousness. This triad commences in the first person with the speaker *being* ("a child of the valley"), *watching* ("rivulets flow"), *listening* ("lullabies," "blues"), and *thinking of convergence:* "If only from this valley we might rise with song! / With singing that is ours." The poem's second section moves into the plural, the collective, the laboring body that defines itself through generations who moved in alienating similarity "in this low valley." That "[d]aily we fill boats with cargoes of our need / and send them out to sea" is Walker's message, contained within the verdancy of the place, the richness of the soil: "We tend the crop and gather the harvest / but not for ourselves do we labor." Walker is resolute in representing estranged labor as it rests fitfully in its haunted valley:

Out of a deep slumber truth rides upon us
and we wonder why we are helpless
and we wonder why we are dumb.

In the poem's third and final stanza, to keep with the language of the landscape, the earth, the "delta" as the poet describes it, Walker interjects the possibility of forces that will disrupt acquiescence and naturalness. Home, where the southern valleys quake with a desire for an insurrection of consciousness, begins with the sleep-shattering questions of the above lines. Seasonal metaphors, eclipsing winters and regenerative springs, are used as linguistic fortifications of a regional restructuring of consciousness. This is evidenced in the way Walker opens the section:

Now burst dams of years
and winter snows melt with an onrush of a turbulent
spring.
Now rises sap in slumbering elms
and floods overwhelm us
here in this low valley.

With the "years" of servility bursting and spring a "turbulent" rather than calming season, elms sapping and "floods" overwhelming the historically docile valley, the poet attempts to denaturalize the longing for home—which in actuality has been a place of degrading hardship, dehumanizing labor, and enforced poverty, as well as ignorance. The valley is not just ripe for growing and harvesting but for "thundering" sounds that will disturb the thought process, with "cannons boom[ing] in our brains / and there is a dawning understanding / in the valleys of our spirits." Walker contrasts the valley's growing season with the awakening of those who make it grow, while the traditionally fertile crescent continues to be represented as a site of intervention: "Into our troubled living flows the valley / flooding our lives with a passion for freedom." What is more, as in "Sorrow Home," she plays linguistically with the idea of organicism. The oppressed bodies of those who have made and are thus the land must reclaim it: "We with our blood have watered these fields / and they belong to us."

While I have articulated Walker's representations of the laboring black body in the black South in poems such as "We Have Been Believers" and "Delta," it is also important to explore the cultural material woven from laboring life, which had also influenced the way Walker saw her southern home. As Walker was writing poems in the vein of Walt Whitman and Langston Hughes, she was also looking to southern oral traditions such as folktales and folk songs as sources of poetic inspiration; these were also traditions from which to borrow in order to reinvent modern poetry from her own perspective as an African American woman. Walker's letters to Richard Wright indicate that she struggled to perfect a series of "folk tales." Although she does not provide any specific examples in these letters, she was most likely referring to the poems that appear in the second section of *For My People*. In these particular poems Walker rearticulates the legacies of familiar folklife characters. Her lyrics describe the exploits of tricksters, conjurers, gamblers, bootleggers, pimps, and laborers, accentuating the nuanced lives of African American folk heroes and heroines.

Walker grew up in a household where the *word* was sacrosanct. Her maternal grandmother's storytelling no doubt introduced her to the rich and varied folklore produced in the antebellum South that would resurface later in the pages of the novel *Jubilee*. Additionally, the African American folktale is an important literary form for Walker, the poet, to be working with in the 1930s. If *For My People* challenges the "Anglo-Saxonness" and class biases of high modernism through its exploration of black consciousness and racial oppression, its appropriation of folk forms is central to this challenge.[21]

In his engrossing study of black culture-building in America, *Black Culture and Black Consciousness,* Lawrence Levine examines the development of the folktale tradition from slavery times through and beyond the period of emancipation. In the twentieth century, he notes, black communities throughout the United States were captivated by "supernatural tales, moral and didactic tales, human and animal trickster tales, tales centering on both real and apocryphal personal experiences . . . the entire range of tales that slaves had told and retold" (368). Storytelling, as art as well as entertainment, remained a significant source of cultural continuity. As Levine also points out, the folk heroes that surfaced after emancipation underwent a significant change from the narrow range of heroes represented in the antebellum period. "[N]ew figures appeared and old ones were frequently altered in aspect or significance. . . . Neither the heroes nor the consciousness that molded them remained static in the century following emancipation" (369–70).

Walker retells ten folk lyrics, including two tales, "Bad-Man Stagolee" and "Big John Henry," whose immense popularity (though as legends they are at odds with each other) have crossed over into mainstream American popular culture.[22] Walker's particular telling of "Bad-Man Stagolee" and "Kissie Lee" suggest important connections to Walker's raced, classed, and gendered poetic articulations. With the poem "Bad-Man Stagolee," Walker reinscribes the Stagolee legend with a complicated twist coupling the policing of black communities with the hero's popularity. Then with "Kissie Lee," Walker rewrites the folktale genre's androcentric bias, as well as the black community's identification of the trickster archetype as male, by answering the Stagolee story with the tale of a knife-wielding female tough.

As legend tells it, "Bad-Man Stagolee" (pronounced Stack'-a-lee, as Walker informs readers in a footnote) shot a man called Billy Lyons after losing to him at cards (or craps). Date, place, and stakes all vary, but in a blues version recorded by Mississippi John Hurt in 1929, "Stagolee shot Billy . . . [for] a five-dollar Stetson hat" (Marcus 76–77).[23] Additionally, according to folk-song collector Alan Lomax, Stagolee is generally arrested for his crimes, executed in some fashion, and sent down to hell.[24] Yet like the many renditions of the Stagolee tale that have circulated, Walker's version also differs. It contains a twist that refashions it for its contemporary urban audience.

That Stagolee was an all-right lad
Till he killed a cop and turned out bad,
Though some do say to this very day
He killed more'n one 'fore he killed that 'fay.

By transforming Stagolee into an "all-right lad" who kills a cop, Walker conflates a number of the versions of the tale into one that identifies Stagolee with violence as an everyday reality for African American communities throughout the nation. The cop, assumed to be white, suggests a fantasy of revenge for the police brutality that black communities have historically had visited upon them. Perhaps the resituated Stagolee was inspired by real events happening in Chicago at the time Walker appears to have worked on the tales. While helping Richard Wright reconstruct the events of the Nixon case (a young black man on trial for murder) on which much of *Native Son* was based, in a letter that included clippings on the trial from the local papers, she comments on the state of affairs between Chicago's black community and the police department:

> You may not know all the brutal attacks of the Chicago Police since last memorial day. Police history in Chicago since that time has been one succession of brutality and intimidation after another. The Maxwell Street Station has become famous for getting confessions by the third degree method and today one Negro boy is permanently paralyzed because of police doings. These rape cases appear annually about this time to increase circulation and I know personally that 56 Negro boys were picked up on the North Side in connection with a murder last fall committed by the woman's sweetheart.[25]

Remaining the stuff of legends, and fashioned with irony in the poem, the figure of Stagolee is a resituated metaphor for what social ills create. Walker's Stagolee contains the same invincible curiosity that all the previous tellers have given him, and she informs us "the tale ain't new," but she stretches the legend from its celebration of Stagolee as mean individualist, to a tale with political undertones. In Walker's telling, Stagolee, after his "bullets made holes no doc could cyo," is able to disappear without being apprehended, eluding the racist taunts and torments which then lead to lynching:

But the funniest thing about that job
Was he never got caught by no mob
And he missed the lynching meant for his hide
'Cause nobody knows how Stagolee died

To highlight Walker's retelling as seemingly political, one must see that the Stagolee story maintained its importance in the black community through its radical symbolism. The myth presents a man whose outlandish and wholly autonomous antics signify the ultimate in freedom in a nation in which that freedom has been most brutally curtailed. Walker's reinterpretation of Stagolee's transgressions further inscribes the story with a hegemonical challenge. Stagolee doesn't just kill a fellow hood, a compatriot gambler, as he does in other versions of the tale: he kills a cop. (He messes with authority; he messes with white America, and he gets away with it.) This is how he becomes a legend.

Bad-Man Stagolee ain't no more
But his ghost still walks up and down the shore
Of Old Man River round New Orleans
With her gumbo, rice, and good red beans!

Yet there is a problem in politicizing the Stagolee tale as well. The legend, apparently built around the careers of two actual turn-of-the-century criminals, Morris Slater and Railroad Bill, is not, according to Lawrence Levine's reading, one that lends itself to romanticization or sentimentalizing.[26] Though Walker's rendition celebrates Stagolee's elusiveness in the face of white authority, he is not Robin Hood nor even Pretty Boy Floyd; his actions never lead to any acts of genuine goodwill within the black community, and the tellers of the tale seem to have been generally conscious of this fact. As Levine maintains, "[these folk heroes] were not given any socially redeeming characteristics simply because in them there was no hope of social redemption" (419). More important, to romanticize folk legends such as Stagolee would be to play with the important dose of reality that Walker, under the tutelage of Wrightian naturalism, perhaps wanted to convey with stories about the more sordid figures of African American folklife, thus reminding her Depression audience of the complicated nature of literary representation.

If "Bad-Man Stagolee" is a tale known far and wide, whose influence has even crossed over into mainstream popular culture, Walker's tale of the female tough "Kissie Lee" recollects a folk hero from the margins. Yet mainstream popular culture, while it is able not only to tolerate but idolize a "bad man" like Stagolee, is apparently not ready to meet his female counterpart in the ballad Walker tells of this good girl turned bad.

> Toughest gal I ever did see
> Was a gal by the name of Kissie Lee;
> The toughest gal God ever made
> And she drew a dirty, wicked blade.

As in "Bad-Man Stagolee" violence in "Kissie Lee" is treated matter-of-factly. What's more, the violence depicted (but not demonized) in these tales is always connected in larger terms to the complex structures of powerlessness found in the communities of their tellers. However, where Walker depicts Stagolee's end in slippery terms as a conscious effort to problematize his legendary import, Kissie Lee lives a life of violence and dies violently as any bad man might.

> She could shoot glass offa the hinges,
> She could take herself on the wildest binges.
> And she died with her boots on switching blades
> On Talladega Mountain in the likker raids.

Perhaps what is most striking is that like the woman of another tale Walker retells, "Yalluh Hammah," in which a female trickster outsmarts a guy who likes to "lay his jive," Kissie Lee's story is about the fierce independence of the female folk hero in a tradition in which the "mens" seem to get all the attention. As with the poem cited in the beginning of this chapter, "Lineage," Walker takes the unsung strength of African American women and provides a space for their recognition inside a literary genre and cultural context in which questions of black women's oppression remained as yet unarticulated. Rather than creating a separate text in which the voices of black women emerge, she acknowledges their labor alongside the men, as well as their legendary transgressions in the case of Kissie Lee, as part of a total dialogue on black structures of feeling that she has attempted to record in *For My People*.

Black folktale culture is decidedly masculine in outlook. Maintaining masculine heroes such as Stagolee and John Henry has been traditionally important in resisting a white racist culture, one determined if not to destroy, at least to stereotype black men through emasculation. The emergence of a folk figure such as Kissie Lee challenges the existing framework in which the bad male folk heroes appear representative.[27] According to Walker's telling, Kissie Lee's abuse at the hands of "a no good shine" is what shapes her character as "the toughest gal God ever made." What is equally striking about Walker's interest in this tale is that like the poem "Lineage," Kissie Lee's turn from victim to agent appears part of a dynamic process controlled by women. Kissie Lee is not the first in line of bad-girl heroes. Her "Grammaw," tired of Kissie's "whinin'," offers the insight that "[p]eople don't ever treat you right," and urges her to do as she has done:

"Whin I was a gal wasn't no soul
Could do me wrong an' still stay whole.
Ah got me a razor to talk for me
An' aftah that they let me be."

Not only does Kissie, within the ironic boundaries of the bad folk hero convention, receive advice through a matrilineal history, but such a historical line suggests the badness of women as a form of self-preservation and pursuit of female agency en suite. Kissie Lee, taking her grandmother's advice, takes this malfeasance a step further: "'Cause when she learned to stab and run / She got herself a little gun." As Kissie graduates from mean gal to "[m]eanest mama you ever seen," she also (in keeping with the superpower suggestions of the bad-man folk legends) loses her status as victim, attains the status of "woman," while at the same time appears to maintain an independence that collapses both stated regions as sites of negotiation: "She could hold her likker and hold her man / And she went thoo life jus' raisin' san'."

The climax of the tale is Kissie's revenge on a man who "done her dirt long time ago / [w]hen she was good and feeling low." Not only does Kissie shoot him "to the floor," but to reveal the determination of her vengeful spirit, she flashes her blade so that "[e]vvy livin' guy got out of her way." Walker tells us that Kissie dies "with her boots on switching blades." As with the other tales, we are given no moral; such is inconceivable in a community that cannot realistically hope that its acts of revenge will not provoke even graver retaliations. Thus as much as Kissie's story invokes female agency, it is not a tale of uplift for black women. Just as judgment on the activity of the men is reserved, so is such judgment reserved for the equally bad women. Walker creates with "Kissie Lee" a presence for black women as tricksters and evildoers as much as she creates a presence for those women (and men) who dared tell their stories.[28]

"Kissie Lee" as transgressor tale bears relation to another important African American aesthetic genre that Walker would have been aware of as she worked on these tales. Blues music, which made much use of African American folktales, was also a cultural phenomenon that women not only participated in but also greatly enriched. Hazel Carby and Angela Davis have lamented the scant scholarship in the area of "women's blues."[29]

The predominant themes in women's blues are related to romantic and domestic preoccupations and therefore seem miles away from the independent individualism portrayed in "Kissie Lee." Yet Angela Davis contends in her essay "I Used to Be Your Sweet Mama" that the romantic and domestic attitudes represented in the blues of pioneers such as Bessie Smith and Gertrude "Ma" Rainey complicate "the prevailing idealization of romantic love in the dominant culture" (237). Blues music, like the transformed African American folklore genre, is a phenomenon of postbellum freedom and celebrates that freedom to the extreme. The ability to work, love, and travel where and how one pleased, for the first time in the history of black America, became the signifying trope of the blues genre. The rough antics Walker describes in "Kissie Lee" are decidedly kin to this exploration of freedom. In many ways Kissie's tale is the reverse of the disheartening tunes of betrayal and abuse that Davis examines in her reading of women's blues. Yet Davis also points to the complex sexual awareness of Smith's and Rainey's music. In fact their frank knowledge and exploration of sexuality and domestic violence are some of the first glimpses we have of the cycle of abuse that women have had historically visited upon them. As previously suggested, Kissie Lee becomes the hero she is because she avenges her own (implied) physical abuse at the hands of a "no good shine." As Davis remarks, with some relevance to Walker's reconstruction of "Kissie Lee":

What is most significant about women's blues as they suggest emergent feminist insurgency is that they unabashedly name the problem of male violence, ushering it out of the shadows of domestic life behind which society dictated it be hidden. (251)

The blues lovingly given to us by Smith and Rainey "allude to rejection, abuse, desertion and unfaithful lovers," but they also persistently explore "independence . . . assertiveness, indeed defiance" (245). "Kissie Lee," though not a tale that directly confronts sexuality or domestic disharmony—the predominant tropes of women's blues—embraces the celebration of a precarious freedom and places "independence," "assertiveness," and "defiance" above all else.

While "Kissie Lee" remains a tale of black female agency, even if from the social margins, Walker leaves her readers with a less sanguine view of black working-class female subjectivity in the poem "Whores," which is part of a sonnet sequence that closes *For My People*. Whether intentional or coincidental, "Whores" represents a closing commentary on black women that is rather different from the representations found in the text's first and second sections. If "Lineage" characterizes black women's contributions to labor history as represented in the first section of *For My People*, while "Kissie Lee," in the second section, entertains readers with the legendary power of the bad female folk hero, "Whores" suggests black women's powerlessness as it depicts real, not mythical, female transgressors.

When I grew up I went away to work
where painted whores were fascinating sights.
They came on like whole armies through the nights—
their sullen eyes on mine, their mouths a smirk,
and from their hands keys hung suggestively.
Old women working by an age-old plan
to make their bread in ways as best they can
would hobble past and beckon tirelessly.

Perhaps one day they'll all die in the streets
or be surprised by bombs in each wide bed;
learning too late in unaccustomed dread

that easy ways, like whores on special beats,
no longer have the gift to harbor pride
or bring men peace, or leave them satisfied.

As a poem by a young black woman, "Whores" is full of contradictions. The prostitute, as she is depicted as a "fascinating sight," is subject to the poet's scrutiny. Yet she is also put under the watchful scrutiny of the social order that demands and purveys her services. The poem's form is important as well. Walker deconstructs the sonnet as it is conventionally associated with the romance tradition by writing about black working-class women's sex work. Walker reappropriates the Petrarchan sonneteer's convention of assessing and praising the attributes of an exalted figure (most notably a lover) by describing sympathetically in the opening octet, and then more judgmentally in the closing sestet, the woman made spectacle by the degrading and exhausting machinations of her trade.

Before analyzing the sonnet at greater length, it is important to look at the historical context that informed the poem's creation. Walker's inspiration for "Whores" came from her work on a WPA-sponsored recreation program for which she volunteered during her senior year at Northwestern. As Walker explained to poet Nikki Giovanni many years later:

> They gave me a group of so-called delinquent girls to pal around with in order to see what kind of influence a person with my background and training would have on them. They were shoplifters, prostitutes, and who knows what else? It wasn't a time when you had a widespread problem with drugs, so the two main problems were shoplifting and prostitution. Division Street was the street for prostitutes. . . . They walked Division Street and . . . *jangled their keys*. (*Poetic Equation* 90)

Not only did Walker's experience with the young prostitutes inspire her to write "Whores," it also gave her background, and later a stipend, to start work on the unpublished novel *Goose Island*. The novel deals with a talented, promising young woman who eventually ends up a Division Street prostitute. The title is the name of the Italian and black neighborhood in which Walker worked with the young "so-called delinquents."[30] Yet the woman of Walker's "background and training" has much to learn from her subjects. The abhorrence of prostitute life that can be gleaned from the poem suggests that the educated young poet may indeed be taught something about social imbalances within patriarchal society by her contact with the Division Street prostitutes. The details of her early attempts at social work that Walker supplies to Nikki Giovanni suggest her naiveté, which might explain the fascination turned to disdain and judgment evoked in the sonnet. Walker explains that her southern, "more provincial" background aroused her curiosity as she began to observe prostitute life in Chicago. "That's when I learned that prostitution and gambling were vices tied up with city politics" (90). Additionally, her introduction to urban social vices was linked to the very program on which she worked, as she implicates her employers: "[o]ne of the straw bosses on the project was a man who was a pimp; his brother was a smuggler dealing in narcotics and everything" (90). Yet while Walker's understanding of sex work appears limited to her work on the WPA recreation project, St. Clair Drake and Horace Cayton's discussion of prostitution in Chicago's Bronzeville sheds some additional light on the traffic in black women articulated in "Whores." During the period in which the poem was probably composed the district's "reputation as a vice area was reinforced by the prevalence of streetwalkers in certain areas" (596).[31] The opinions of social workers and policemen concurred. Race discrimination made the women of Bronzeville more obvious targets for arrest. While young girls without opportunity became more susceptible to the "trade," black women who were not prostitutes were picked up because of their close proximity to it. As Drake and Cayton observe:

> During the Depression years the boldness of [prostitutes'] solicitations drew bitter comments from lower-class women who were trying to maintain stable relations with their men or *raise children right*. Thus one lower-class housewife, when asked about the building in which she lived, replied: "Honey, this place is full of whores. They are the cheapest, nastiest set in Chicago. If I could get me another place I wouldn't be here."
> (596)

A close analysis of "Whores" suggests that Walker's sympathies lay with Drake and Cayton's disgruntled housewife. The poem maintains a sharp distance from its subject, connected, as previously suggested, to Walker's southern, middle-class, educated perceptions of the northern urban prostitute. Her religious upbringing perhaps instilled in her a sense of judgment about the uses of sexuality. Yet Walker may also be limited in her understanding of the contradictory elements at stake with regard to sex work by the rampantly uncomplicated attitude toward the prostitute she would have been exposed to in Chicago leftist circles at that time. For example, stridently accusatory tropes that linked prostitution with capitalism were popular features in Depression-era radical reportage and proletarian writing. Indeed, rather than revealing an understanding of African American social and economic disenfranchisement, "Whores" reads as a pitying response to black women's transgressions. As historian Kevin Mumford notes in his work on black/white sex districts in Chicago and New York in the early twentieth century, "Racism in the market—black women's relegation to domestic service, their vulnerability to sexual harassment, and segregated service in brothels—combined to increase the probability that African-American women would enter prostitution." As Mumford adds to this already discouraging scenario, "[a]t the same time racism operated within the markets of commercialized sex, forcing women of color to negotiate yet another set of racial stigmas and hierarchies" (96). While Walker would most certainly have gathered that the prostitute's underemployment was due to race and gender prejudice in the North and was inextricably linked with her decision to work as a prostitute, the sympathetic gaze she gives to workers in her other poems is decidedly absent from "Whores."

Like a number of the other sonnets in this final section, "Whores" is constructed as a memory. Not only are these prostitutes removed from the poet because of differences in lifestyle and opportunity, they are described from a historical distance—a past memory. Thus interesting ambiguities arise in the speaker's voice. The poet's naiveté makes these women "fascinating sights"; she is encountering the northern prostitute for the first time, and her work on the recreation project requires her to tune into the concerns and desires of young women whose lives and hers would not otherwise intersect. Yet the gaze Walker constructs in this poem also suggests the male gaze the prostitute receives as she presents her wares in the marketplace. "Their sullen eyes on mine" with their "keys hung suggestively" describe them the way they are seen by their potential purchasers—men whose race and class are unknown to us. The poem's disengaged tone suggests more than one possible speaking voice; however, imagining the young, college-educated Walker as speaker, we are offered an interesting contrast between the poet's intellectual work and the belittling sex work performed by the Division Street prostitutes. After all, the poet's work with young delinquent girls who have, among other things, been picked up for prostitution, prepares her to see "whores" through the eyes of a reformer. She represents, ironically in the midst of Depression, the world of real work— social work. These women are also removed from the speaker by age and class: "Old women working by an age-old plan / to make their bread in ways as best they can."

The poem's closing sestet is more ambiguous, while retaining its judgmental tone. Walker imagines her subjects dead "in the streets" or "surprised by bombs," which suggests a call for their destruction. To rearticulate an important point, in the poems previously discussed in this chapter, Walker explores the complicated relations of her subjects to the social praxis inscribing them. This particular poem rather dispassionately observes the labor of black women without spending much energy on the alienated confines in which they have been scripted. However, the reference to "whores on special beats" suggests an important dichotomy of prostitute life, the body that is negotiated between the police and the pimp. Walker reflects upon the complicated relationship between prostitution and the economic and social surveillance of black women by connecting the illegal trade of prostitution with the law itself. The police, those other beat walkers, become "whores on special beats"; thus Walker alludes to police involvement in the city's underworld activities, in which these women and their pimps are also intimately linked.[32] These "special beats" also suggest the prostitute working the turf controlled by her pimp. She does not control her own means of employment (and production), her body. Whether on the police or pimp's "special beats," these women "no longer have the gift to harbor pride / or bring men peace." These final lines, which in the traditional sonnet are executed to suggest a resolution about love, negate such a possibility: the traffic in (black) working-class women continues; black intellectual workers like Walker can only observe.

If "Whores" settles upon a bleakness of experience symbolized through the prostitute and her marks upon the pavement, two poems that close *For My People* suggest a kind of dialectic between resignation and struggle that is also signified in the text as a whole. "Our Need" and "The Struggle Staggers Us" are sonnets of hope, even as they embrace the dismal reality of a world moved out of Depression into war. In "Our Need," Walker hopes for "a wholeness born of inner strength," and "the friendly feel of human forms." Thus the humanity stripped from "Whores" returns even if, as she laments in the title of the collection's final poem, "the struggle staggers us." *For My People* is a book about struggle. Given the larger social questions that Walker's years in Chicago provided her with, the struggle she acknowledges may be collective, but it is also one of daily survival and the personal, ordinary claims that inscribe the "struggle between the morning and the night." This need and this struggle that Walker hopes to see fashioned into a "journey from the me to you" and a "journey from the you to me," in fact anticipates the conscious rumblings of the Civil Rights era. It is rather significant that *For My People* appears in 1942, toward the close of a historic period that has been characterized as the end of European dominance (1492–1945). It is a text about domination, about the resistance to domination, and about the possibility of transcending domination even as "the struggle staggers us." *For My People* is a collection of poems that has named and claimed a history and a movement for African American struggle before a large-scale agenda had been inaugurated. It is interesting, though not surprising from an author who was also a working mother, that Walker did not follow *For My People* with another book of poems until the mid-1960s. Like the 1930s and early 1940s, the period in which Margaret Walker began to publish her first important social poems, the 1960s was a time of social passion and protest. It seems that Walker's writing ground, her place to articulate the aesthetics of race and class, not to mention her interest in rearticulating the tropes of psychology, religion, and science mentioned at the opening of this chapter, were to be once again inspired by what was happening in the streets of America's cities (like Chicago) in the 1960s.

Afterword

The reason I write history is that I am interested in other practices, less cut off and abstract, which once existed and might still be learned from.

T. J. Clark, *Farewell to an Idea*

About the time I completed this book the Library of America published volumes one and two of *American Poetry: The Twentieth Century* (the first two of a series that will cover the entire century). Organized chronologically by birth date, volume one contains work by major and "minor" poets from Henry Adams to Dorothy Parker. Volume two includes major and minor poets from e. e. cummings to May Swenson. This anticipated multivolume text appears to represent itself as a corrective document to the narrowly constructed poetry anthologies that were published under the aegis of the New Criticism. In a sense it attempts to be inclusive in the way the anthologies of the 1920s and 1930s managed to be. It includes not only the work of major and minor poets but also anonymous ballads, as well as lyrics by blues and popular song composers.[1] The Library of America's fall 2000 catalogue generously describes the anthology's distinctiveness: "folk ballads on current events, erotic sonnets, visionary landscapes, exercises in Chinoiserie, blues lyrics, humorous verse, Dadaist experiments, and the neo-traditionalism of the Fugitives" (of course!).

With regard to my study of Lola Ridge, Genevieve Taggard, and Margaret Walker in particular, and women poets on the left in general, *American Poetry* is problematic. This text is an impressive compendium of the enormous range and activity of America's modern poets; yet like any anthology it is very much a reflection of the tastes of its editors.[2] While there is nothing wrong with the text's representative tastes, the anthology's broad emphasis and grand scheme is bound to fail poets like Lola Ridge and Genevieve Taggard. The power of their social poems, and hence their positioning as social poets, collapses under the weight of the text's grand design. Their work appears in essentially the same position as it has been previously represented vis-à-vis the modernist canon. *American Poetry* presents the problem of seeing twentieth-century American poetry in one grand sweep. My efforts in this study have been to place Ridge, Taggard, and Walker in a rather more complicated position, by recovering and/or reevaluating them through the social and political contact zones that produced their voices of resistance.

Lola Ridge appears in volume one, thus righting her neglect by previous postwar anthologies. Yet the examples of her work are hardly representative, particularly if one wants to read Ridge as a feminist or radical poet. Two excerpts from "The Ghetto" are included in the five pages devoted to her work. Sections one and six of the poem show Ridge as a skilled imagist poet. However neither section reveals the attention to gender that is a central feature of this dynamic work. (One might question whether it is even fair to take this important poem out of context as the editors have done.) The other two poems, "Fifth-Story Window" and "Kerensky" are interesting, but come from perhaps Ridge's weakest book, *Red Flag*. These two poems certainly illustrate the poet's political consciousness, but their inclusion also reflects an attitude about "literariness" that typifies the anthologies published under the influence of the New Criticism. They are descriptive narrative poems that speak more about language than they do about the social and historical spaces that produced them. They also lack the directness—a bold feature of much of Ridge's work—that can be found, for example, in "Electrocution" and "Morning Ride," the two poems from this same collection that I discuss in detail in chapter 2. Each poem's direct embrace of the social world, each poem's use of imagery to lay bare the bodily manifestations of pain to readers generally accustomed to poems about love, the natural world, or the artist's erudition or alienation, are left out of Ridge's contributions to *American Poetry.* As a result, her power as a poet is weakened. While the anthology format as a given stunts artistic expression by taking a writer's work out of context, Ridge's directness, her power to expose and expose bluntly, is buried. One might ask what Ridge's legacy would look like in *American Poetry* if poems like "Electrocution" and "Morning Ride" had been included as well. The timeliness of these works is one consideration; the subjects of these poems—the death penalty and racially motivated murder—are live issues in America at the dawn of the twenty-first century.

Genevieve Taggard's work appears in the second volume of *American Poetry.* Twelve of her poems were selected—a total of seven pages. Three poems from her most "class-conscious" book, *Calling Western Union,* are included. Yet two of these three poems, "Everyday Alchemy" and "Try Tropic," were composed in the 1920s and were reprinted in *Calling Western Union* from earlier books. The editors exclusion of the "original" poetry in *Calling Western Union* de-emphasizes Taggard's social vision as a Depression-era writer. Taggard's overall representation in *American Poetry* de-emphasizes her socialist and feminist leanings. Nonetheless, "Try Tropic" and "All Around the Town" are interesting inclusions for this anthology; as bit-ing satire they also reveal Taggard's critique of capitalism. "All Around the Town" ingeniously equates the unequal distribution of wealth evidenced in Manhattan real estate with the American poetry scene in the 1930s. "Eliot Park" is for "key holders only," and devoid of the life provided by "roller skaters" and "hurdy-gurdies," not to mention other aspects of pop culture implied in the poem's title—a phrase taken from a music hall song. As the poet comments how "unusually high" rents are in the "Tate section," she also pays homage to fellow marxist poet, Kenneth Fearing (who after decades of neglect has a hefty representation in *American Poetry*): "I like Fearing Sq., myself. It is so central." As Taggard rewrites the history of modern American poetry by placing herself at its center with fellow radical Fearing, she does an ironic justice to the characteristic omissions found in most poetry anthologies, including this one. She leaves for posterity to readers who will come across her work probably for the first time a critique of the very poetry industry that demolished Fearing Sq. only to reconstruct it at century's end when its central location (read as representative of left culture and ideology) has disappeared from the public imaginary.

Born in 1915, Margaret Walker misses inclusion in volume two of *American Poetry* by two years; it ends with May Swenson who was born in 1913. Walker will no doubt appear in volume three, and we will have to wait for its publication to assess the poems selected to represent her.

Other female social poets such as Ruth Lechlitner, Lucia Trent, and Marie de L. Welch are notably absent from *American Poetry*, while other forgotten and/or rediscovered poets have been included. Anyone reading the *New Masses* in the late 1920s and 1930s would be familiar with Lechlitner, Trent, and Welch, but this identification alone is not enough to justify inclusion in broadly defined anthologies such as *American Poetry*.[3] As no single anthology can represent every aspect of literary and cultural production when it comes to modern American poetry, we must read between the lines. Part of the task of *Women Poets on the Left* has been to suggest another place to begin reading.

As I pointed out in chapter 1, two generations separate Ridge, Taggard, and Walker; thus *American Poetry* represents each poet accurately according to "her time." Yet there is something inaccurate about describing (women) social poets as part of a particular time. Of course, as I have pointed out, the Depression was a period in which the social voice in literature burgeoned.

Yet if we think of these poets' value largely in the context of Depression-era activism and social commitment then we lose other aspects of their creative lives that came before and extend beyond this period. I hoped to complicate the idea of grouping poets together by writing about poets who in the traditional sense of a *literary period* belong to different generations, yet at the same time share a sustaining radical spirit that is not limited to age or generational sensibility. Generational differences are reinforced in *American Poetry*, for we find Ridge, Taggard, and Walker separated into volumes in this multivolume text. Separated from one another, Ridge, Taggard, and Walker become voices of distinct literary periods, rather than creators on a continuum of radical expression.

The canonical poet W. H. Auden wrote in his memorial poem to W. B. Yeats that "poetry makes nothing happen" (197). This statement seems even more appropriate today as we witness the triumph of late capitalism at the dawn of a new millennium. Poetry! What could be more inconsequential? Okay, so poetry can't change the world, yet while poetry made nothing happen for the text of white male modernism, women poets made themselves happen, and women poets on the left, wielding a twice threatening ax, attempted to change the world through the word. Nothing may have happened as a result, and it is doubtful that poets like Lola Ridge, Genevieve Taggard, and Margaret Walker thought themselves capable of much more than expressing themselves and irritating the status quo. As women poets, though, they made themselves happen. They created a social and intellectual space distinct from the spaces inscribed within the text of white male modernism. American women social poets of the modern period changed the poem, and poems, as we know, exist in the world. I believe that women poets on the left such as Lola Ridge, Genevieve Taggard, and Margaret Walker knew that the poet cannot exist in social isolation, even if, as Auden suggests in his poem to Yeats, poetry does. I hoped to suggest that poetry (and women's poetry at that) can address questions other than purely aesthetic ones and that poetry itself can be part of a greater social dialogue (in good times as well as bad times). It can engage us, inform us, fire us up (even if the idea of sustained social action seems rather quaint to us now).

In *Women Poets on the Left* my task has been to show how a group of women poets responded to the massive social changes of the early twentieth century and the resultant upheavals and injustices such changes produced. I also hoped to intervene in a discussion about modernism that has privileged a group of largely white, male, conservative poets, and to intervene yet again in the discussion of a gendered modernism that is almost equally as narrow in its attention to women poets. While I lament that the feminist aspects of Ridge's and Taggard's contributions are missing from *American Poetry,* I am reminded of Ridge's, Taggard's, and Walker's complicated position vis-á-vis feminist poetics, particularly with regard to my discussion of their work in this book.

Their poetry does not easily fit into feminist readings in which gender representations and gender relations are the central focus. The historical moments that produced these writers and the political life that shaped them made gender discrimination one of many flaws in the social fabric that each poet wove into her work. Class, race, place of birth: these too determine what the woman poet will imagine. Yet where necessary I have attempted to draw close attention to feminist themes in my study. I have suggested how Lola Ridge represents ghetto life through a gendered lens. I have examined how Genevieve Taggard particularizes women's struggles during the Depression. I have also shown how Margaret Walker represents female agency in poems about African American life and culture. Still my readers may wonder why I did not focus more on how gender relations affected the careers of each poet I examined, or why I did not make more use of contemporary feminist theory in my readings of the poems in this book.

Lola Ridge and Genevieve Taggard can wear the classification of new woman poet (an exceedingly important yet loaded category for women writing in the 1920s). Both women witnessed the ratification of the Nineteenth Amendment and explored bohemian life in feminist Greenwich Village. I have maintained that feminist themes and gender relations are not exclusive or necessarily defining tropes in their work, however.

In *The First Wave: Women Poets in America,* William Drake may be correct in suggesting that postsuffrage empowerment ignited in Ridge and Taggard a "quest for an alternative vision."[4] Yet he never addresses Ridge's most complex means of representing this empowerment. Her depictions and suggestions of the exploited and tortured human body—adjunct of the immigrant's and worker's everyday battles—complicates the contradictory separation of human beings into gendered carceral bodies. I look at a variety of poems in which her images of bodily harm point to a social rather than gendered inscription of the human body in pain.

Taggard's exploration of gender relations has been examined in painstaking detail by Nina Miller in *Making Love Modern,* but no literary historian has drawn sufficient attention to Taggard's wedding of verse to social action. As a result I found it necessary to examine Taggard's early poem "Everyday Alchemy" as it was reprinted during the Depression. In its shift from love lyric to critique of poverty it spoke to a larger audience and addressed perhaps the greatest social problem of its time.

Walker is too young to have been influenced by the new woman politics that shaped the careers of Ridge and Taggard. She was not, however, unmoved by the double burden experienced by black women historically, and especially during the Depression. The rather awkward "Whores" renders prostitution as both spectacle and call to judgment; it also reveals in some ways how both black and left politics at that time turned a blind eye to gender specific problems such as women's underemployment. While I tried to point to the contradictory position of women (and women artists) within the organized left, my main preoccupation has been to read the poetry of Lola Ridge, Genevieve Taggard, and Margaret Walker within the social and political contexts that inspired its creation. Lacking a movement that named the particular problem of gender discrimination, Ridge, Taggard, and Walker instead made their beef with that ol' devil capitalism. I am of course thankful for their political (mis)adventures. It has helped to place them outside the mainstream and thus given me an opportunity to stake out new territory in the study of modern American poetry.

While the diverse group of women I have brought together in this study were definitely "of their time" as some would say, their time is one that we should not forget. Yet what their time could possibly have to do with our time is a question we might need to ponder. If modernism and socialism were twin projects, as T. J. Clark has argued, and these projects are representative of a "ruined past" from which we presently stand at a great distance, these two projects directly influenced the writing lives upon which this book focuses. As I have hoped to point out, this mix of modernism and radicalism constitutes a useful past. It is a past to learn from, which looms larger than the mere scribblings of lines of verse on a page and is indicative of a structure of feeling close to a community of artists and activists ("the desire of worlds moving unmade," in the opinion of socialist, feminist, and modernist Muriel Rukeyser).

As I hoped to retrieve the voices of radical women poets out of the "ruined past," I am reminded of two examples from the annals of white male modernism in which Lola Ridge's memory is invoked. To me these examples characterized the social and political silences of the 1950s, which was also a death knell to an entire generation of cultural innovation and resistance.

In chapter 48 of William Carlos Williams's *Autobiography*, he reminisces about his last encounter with Ezra Pound and a subsequent visit from the F.B.I. Political differences created a wall of silence between the two master moderns—friends since college. Williams uses Pound's postwar imprisonment in a "hospital for the insane" (318) to head up a long list of what had happened to those renegade artists of the modern period. The dead Lola Ridge is sandwiched between a reclusive Henry Miller and a silent, impoverished Djuna Barnes.

The other example is Kenneth Rexroth's memorial rant to Dylan Thomas, "Thou Shall Not Kill," in *In Defense of the Earth*. "They are murdering all the young men," the poem begins. Barring the sexist exclusion, Rexroth blames Thomas's death on postwar capitalist culture and its complacent corporate tool in his Brooks Brother's suit. He also suggests that Thomas's death signifies the disappearance of a highly diverse culture of modern poetry, and in the poem's second section he makes his list of the disappeared. Lola Ridge in her "icy furnished room" is wedged between (the forgotten) James Oppenheim and (the forgotten) Orrick Johns (ironically, a place where the critical text of white male modernism has liked to situate her).

Williams and Rexroth suggest the limitations of the conventional postwar modernist critique. Yet, whether resigned in tone like Williams's, or angry yet helpless as Rexroth's, these poets present personal testimony to the cultural repression that would result in the burial and neglect of countless creative artists.

In the postwar period there would no longer be room to remember the fiery musings of an anarchist poet like Lola Ridge. Nor would there be room to remember Genevieve Taggard, another casualty from that generation of resisters; she died as the House Un-American Activities Committee saturated the nation with its paranoid ravings. As the surviving member of the trio, Margaret Walker dusts off the vestiges of her youthful, radical, modernist past to become an important Civil Rights–era poet.

It would of course take another book—maybe my second volume—to discuss the social poetry of the postwar period, from the Black Arts movement to the antiwar, women's, Chicano/a, Asian American, Native American, and gay and lesbian movements that created politically engaged poetry. Whether or not these poetries can be easily linked to the radical poetry produced by American women during the modern period is a question worth exploring. As the radicalisms of the 1960s become history, and the technologies of the twenty-first century are pervasive reminders of a whole new world out there, we may begin to see new forms of resistance and new types of poetry (and poetry slams and webzines have already made their mark). Curiously anarchism, Lola Ridge's political education in America, has been adopted by a new generation of computer-age college students (as recent events in Seattle and Los Angeles have revealed),[5] while the organized communist left that was an important feature in Genevieve Taggard's life and career has all but vanished. Margaret Walker began one of the first African American studies centers, which now bears her name, at Jackson State University in Mississippi. Since the founding of Jackson State's center over thirty years ago, there has been a proliferation of black studies programs all across the United States. Even Harvard, the reactionary "Hangman's House" of the Sacco and Vanzetti case (see chap. 2, n. 30), now has its own African American research and study center, the W.E.B. DuBois Institute. I don't want to focus too much on the mainstream, however. Ridge, Taggard, and Walker were never mainstream poets; they wrote against the grain of conventional American life and its institutions. We need to remember this fact about the women (and men) who wrote political poetry during the modern period. Whatever the creative uses of the political are at the millennium, we have a newly articulated group of women poets to think back on as we contemplate what lies ahead.

Notes

Chapter 1. Introduction: "The Buried History within the Buried History"

1. Susan Stanford Friedman's *Psyche Reborn: The Emergence of H.D.* explores "H.D.'s interactions with psychoanalysis and esoteric religion as a . . . [c]lear instance of a larger debate in modern thought between scientific and artistic modes of creating meanings" (ix). In fact, the emergence of feminist psychoanalytic criticism has had a tremendous influence upon modern poetry criticism; it may even explain some of the neglect of radical poetry. Carolyn Burke's exhaustive research on Mina Loy over the past twenty years culminated in the biography *Becoming Mina Loy* in 1996. The feminist literary investigations of volume 1 of Sandra Gilbert and Susan Gubar's *No Man's Land: The Place of the Woman Writer in the Twentieth Century* is primarily engaged in an argument the authors take from Virginia Woolf's *A Room of One's Own:* "The history of men's opposition to women's emancipation is more interesting perhaps than the story of that emancipation itself" (quoted in Gilbert and Gubar viii). *Shakespeare's Sisters: Feminist Essays on Women Poets* is an early collection of essays edited by Gilbert and Gubar. With the exception of Gloria Hull's essay on black women whom she does not describe as Shakespeare's sisters, the text reveals an extremely narrow vision of modernism.

2. In addition to Nelson's and Kalaidjian's examinations of the radical culture highlighted in little magazines, journals, and newspapers, Jayne Marek and Alan Golding have respectively maintained the significant place of the little magazine in the making

of modernist culture. See Marek, *Women Editing Modernism: "Little" Magazines and Literary History* (Lexington: University Press of Kentucky, 1995); and Golding, *From Outlaw to Classic: Canons in American Poetry* (Madison: University of Wisconsin Press, 1995) (in particular 114–43).

3. Some attempt at correcting these exclusions has been made in literature anthologies. The fourth edition of the *Norton Anthology of American Literature* (1994) includes eleven poems by Genevieve Taggard, seven of which come from Taggard's most fervent period of radical activity. *The Oxford Anthology of Modern American Poetry* (2000), edited by Cary Nelson, includes the work of Lola Ridge, Genevieve Taggard, and Margaret Walker, as well as other notable female social poets.

4. Rukeyser's brilliant and powerful work has been the recent subject of a number of scholars. Anne Herzog's dissertation, "Faith and Resistance: Politics and the Poetry of Muriel Rukeyser" (Rutgers University, 1995) is devoted exclusively to Rukeyser's leftist, feminist aesthetic. See also Anne F. Herzog and Janet E. Kauffman, *How Shall We Tell Each Other of the Poet: The Life and Writing of Muriel Rukeyser* (New York: St. Martins Press, 1999). Poet Jan Heller Levi is at work on a biography of Rukeyser to be published by Alfred Knopf. The Paris Press of Massachusetts has recently reissued Rukeyser's 1949 book of criticism *The Life of Poetry.*

5. James O. Young's *Black Writers of the 1930s* (Baton Rouge: Louisiana State University Press, 1973) expresses a disdain for proletarian poetry of the period that carries over into his criticism of black radical poets, including Walker.

6. For a recent discussion of Davidman's radical poetry see Donna Allego's dissertation, "The Construction and Role of Community in Political Long Poems by Twentieth Century American Women Poets: Lola Ridge, Genevieve Taggard, Joy Davidman, Margaret Walker, and Muriel Rukeyser" (Ph.D. diss., Southern Illinois University, 1997).

7. Marie de L. Welch (1904–1976) published three collections of poems: *Poems* (1933), *This Is Our Own* (1940), and *The Otherwise* (1977). Welch's early poems explore urban life as well as the natural world. As Alan Filreis points out in *Modernism from Right to Left: Wallace Stevens, The Thirties, and Literary Radicalism* (New York: Cambridge University Press, 1994) *Poems* was criticized by radical writers such as Stanley Burnshaw and Willard Maas for not being revolutionary enough. While her poetry may not bear the mark of a "revolutionary," Welch apparently spent most of the 1930s close to the California branch of the Communist Party U.S.A. (see Muriel Rukeyser's introduction to *The Otherwise*). *This Is Our Own* merits attention because it moves from conventionally wrought poems that explore the natural world through a subtle leftist bent to free verse poems about labor strikes and the civil war in Spain.

8. For example, Margaret Anderson published articles by Emma Goldman and Alexander Berkman in the *Little Review,* as well as her own in support of Goldman. She also published news on Goldman's arrest on sedition charges, as well as a letter Goldman wrote from prison. Anderson often printed her "anarchistic" opinions such as her dis-

appointment that someone hadn't shot the governor of Utah before he shot Joe Hill. She also expressed her views on art and anarchism in a 1916 *Little Review* article.

9. For a discussion of "Ice Age," see Nina Miller, *Making Love Modern.*

10. As Constance Coiner writes: "In 1935, responding to Hitler's rise to power, the Communist International reversed its strategy to the 'Popular Front,' calling for coalitions between workers' parties and liberal capitalist parties. The CPUSA changed its course accordingly, helping form the CIO and allying itself with the New Deal. Opposing fascism rather than agitating for socialism became its central strategy" (*Better Red* 29).

11. I do not concern myself here with right-wing journals.

12. Quatermain's critical/biographical sketch of Ridge in the *Dictionary of Literary Biography* (54) is not particularly complimentary to Ridge, largely because of its author's narrowly conceived idea of modernism.

13. This text compiled by Cynthia Davis and Kathryn West was published by Oxford University Press in 1996. "*Women Writers of the United States* weaves [a] rich and multi-hued historical fabric out of political and world events, everyday occurrences, medical advances, founding moments, lifestyle changes, demographics, conferences, crusades, statistics, inventions, survey results, crazes. . . . These in turn encompass the broad spectrum of women's writing that serves as the core of this timeline" (x). The book started as research assistance its authors performed for Cathy Davidson and Linda Wagner-Martin's edition of *The Oxford Companion to Women's Writing in the United States.*

14. The anthology is targeted toward the survey course of American literature from the Civil War to the present. The work of Lola Ridge and Genevieve Taggard appears in a special section within the modern period 1910–1945 (edited by Cary Nelson) entitled "A Sheaf of Political Poetry." Margaret Walker's poetry and an excerpt from her novel *Jubilee* appear in a section, "Issues and Visions in Modern America." In this section she shares interesting contradictory space with John Dos Passos, Michael Gold, Meridel LeSueur, John Crowe Ransom, Anzia Yezierska, Saunders Redding, Pietro Di Donato, Mourning Dove, the anonymous poetry of early Chinese immigrants, etc. See also Paul Lauter, *Canons and Contexts* (New York: Oxford University Press, 1990); and Lillian Robinson, *In the Canon's Mouth* (Bloomington: Indiana University Press, 1997).

15. Marxist and socialist-feminist criticism has had far greater appeal in Great Britain. Michele Barrett's *Women's Oppression Today* (London: Verso, 1980; rev. ed. 1988), Juliet Mitchell's *Woman's Estate* (Harmondsworth: Penguin, 1971), and Sheila Rowbotham's *Woman's Consciousness, Man's World* (Harmondsworth: Penguin, 1973) are considered classics of socialist-feminist criticism. Nonetheless, American feminists have produced socialist-feminist criticism that has influenced a younger generation of Americanist scholars like myself: see Tillie Olsen, *Silences* (New York: Delta, 1979); Lillian Robinson, *Sex, Class, and Culture;* Jane Marcus, *Art and Anger* (Columbus: Ohio State University Press, 1988); Judith Newton and Deborah Rosenfelt, *Feminist Criticism and*

Social Change (New York: Methuen, 1985); and Cora Kaplan, *Sea Changes: Essays on Cultural Politics* (London: Verso, 1986). A recent book that reexamines marxist and socialist-feminist criticism in the advent of postmodernism is Donna Landry and Gerald MacLean, *Materialist Feminisms* (Cambridge, Mass.: Blackwell, 1993). Landry and MacLean cite the work of Gayatri Spivak as remapping marxist-feminist criticism from a postmodernist perspective. Two recent critiques of modernism typify this difference between British and American feminist perspectives. In *Men and Women Writers of the 1930s: The Dangerous Flood of History* (New York: Routledge, 1996), Jan Montefiore devotes an entire chapter to issues of gender and class in British radical poetry of the 1930s, not to mention giving voice to "underservedly" [*sic*] forgotten poets. Margaret Dickie and Thomas Travisano (*Gendered Modernisms: American Women Poets and Their Readers* [Philadelphia: University of Pennsylvania Press, 1996]) have compiled a series of essays on Stein, Moore, H.D., Millay, Laura Riding, Bishop, Rukeyser, and Gwendolyn Brooks. Though the collection's aim is to look at modern poetry from a gendered lens, class and political subjectivity are treated as secondary at best.

16. See Laclau and Mouffe, *Hegemony and Socialist Strategy: Towards a Radical Democratic Politics* (London: Verso, 1985).

17. This fact is important when considering the outpouring of radical, class-conscious poetry produced by women of color since the late 1960s. Poetry by Margaret Walker, Alice Walker, Audre Lorde, June Jordan, Sonia Sanchez, Jayne Cortez, Paula Gunn Allen, Joy Harjo, Mitsuye Yamada, Janice Mirikitani, Jessica Hagedorn, Marilyn Chin, Cherrie Moraga, Gloria Anzaldua, Sandra Cisneros, Judith Ortiz Cofer, and Aurora Morales Levins, for example, problematizes race, class, and gender as a trajectory that cannot be divvied up or watered down by suggestions that one category has primacy over another.

18. See Jerry Ward's interview with Walker, "A Writer for Her People: An Interview with Dr. Margaret Walker Alexander," *Mississippi Quarterly* 41 (Fall 1988): 515–17.

19. See Studs Terkel's interview with Cayton in *Hard Times*.

20. See Walker's essay "Black Women in Academia" in *How I Wrote* Jubilee (26–32).

21. Information about this interview and about Hayden's early "African-American Marxism" comes from Alan M. Wald, "Belief and Ideology in the Work of Robert Hayden" in *Writing from the Left*.

22. All three poets signed the 1936 "call" for the formation of the League of American Writers. The organization was founded as a support for the Communist Party's Popular Front agenda, though many nonparty members were active in the league.

Chapter 2. Writing the Radical Body of Modernism: Politics and Pain in Lola Ridge's Poetry

1. In the same letter to Abbott from which the opening epigraph is taken (Carl Zigrosser Papers, Van Pelt Library, University of Pennsylvania), Ridge complains of the more mainstream direction in which she feared the magazine was heading: "I have just

read the new *Modern School* from cover to cover, and am surprised and disappointed by the semi-political, quasi-radical tone of the greater part of it."

2. In a later quote printed in *Living Authors,* a reference book published in the early 1930s, Ridge connects the political statement to her poet's task of revealing and representing one's deepest emotions. "Let anything that burns you come out whether it be propaganda or not. . . . I write about something that I feel intensely. How can you help writing about something you feel intensely?" (341).

3. For comments on Ridge by those who knew or admired her see Williams, *The Autobiography of William Carlos Williams,* New York: New Directions, 1967; Linda Hamalian, *A Life of Kenneth Rexroth,* New York: W.W. Norton, 1991; Nellie McKay, *Jean Toomer, Artist: A Study of His Literary Life and Work, 1894–1936,* Chapel Hill: University of North Carolina Press, 1984; Joan Mellen, *Kay Boyle: Author of Herself,* New York: Farrar, Straus and Giroux, 1994; Bonnie Costello, general editor, *The Selected Letters of Marianne Moore,* New York: Knopf, 1997.

4. From the introduction to *Against Forgetting: Twentieth Century Poetry of Witness,* 31. Forche's work underestimates the complicated role gender plays in what she and other contemporary writers and critics have termed the "poetry of witness." This collection, international in scope, contains one late poem by the important socialist and feminist poet, Muriel Rukeyser. It also includes Ezra Pound and e. e. cummings as "poets of witness." One wonders if Forche has ever read any of Ridge's poetry.

5. This poem, which appears in Ridge's first collection *The Ghetto and Other Poems,* appeared in a number of early-twentieth-century poetry anthologies. Various kinds of mixing of poetry genres occurred in these early anthologies, as opposed to those that began to appear in the postwar period. "Reveille" was published in anarchist Marcus Graham's *Anthology of Revolutionary Poetry* (1929) and Alfred Kreymborg's collection, *Lyric America* (1919), which included many poets from the *Others, Dial, Poetry* and *Little Review* circles.

6. This statement is from William Carlos Williams, whom Lola Ridge knew well. To refer to it as "dogma" is not to denigrate its sentiments, but to suggest its rhetorical nature. Advice is advice.

7. See the introduction to Taggard's *Collected Poems: 1918–1938.*

8. In the case of Furman versus the State of Georgia (1972), the Supreme Court ruled that the death penalty, even in a murder conviction, was unconstitutional because it violated the Eighth Amendment's protection against "cruel and unusual punishment." Brennan and Marshall wrote the lead opinions. (See *U.S. Reports,* vol. 408.)

9. While citing Foucault on the condemned body, it is necessary to note his rejection of "agency," which Ridge attempts to utilize in much of her poetry. For Foucault nothing is free of totalizing, rationalizing, or conceptualizing domination; no social agent can loosen its power over society. However, Foucault is useful again in noting Ridge's representation in a number of her poems of the abusive power of "disciplinary technology," not to mention the ultimate fate of the "condemned body" in "Electrocution."

10. See Rebecca Zurier's *Art for the Masses: A Radical Magazine and Its Graphics, 1911–1917* (Philadelphia: Temple University Press, 1988).

11. Whether by Ridge's intention or not, an additional reference surfaces with the word *Hill*. Her contemporary readers would have been reminded of another labor activist and Wobbly martyr, Joe Hill, who met a similar fate to Little's. Howard Zinn's characterization of Hill's plight in *A People's History of the United States* (New York: Vintage, 1980) merits mention:

> In November 1915, Joe Hill was accused of killing a grocer in Salt Lake City, Utah, in a robbery. There was no direct evidence presented in the court that he had committed the murder, but there were enough pieces of evidence to persuade the jury to find him guilty. The case became known throughout the world, and ten thousand letters went to the governor in protest, but with machine guns guarding the entrance to the prison, Joe Hill was executed by a firing squad. He had written Bill Haywood just before this: "Don't waste time in mourning. Organize." (327)

12. Europe went to war in 1914, after the assassination of Archduke Francis Ferdinand of Austria-Hungary by Gavrilo Princip, a Serbian Nationalist. The war had been mostly precipitated by the imperialistic and territorial struggles of Germany, France, Great Britain, and the Austro-Hungarian empire. The United States remained neutral. However, when a German submarine sunk the ship Lusitania and 128 U.S. citizens died, the U.S. began to rethink its policy of nonintervention. As Germany made submarine advances against British sea control, the U.S. broke off relations with Germany. Then in April 1917, the U.S. entered the war. Antiwar intellectual Lola Ridge would no doubt have argued that the U.S. entered the war because there was money to be made from it; her nickname for war was "the male dance." The war ended in November 1918. A conservative estimate of the total war dead is about ten million, with an additional twenty million wounded.

13. A particularly important connection to wartime politics that DuBois and Gruening make is their comparison of the reports of German terror abroad to the activities of whites in East St. Louis. They write: "In all the accounts given of German atrocities, no one, we believe, has accused the Germans of taking pleasure in the sufferings of their victims. But these rioters combined business and pleasure. These Negroes were 'butchered to make' an East St. Louis 'holiday'" (220–21).

14. Coincidentally, the poem also recalls a famous, and very disturbing, nursery rhyme from the *Mother Goose* collection:

> Lady bird, lady bird
> Fly away home.
> Your house is on fire,
> Your children all gone.
>
> All except one
> And that's little Ann

And she has crept under

The warming pan.

15. Undated letter, *Broom* correspondence, Harold Loeb Papers, Princeton University Library.

16. Letter of March 1922, Harold Loeb Papers, Princeton University Library. Much of Ridge's correspondence with Loeb suggests an unusually zealous devotion to getting the journal out and doing it right. The correspondence also suggests a fairly smooth reciprocal relationship between the two; however, Ridge and Loeb eventually came to loggerheads over the material Ridge collected for an "All American number" in which she resigned on Loeb's insistence that Gertrude Stein be included. Ridge informed Loeb that Stein "has only an occasional gleam—[it is] mostly—blah! Blah! . . . In a few years her work will be on the rubbish heap with the rest of the literary tinsel that has fluttered its little day and grown too shabby even for the columns of a daily" (letter of July 11, 1922, Loeb Papers).

17. This particular statement suggests a reference to Ridge's own body as an object of lynching.

18. Letter in the Lola Ridge Papers, Sophia Smith Collection, Smith College Library.

19. Some explorations on the case are Felix Frankfurter, *The Case of Sacco and Vanzetti* (1927); Francis Russell, *The Tragedy in Dedham: The Story of the Sacco and Vanzetti Case* (1962); and Herman Ehrmann, *The Case That Wouldn't Die* (1969). Upton Sinclair's *Boston* (1928) is a "documentary novel" of the case. Sacco and Vanzetti in their own words can be found in Marion Denman Frankfurter and Gardner Jackson, eds., *The Letters of Sacco and Vanzetti* (1980).

20. Joughin writes at the end of his chapter on the Sacco and Vanzetti poetry that though other poets wrote about the case with equal force, none "gives any sign of having worked at his [*sic*] material for as many hours and with as intense a desire for final artistic perfection." He continues with a claim that Ridge's poems "almost certainly deserve a permanent place among the chief American poems" (391–92).

21. The other poems are by Witter Bynner, Countee Cullen, Edna St. Vincent Millay, E. Merrill Root, Malcolm Cowley, Arthur Davison Ficke, and James Rorty. Interestingly the other "best work in verse," besides Ridge, was the poem "For the Honor of Massachusetts" by a "regional" poet, Brent Dow Allinson. Allinson's poem appeared respectively in *Locomotive Engineers Journal, La Follette's Magazine,* and a religious publication, *Unity.*

22. Luigi Galleani (1861–1931) was a leading agitator and propagandist of the Italian anarchist movement. He had considerable influence over Italian workers in both Italy and the United States. Galleani spurned individualistic anarchism in favor of a proletarian based anarcho-communism. He also believed that social revolution could only come about through violence—through complete destruction of the existing social order. Galleani's main mouthpiece for his ideas was *Cronica Sovversiva,* which he published from 1903 to 1918. In the summer of 1919, during the famous red scare, Galleani

was deported. A compelling biographical sketch of him can be found in Paul Avrich's *Anarchist Portraits.*

23. Porter provides an intriguing portrait of Ridge here, and the incident described has been confirmed by other writers, for example, Robert McAlmon and Kay Boyle in their memoir *Being Geniuses Together, 1920–1930* (Garden City, N.Y.: Doubleday, 1968). However, later in the passage, perhaps for dramatic effect, Porter inaccurately tells us that Ridge "had not long to live." Lola Ridge died in the spring of 1941, thirteen and a half years after the execution of Sacco and Vanzetti.

24. Monroe was founder and editor of *Poetry: A Magazine of Verse,* to which Ridge contributed a number of poems and reviews. Not only was *Poetry* an influential journal throughout Ridge's career; it was also particularly supportive of women poets. Monroe begins her review of *Firehead,* a book-length poem about the Crucifixion that also allegorically represents the case of Sacco and Vanzetti, with the following commendation:

> Lola Ridge has always been fascinated by the heroic. Courage, protest, revolt—these she has celebrated in her poems and practiced in her life, impatient of humdrum, of the neatly organized processes of ordinary society. The exceptional allures her, the tragic, the sublime; in the utmost reaches of these she has full faith, reserving her doubts for incredibilities at the other end of the scale—for humanity's littleness, meanness. (36)

25. Ridge is not alone in connecting Sacco's and Vanzetti's executions with Christ's crucifixion. Joughin cites a number of poems that employ this trope. Visual artists also created comparisons with the Crucifixion. Ben Shahn, in his twenty-three painting series exhibited in 1932 under the title, "The Passion of Sacco and Vanzetti," remarked the following:

> I got to thinking about the Sacco-Vanzetti case. They'd been electrocuted in 1927, and in Europe of course I'd seen all the demonstrations against the trial. . . . Ever since I could remember I'd wished that I'd been lucky enough to be alive at a great time—when something big was going on, like the Crucifixion. And suddenly I realized I was! Here I was living through another crucifixion. Here was something to paint. (Quoted in Frances K. Pohl's *Ben Shahn* [San Francisco: Pomegranate Artbooks, 1993] p. 12)

26. "Denied the usual privilege of physical labor because of a technical rule governing the handling of unsentenced prisoners charged with murder, Sacco discovered that daily exercises in his small cell were a poor substitute" (Frankfurter and Jackson 5).

27. Robert D'Attilio's entry "The Sacco and Vanzetti Case" in *The Dictionary of the American Left* describes the effect of Fuller's consideration of clemency:

> [Fuller] appointed an advisory committee, the "Lowell Committee," so called because its most prominent member was A. Lawrence Lowell, president of Harvard University. The committee, in a decision that was notorious for its loose thinking,

concluded that the trial and judicial process had been just "on the whole" and that clemency was not warranted. It only fueled controversy over the fate of the two men, and Harvard, because of Lowell's role, became stigmatized, in the words of one of its alumni, as "Hangman's House." (669)

28. This "white . . . agony" is the same descriptive phrase Ridge uses in "Electrocution" to suggest the moment of contact between the volts of electricity and its human subject. Curiously the word *agony* appears in a much quoted statement Bartolemeo Vanzetti made upon receiving his death sentence. This statement also appeared in one of Ben Shahn's serigraphs made in 1958:

> If it had not been for these thing, I might have live out my life talking at street corners to scorning men. I might have die, unmarked, unknown, a failure. Now we are not a failure. This is our career and our triumph. Never in our full life could we hope to do such work for tolerance, for joostice, for man's onderstanding of man as now we do by accident. Our words—our lives—our pains—nothing! The taking of our lives—lives of a good shoemaker and a poor fish-peddlar—all! That last moment belongs to us—that agony is our triumph.

29. Two other sources I consulted were a biography, *The Gentle Dynamiter* by Estolv Ethan Ward, a Mooney admirer who was the court reporter at the time the Mooney-Billings case first went to trial; and Hugo Bedau and Michael Radelet's *In Spite of Innocence,* which provides a chapter on the Mooney-Billings case, rereading it in the light of a century's worth of fallacious judicial decisions.

30. Langston Hughes, probably the world's best known black writer, also wrote a poem for Mooney. Hughes visited Mooney in prison in 1932, and in that same year the *New Masses* published his poem "To Tom Mooney." An important, largely ignored fact about Hughes is that he spent most of the 1930s writing radical verses for left-wing magazines. See Langston Hughes, *Good Morning Revolution* (New York: Lawrence Hill, 1973).

31. The Beinecke Rare Book and Manuscript Library at Yale University retains a copy of this poster, which is catalogued under the title "Labor Martyr Immortalized in Poem." Under Mooney's photograph, which identifies him by name, is the caption: "A very sick man in San Quentin Prison, May 1928." Between this caption and the Lithographic Union logo at the bottom right is an advertisement: "Order this POSTER, 28 x 34 inches, for Labor Day, May Day, Working Class and Mooney parades and demonstrations, mass meetings, Union's halls and Workers' headquarters. Price: Single copy 15¢, 10–$1.00 . . . 1,000–$50.00. Payable in advance to the TOM MOONEY MOLDERS' DEFENSE COMMITTEE."

32. Ironically, another magazine called *Blast* was published in England in 1914 and 1915 by Wyndham Lewis. Lewis, a novelist, poet, and father of vorticism, was a fascist politically.

33. Accounts of the activities of Tom Mooney's defense committee appear in Frost, *The Mooney Case,* and Ward, *The Gentle Dynamiter.*

34. Feminist and activist Miriam Allen de Ford described Mooney in the following way: "It may well be admitted that Mooney is not a gentle, tolerant saint. . . . I have been rather amused to find that people outside California, who are indignant at the injustice done him, picture him as a mild-eyed martyr. Mooney is an aggressive, stubborn fighter; a sensitive, self-willed, touchy individual, not broken but embittered" (Frost 364).

35. To understand Ridge—a radical poet, as well as feminist—and the importance of working-class politics in her writing, we need to consider a viewpoint that may have been close to her. It also might help explain why representations of female activism (other than her own) are not found in most of the poems so far discussed. In *Women, Resistance, and Revolution,* Sheila Rowbotham presents an important difference in feminist thought between the American-born suffragists and immigrant radical feminists like Emma Goldman (with whom Ridge was allied during her years working for the Ferrer Association). "Goldman showed how the Stanton-Anthony tendency within feminism remained deliberately blinkered about labor movement struggles even to the point of supporting strike-breaking by women. This earned them the antagonism not only of male but female-workers" (109). If Ridge was siding with male (and female) workers, it would be difficult at this point to find her embracing a suffragist agenda that condoned strike breaking, whether by women or men.

36. For a discussion of the background pertaining to this lecture, and the book Ridge had planned to write from it, see Elaine Sproat's introduction to "Woman and the Creative Will," *Michigan Occasional Papers* 18/19 (Ann Arbor: Women's Studies Program, University of Michigan, 1981).

37. The cover of the April 13, 1918 issue of the *New Republic,* the then-four-year-old liberal opinion magazine, announced Lola Ridge's arrival onto the literary scene, as it were. Beginning with an announcement of its lead article "Politics During War," the titles finish off in triangular fashion, "What Democracy Means," by H. G. Wells and "The Ghetto," by Lola Ridge. While the magazine debated issues related to the United States' entrance into World War I, which the *New Republic* ultimately endorsed despite the room it gave to antiwar intellectuals like Ridge and critics Randolph Bourne and Van Wyck Brooks, Ridge's poem explored a social phenomenon that wartime fervor strived to bury. The full text of the poem appeared in Ridge's first collection, *The Ghetto and Other Poems,* published in the fall of the same year.

38. The phrase "labor and desire" comes from Paula Rabinowitz's brilliant study on women's revolutionary fiction of the 1930s. She looks closely at how gender difference and women's writing resituates the arena in which radical politics were articulated in Depression-era America.

39. This statistic comes from Susan A. Glenn's engrossing social history of immigrant Jewish women in the United States *Daughters of the Shtetl.*

40. The Jewish ghetto in fact had a number of its own poets who wrote in the Yiddish language and published in Yiddish newspapers like the *Forverts.* Morris Rosenfeld (1862–1923) is especially noteworthy for this particular discussion since he

was nicknamed the "pants-presser poet." His *Songs from the Ghetto* (Boston: Copeland and Day, 1898), was published in a bilingual edition. His poetry, though maudlin and stylistically representative of an earlier era, expressed the harsh realities of sweatshop life.

41. Agnes Nestor wrote about her experiences as a glove-maker and union organizer in *Life and Labor,* the publication of the Chicago-based National Women's Trade Union League, which was edited by Alice Henry. The League was instrumental in supporting and aiding the 1910 shirtwaist-makers' strike in which more than 20,000 mostly teen-aged girls walked off their jobs in protest of poor wages, long hours, and unsafe working conditions. Most of this work about which the young women protested was per-formed in and around "the ghetto." One year later, 146 people, mostly women and girls, died in a fire at the Triangle Shirt-Waist Company. The Triangle Company had been a 1910 strike target.

42. The statement is not a direct quote from Goldman. It appears to be rather an encapsulation of a passage from her autobiography in which Goldman describes her anger at her comrades for suggesting that her love of dancing was frivolous and unbe-coming of a revolutionary. As Goldman remarks in *Living My Life:* "I want freedom, the right to self-expression, everybody's right to beautiful, radiant things. . . . Anarchism means that to me" (56).

43. Ridge most certainly would have been familiar with James Oppenheim's poem "Bread and Roses," written in 1912 to honor the striking women and girls in Lawrence. Oppenheim (1882–1932), a founding editor of the important but short-lived magazine the *Seven Arts,* wrote poetry, as Cary Nelson estimates, which combined genteel values and socialist ideals (135). See Oppenheim's *Songs for a New Age* (New York: Century, 1914).

44. The use of the word *notion* is interesting here, in addition to the phrase, "the notions of the hour." Notion, though meant here in reference to sewing notions, also means "idea." Ridge's ghetto is full of "the notions of the hour" in terms of the new ideas adopted by the young and in circulation in the sweatshops, cafes, clubs, etc. Thus one who peddles notions is not someone who is merely employed in the sewing trade, but is someone who passes on the latest ideas to those he encounters. The pronoun *he* is used because peddlers and ragpickers were almost always men.

45. Annelise Orleck partly addresses this contamination by stressing the important tension between traditional Jewish biblical values and the nineteenth-century radical philosophies of which Eastern European Jews became aware:

> Jewish religious leaders were, at most, lukewarm to Socialism. But in the Jewish Socialism of the time there was a cross-fertilization of Biblical and Marxist imagery that made even men and women from religious homes feel comfortable with Social-ist ideas and activism. Immigrant Jewish Socialism had its own language and sym-bols, a mixture of the ancient prophets and nineteenth-century revolutionaries. (27)

46. Max Stirner (1806–1856) was a German anarchist and author of *The Ego and Its*

Own. This text, which appears in Ridge's book collection in the Bryn Mawr College Library, and which she had probably read shortly before "The Ghetto" first appeared, was published in 1846 and translated into English in 1897. Though the book caused a stir at the time of its publication and an interest in Stirner was revived after the book was translated into English, his absolute egoism and individualist stance put off even most anarchists. According to Stirner: "Nothing is higher than myself"; "Every higher being whether God or man weakens the feeling of my own individuality"; "I don't do anything for God's sake, for man's sake, but for my own sake." Though Ridge was active in anarchist circles for a number of years, it is not clear what, if any, influence Stirner had on her thinking about individual liberty. The quick manner in which the "maimed" fellow who "garbles" Stirner is shouted down suggests that, at least in Ridge's observation, he was not all that popular among the young Jewish anarchists. (I am indebted to Paul Avrich for these quotes.)

Chapter 3. *Calling Western Union*: Party Lines and Private Lines in Genevieve Taggart's Poetry

1. Cary Nelson and Karen Ford are at work on a selection of Taggard's poems to be published in the University of Illinois Press's "American Poetry Recovery Series."

2. The narrative line is also crossed by Meridel LeSueur in a work of short fiction from the 1930s, "I Was Marching." In the story, based on the 1934 Minneapolis teamsters' strike, a middle-class woman goes to volunteer at the local union headquarters in order to support the "men." As she helps out, she begins to feel that her life has never been more useful. When she marches, she feels she is part of no greater thing on earth than this struggle to preserve workers' dignity. Like Taggard's poem, in whose final lines the middle-class marcher admits that she has "come" for her "class," LeSueur's final lines announce her protagonist's giddiness at the class lines she crosses in order to feel part of the struggle: "I felt my legs straighten. I felt my feet join in that strange shuffle of thousands of bodies moving with direction, of thousands of feet, and my own breath with the gigantic breath. As if an electric charge had passed through me, my hair stood on end, I was marching" (191).

3. See Charlotte Nekola's "Worlds Moving: Women, Poetry, and the Literary Politics of the 1930s," in *Writing Red,* ed. Nekola and Rabinowitz.

4. Mike Gold (1893–1967) presented his ideas about proletarian realism in the April 1930 issue of the *New Masses.* He founded and edited the magazine along with Joseph Freeman. Gold, who grew up in poverty on New York's Lower East Side and wrote about it in his immensely popular autobiographical novel *Jews without Money* (1930), advocated a "proletarian realism [that] deals with the *real conflicts* of men and women who work for a living." He set this desire for a working-class literature against a "literature for its own sake." He argued that "workers will scorn any vague fumbling poetry, much as they would scorn a sloppy workman." Literature should be "useful" and have a "social function," with "as few words as possible"—no "verbal acrobatics." Gold

might encapsulate proletarian realism as "swift action, clear form, the direct line, cinema in words." The world should not be represented with "pessimism," as the bourgeois writer does, but with "revolutionary élan" (all quotes from Coiner, *Better Red* 23–24). For a current, detailed discussion of Gold's political and aesthetic project see James Bloom's *Left Letters: The Culture Wars of Michael Gold and Joseph Freeman* (New York: Columbia University Press, 1994).

5. Gold's masculine reading of 1930s' culture is shared by a number of male poets of the period. Two writers whose work appears in the 1978 anthology *Social Poetry of the 1930s: A Selection* (Jack Salzman and Leo Zanderer, eds. [New York: B. Franklin, 1978]) signal the sexist and homophobic outlook found in literary radical circles. The Missouri farm poet H. H. Lewis, in poems of praise written to the Soviet Union, metaphorizes "mother Russia" as a robust "masculine" woman. He idealizes the Soviet woman as a strong, laboring mother who has no time for the "femininity" constructed by the bourgeois world. Robert Gessner, later to become a New York University film professor, in "Upsurge," a quintessential Depression poem, depicts destitute, unemployed men who have "gone to other men" in their despair. Homosexuality becomes the ultimate symbolic trope through which the poet represents a man's degradation at this historical crisis point. The Communist Party's antigay agenda made sexual radicalism taboo. *Out* in the Communist Party meant, *out* of the party.

6. Rabinowitz's critical, theoretical, and historical study *Labor and Desire,* is an answer to the left literary history coming out of the late 1950s and 1960s that managed to leave out the work of radical women prose writers. She explores dozens of novels and suggests how they answered the androcentric analyses of male left culture in the 1930s. Using primarily the intellectual material of poststructuralism, feminism, and marxism, Rabinowitz asks difficult questions about the undervalued work of women's working-class fiction and women's roles as radical intellectuals.

7. The use of sloganeering in modern American poetry is wonderfully synthesized and problematized by Cary Nelson in his essay "Literature as Cultural Studies: 'American' Poetry of the Spanish Civil War." He maintains that the poetry produced internationally in solidarity with the Spanish Republic during the war years (1936–1939) implicitly, rather than explicitly, integrated sloganeering. The worldwide support of the Spanish Republic inspired a poetic discourse that "circulate[d] from street and newspaper into poems and back to the street again." It merged with the transitional public dialogue on the fight against fascism. "In the process the slogans are infused with all the values poetry itself has historically acquired, and the slogans become not merely instrumental but also literary, lyrical signposts of a history already eternal and monumentalized. And their deployment in the street thereafter has the feel of poetry at work in public life" (85).

8. It would be impossible to mention all the forgotten American verse of the period 1915 to 1945 that contained elements of song, which also included social messages. For example, James Oppenheim's "Bread and Roses" was inspired by the women marchers

during the 1912 textile strike in Lawrence, Massachusetts. The Italian-American anarchist poet Arturo Giovanitti also wrote ballads while in prison for his activism on behalf of the Lawrence strikers. Sarah Cleghorn's *Songs of Peace and Freedom* was penned as part of a resistance campaign against World War I. Ralph Chaplin, poet laureate of the IWW, authored "Solidarity Forever," a ballad still sung today in AFL-CIO circles. Langston Hughes's first book of poems, *The Weary Blues,* mixes the folk idioms of blues music with chants against racial inequality.

9. Taggard's article "Bolshevik Sweethearts," a review of Alexandra Kollantay's novel *Red Love,* appeared in the June 1927 issue of the *New Masses.* In keeping with the tenor of Third Period revolutionism, it praises the sexual emancipation of the Soviet woman.

10. A copy of the report is in the Genevieve Taggard Book Collection at the Dartmouth College Library. Other noted sponsors of the United Committee to Aid Vermont Marble Workers included: Roger Baldwin, Sarah Cleghorn, Malcolm Cowley, Martha Gruening, Josephine Herbst, Alice Mary Kimball, Archibald MacLeish, and Lewis Mumford.

11. It is worth noting that names of the women interviewed, Mereau and Bujak, suggest that they, their striking husbands, and starving children were immigrant "strangers" in the WASP land of the Proctors.

12. Images of the grieving, impoverished, or determined mother circulated in much Depression-era art and literature. In America one recalls feisty Ma Joad in *The Grapes of Wrath* or Dorothea Lange's famous WPA photograph of the California migrant mother, who at thirty-three looked closer to fifty-three. In Germany, Brecht's *Mother Courage* complicated the idealization of the destitute mother by portraying her as earning her keep through the ravages of war. Käthe Kollwitz's bronze sculpture "Tower of Mothers" depicts a grouping of babushka-wearing women protectively encircling many young children. Moreover, the trope of "Mother Russia" was used in much Popular Front art and literature.

13. The search for dignity is revealed in a comment made by committee member Isadore Polier in his research into the living conditions in the region:

> In the course of a half hour this morning I interviewed people from several towns and found uniformly a story of inadequate diet. As to houses, one witness said the house used to be a barn. I said, "a real barn?" She said, "Yes, it is still painted red." (29)

14. The majority of the workers at the Vermont Marble Company lived in houses owned by the company. It was revealed in Mrs. Bujak's testimony and by committee members that this overseer, Mr. Dwyer, had been tried and convicted of not providing relief to those in need. He was fined $60. His lawyer was the same lawyer who represented the town of Central Rutland and the Vermont Marble Company.

15. The essay, a response to poet Horace Gregory's defense of certain middle-class writers' decisions not to join the Communist Party, appeared in the February 14, 1935 issue of the *New Masses.*

16. Paul de Kruif (1890–1971) wrote on a variety of health-related issues from individuals who made medical history *Hunger Fighters* (1928), *Men Against Death* (1933), and *Kaiser Wakes the Doctors* (1943)—about industrialist Henry Kaiser's employee health care plan that gave birth to the first HMO—to a history of public health in the United States, *The Fight for Life* (1938). In 1962 he published a memoir, *The Sweeping Wind*.

17. Crystal Eastman (1881–1928) was an outspoken feminist, socialist, pacifist journalist, and legal scholar. See Blanche Cook's introduction to *Crystal Eastman on Women and Revolution* (New York: Oxford University Press, 1979).

18. Though Taggard was, as a child, aware of the plantation system developing around her in Hawaii, she has only one small reference to it in this particular memoir. Yet in an article she wrote for the *Yale Review* shortly after the end of World War II, she attempts to link the islands, most recently associated with the Pearl Harbor bombing, to their early days as an American colony. In the following description Taggard reacts to the system that has controlled and classified the island's multicultural work force:

> The big "heathen" [here she appropriates WASP terminology] worked in the sugarcane fields and in the mill. The little heathen came to school. . . . At the mill the white men who worked the heathen wore boots and carried whips and clubs in their belts. The Japanese and Chinese coolies were docile; they worked long hours, sent their children to learn English, put our kind of clothing on them, encouraged them to mind their teachers. The races of children did not fight among themselves; they were affectionate and pliable. Silence and timidity were the only obstacles the teachers ever encountered. Now and then, a mother or a father said, "Sayo Nara," or "Hello," to the teachers. Who could complain of the heathen? ("Plenty Pilikia" 53)

19. The theater of repression Taggard evokes through these negative passages is further explored when she equates the provincial mores derided in the works of Sinclair Lewis, Sherwood Anderson, and Edgar Lee Masters with her own impressions of provincial Washington State:

> The broken finger nails on the stubby hands of those people! The envy and scorn for all trades that differed from their kind of toil; the disgust for all other skills; the malignant hatred of all desire that did not have money for its object! Was it for this that the intrepid crossed the plains and the Rockies? To make this life! What a sorry life! Based on mass panic and fear of a whole complex of things in a civilized world. Foreigners, first and foremost; Chinks, Wops, Polacks, Swedes, Huns, Frogs—ridicule at one end, lynching at the other. City people, smart folks, gentle folks, stuckup people—freeze 'em out. Book learning, scientific ideas, the higher criticism—down with it, it's immoral. Innocent pleasures, beauty, joy of life, wine, pictures, music. So you're getting too good for us plain folks, are you! (xxxvi)

20. Taggard's first husband was Robert Wolf, a novelist and radical like herself, whom she married in 1921. That same year her only child, Marcia, was born. Her

marriage ended in 1931 when Wolf was institutionalized. In 1935 Taggard married journalist Kenneth Durant. Durant, who had been a Harvard classmate of John Reed's, headed the New York office of the Soviet News Agency TASS, which he helped open in the mid-1920s.

21. The biography was received more or less positively by critics, who focused upon the speculative and "mannered" style of the text. Taggard anticipates postmodern practice by embellishing and reading into much of her character descriptions. Taggard's "projecting" a self, and indeed a romantic self, onto an individual about whose life so little is known, anticipates the interruptions of recent theories of biography and autobiography, which challenge the notion that the genre produces objective, accurate "lives," rather than creates additional fictions. Note the following description of Dickinson's relationship with her family: "When it came out in speech, her family found her wit a little too witty; father would silently leave the table when Emily's talk escaped bounds—his displeasure numbed her manner, but could not change its flavour" (11).

22. Nancy Walker, in an essay on Dickinson, Alice James, and Virginia Woolf, remarking on Dickinson's life of "extreme privacy" ("Wider Than the Sky" 272) describes the poet as having lived "the life of the mind," yet she makes no reference to Taggard's articulation of that very thesis nearly sixty years earlier. Suzanne Juhasz's study of Emily Dickinson's "life of the mind" begins by tracing the genesis of Dickinson scholarship. "[That Dickinson] lived primarily in the mind . . . has long been acknowledged as a factor central to her biography and to her art" (*The Undiscovered Continent: Emily Dickinson and the Space of the Mind* [Bloomington: Indiana University Press, 1983] pp. 1–2). One can't blame either Walker or Juhasz for their oversight, when the work of Genevieve Taggard both as poet and feminist intellectual has all but disappeared from cultural and historical memory.

23. It is worth noting that Taggard begins her biography with a description of the scene of Dickinson's one great "public" act: she picks up her pen, writes, and posts four poems to Thomas Higginson. Taggard pointedly wonders whether the commencement of the Civil War could have had something to do with Dickinson's call to action:

> Let us use the usual language regarding Emily Dickinson: she was an eccentric, a recluse, an old maid, one of the many in New England. She had been living in an enclosed universe and now found the new styles of living and dying troublesome and disorderly. . . . As would be said of any such person, the war gave her something to think about. (6)

24. Also see Paula Rabinowitz's reading of the poem in *Labor and Desire,* 42.

25. For a reading of Taggard's work within the love lyric tradition of the new woman bohemia of New York's Greenwich Village, see Nina Miller's *Making Love Modern.*

26. In the essay Eliot praises Donne and the other metaphysical poets for their ability to synthesize dissimilar aspects of experience and their artistry in fusing thought and feeling. It is also in this essay that Eliot coins his famous term "dissociation of sensibil-

ity," referring to separation of the emotion and the intellect as practiced by poets between the last part of the seventeenth century up until the early twentieth. Eliot, and other modern poets, pointed particularly to Victorian poets such as Tennyson and Browning as exemplars of this dissociated practice.

27. Taggard's own interest in these poets resulted in her editing and publishing an anthology, *Circumferences: Varieties of Metaphysical Verse* (1930). In *Circumferences*, Taggard traces the tradition from the metaphysical poets themselves up to the time of the text's publication, as noted by Lola Ridge in her review of the book: "John Donne and Emily Dickinson Constrained into a Curious Marriage at Its Center" (*New York Evening Post* April 5, 1930). Taggard's varieties of metaphysical verse are just that: types, or as she refers to them, "approximates" of the tradition that began with Donne and whose influence extended into her own generation of poets. Although Taggard's own work does not appear in this anthology, as a poet she identified with the metaphysical tradition. However, the exigencies of *Calling Western Union* indicate the poet's feeling that the social crisis in America in the Depression required a different kind of verse altogether.

28. The feminist concerns of "Everyday Alchemy" are at best problematic. An important trope for leftist and feminist writers of the 1930s was the woman who offered comfort as she struggled to resist oppression and worked to build a new world alongside her man. Taggard, reviewing Alexandra Kollantay's novel *Red Love* for the *New Masses* (see chap. 3, n. 9), attempts to problematize the nurturing as well as social roles of women and men: "I believe in endowment of motherhood, taxation of men by the state, and babies born any nine months their mothers desire. But Kollontay is a little hipped as all feminists are, in thinking that what we want is woman's freedom from men, rather than freedom with them. Men need endowment of motherhood as much as women and children do; the need is a social one, not a sex affair all alone in a vacuum" (29).

29. It is even possible that Taggard knew Käthe Kollwitz's drawings of mothers holding their sons' slain corpses. Kollwitz lost a son in World War I and a grandson in World War II.

30. Rabinowitz's discussion of Daniel Aaron's *Writers on the Left* and Walter Rideout's *The Radical Novel in the United States, 1900–1950* is in *Labor and Desire*. See Wald's new introduction to the Morningside edition of Aaron's *Writers on the Left*. Perhaps one of Aaron's most valuable points, especially with regard to this study, is this remark from his preface: "Without including the fellow travelers or liberals or non-party radicals the story of literary communism would be very thin indeed, for the Communist Party had far less influence on writers than the idea of communism or the image of Soviet Russia" (ix).

31. For a discussion of women and technology in the 1920s see Elaine Showalter's introduction to *These Modern Women: Autobiographical Essays from the Twenties* (1979; New York: Feminist Press, 1989); and Ruth Schwartz Cowan's *More Work for Mother:*

The Ironies of Household Technology from the Open Hearth to the Microwave (New York: Basic Books, 1983).

32. The other questions that the fourteen authors responded to were: "why they wrote and for what audience; their definition of literary prostitution; their opinion of American culture; the feasibility of writers united to secure artistic and economic advancement; whether society had the right to make social demands on the writer; and what attitude, if any, the writer should take toward the revolutionary labor movement" (165). Taggard's essay was a rather negative review of the Machine Age Exposition, organized by Jean Heap and held on May 16–18, 1927, in New York. ("After the show we went outside to a comparatively better show, the city of New York" [*New Masses* 18].) She drew criticism from Lewis Mumford in a later issue for not being appropriately critical of the technological age and its crowded subways and massive skyscrapers. However, Taggard's response to Mumford, in which she disclaimed any opinion that the machine age was "good or perfect," suggests that his fear of "congestion," which technological development encouraged, was not all that different from Taggard's essential dislikes. Taggard was, nonetheless, better humored in her criticisms (418, n. 12).

33. The feminine analogies used in this comment are rather interesting. Artists are associated with "fecundity" and "crop[s]." They are also represented as children who know better than to interfere with "mother" and her "housework." The fact that Taggard was at this time juggling being an artist, a mother to a six year old, and a "public intellectual," is an appropriate connection to such analogies.

34. A recent PBS documentary on Anderson provides an ironic anecdote paralleling Jim Crow America and the Nazi regime that American soldiers (including blacks) were off fighting. Anderson's German refugee accompanist Franz Rupp recalls the Anderson entourage going to the train station after a performance in Birmingham, Alabama (to a segregated audience no doubt). German prisoners of war, who were in transit to internment at a nearby army base, were given first-class meals in the whites-only waiting room, while Anderson, a world-class diva, ate a sandwich on a bench in the rear outside the station.

Chapter 4. The Girl Who Went to Chicago: Political Culture and Migration in Margaret Walker's *For My People*

1. As Walker told Claudia Tate in an interview published in 1983, it actually took her three tries to win the award and get Yale to publish her manuscript: "Stephen Vincent Benét [himself an award-winning, neglected poet], the editor at that time, wanted to publish it the first time I sent it to him from the University of Iowa." Walker completed a master's degree at the University of Iowa Writer's Workshop in 1940. In 1965 she completed a doctorate there. Her thesis was *Jubilee,* which was published a year later. Walker also informs Tate that Benet had to stage a virtual coup in order to get her book published; he refused to nominate any other book. What is more, Benet came to edit the series no doubt because of the success of his Pulitzer Prize–winning, book-length

Civil War poem, *John Brown's Body.* "I think [Benet] felt they were refusing [to publish *For My People*] purely on the basis of race" (192).

2. Walker's thirty-year struggle with *Jubilee* is exemplified in Tillie Olsen's feminist classic, *Silences:* "It is humanly impossible for a woman who is a wife and mother to work on a regular teaching job and write" (209). By quoting Walker's experience writing her novel, Olsen depicted one of the many "silences" belonging to women writers as part of a shared history. It is only fitting that a creative work detailing the life of a female slave should have faced so many obstacles on its road to completion.

3. An unpublished essay by Jim Werner, "Let a New Earth Rise: Landscapes of Mystery, Sorrow and Hope in Margaret Walker's *For My People,*" focuses upon the landscape. Eugenia Collier explores the influences of Southern black folklife and the natural world in her essay "Fields Watered with Blood: Myth and Ritual in the Poetry of Margaret Walker," in *Black Women Writers, 1950–1980: A Critical Evaluation,* ed. Marie Evans (New York: Anchor/Doubleday, 1984). Richard K. Barksdale's "Margaret Walker: Folk Orature and Historical Prophecy," in *Black American Poets between Worlds, 1940–1960,* ed. R. Baxter Miller (Knoxville: University of Tennessee Press, 1986) details myth and religion in *For My People.* All three essays focus on Walker's evocation of racism, but do not emphasize the ideological influences of the Great Migration and the Depression on her work. A new collection of essays edited by Maryemma Graham and devoted to Walker's work is forthcoming from the University of Georgia Press. It is hoped the collection will include new readings of Walker's work within the context of race, class, and gender politics.

4. Obviously to ignore the segregated South is to deny Walker a sense of place in both the literal and figurative sense. As she wrote in the late 1980s: "The South is my home, and my adjustment or accommodation to it—whether real or imagined (mythic and legendary), violent or non-violent—is the subject and source of all my poetry. It is also my life" (*This Is My Century* xvii).

5. In a letter to Richard Wright dated October 9, 1937 (Richard Wright Papers, Beinecke Rare Book and Manuscript Library, Yale University), Walker excitedly remarks that a friend won a scholarship to the Workers' School and gave it to her. (Walker appears to have participated in the organizing of its "Writers and Artists" unit.) The scholarship enabled the young poet, seeming to be constantly without means, to take two courses, fundamentals of political education and political economy.

6. Walker discusses *Goose Island* in her book-length conversation with Nikki Giovanni, *Poetic Equation,* as well as in her biography of Richard Wright, *The Demoniac Genius of Richard Wright.* A copy of the manuscript is housed in Walker's archive at the Margaret Walker Alexander Center for Black Studies at Jackson State University in Jackson, Mississippi.

7. A fuller articulation of this argument can be found in the anthologies, *This Bridge Called My Back: Writing by Radical Women of Color* Gloria Anzaldua and Cherrie Moraga, eds. (Watertown, Mass.: Persephone Press, 1981); and *All the Women Are White,*

All the Blacks Are Men, but Some of Us Are Brave: Black Women's Studies, Patricia Bell-Scott, Gloria T. Hull, and Barbara Smith, eds. (Old Westbury: Feminist Press, 1982).

8. It is important to mention the work of Gwendolyn Brooks, a Chicago poet whose first book of poems, *A Street in Bronzeville* (1945), is an important evocation of black Chicago. It is not clear how well Walker and Brooks knew each other in those days, and whether any rivalries existed between them as young, talented black women. Brooks's second book, *Annie Allen,* published in 1949 and winner of the Pulitzer Prize, contained a number of sonnets, and according to Walker herself, the technical polish of these poems evidenced "racial vindication" for black poets under the scrutiny of white critics who thought their work lacked "form and intellectual acumen" (110). See Walker's essay originally published in *Phylon* in 1950, "New Poets of the Forties," in *How I Wrote Jubilee.*

9. To suggest the importance of this book of poems to the African American community, this interview accompanied photographs taken by Ronald Freeman in honor of the text and its author.

10. Walker claims that it was Nelson Algren, whom she knew from the Chicago Writers' Project, who suggested the urgency of the last stanza and urged her to state her vision of the future. The use of the word *earth* to begin the final stanza also merits mention, for it is a word connected to people's fights for land, for resistance to domination. Thus Walker suggests with it a kind of self-determination for African Americans. One might also recall texts like Pearl Buck's *The Good Earth,* about the plight of Chinese peasants, or Joris Ivens's cinematic portrait of the Spanish Republic's resistance to Franco, *The Spanish Earth.*

11. For a discussion of Walker's friendship with and admiration for Langston Hughes, see her essay "A Literary Legacy from Dunbar to Baraka," in *How I Wrote Jubilee.*

12. Walker continues with an important contradiction:

Imagine my amazement to hear a white girl tell me she was forced to leave Northwestern because she had no money. But I, a poor Negro girl, had stayed even when I had no money. They never threatened me with expulsion. Yet I did not find a white school in the Middle West free of prejudice. All around me was prejudice. To understand the issues out of which it grew became my life's preoccupation. ("Growing Out of Shadow," *How I Wrote* Jubilee 7)

13. Richard Wright's ethnic construction of Chicago is examined in Carla Capetti's *Writing Chicago: Modernism, Ethnography, and the Novel* (New York: Columbia University Press, 1993). The book also explores the ethnic identification of two other Chicago radical writers, Nelson Algren and James T. Farrell.

14. Because she is writing in an age before a specific consciousness about inclusive language had developed, Walker uses "men," though she implies women too. Walker was certainly aware of the sexism within her own community, but was also fully aware of the improbability of making any social gains without the full participation of both

sexes. Yet it is also worth noting again that the influence of the white male left and the absence of an articulated feminist consciousness amongst its female members may have led the poet to disregard whether the new race of "men" in control would be willing to share its power with women, particularly black women.

15. In the early 1930s, during the Communist Party's Third Period dedication to the revolutionary working class, calls for a new black nation in the South influenced a number of pro-party black intellectuals and workers. For differing views on blacks and the Communist Party see the revisionist histories of Robin D. G. Kelley, *Hammer and Hoe*, and Mark Naison, *Communists in Harlem during the Depression* (Urbana: University of Illinois Press, 1983). For an anticommunist perspective see Harold Cruse, *Crisis of the Negro Intellectual* (New York: William Morrow, 1967).

16. Horace Cayton remarks to Studs Terkel, years after he co-authored *Black Metropolis,* about the significant impact the black church had on sustaining its community. He claims the Communist Party "raised issues that Negroes were interested in," but they "made very little inroads." According to Cayton, "[o]ne of the reasons the Communists flopped is they didn't know how to deal with the Negro church. The church was the first Negro institution, preceding even the family in stability" (quoted in Terkel 434–38). While Cayton is critical of the Communist Party in *Black Metropolis,* he maintains the important role the communists played in promoting black leadership within the CIO and pushing the organization's commitment to racial equality.

17. Race politics and the industrial unions have been a subject of much debate, especially in reference to the United Auto Workers. See Michael Goldfield, *The Color of Politics* (New York: New Press, 1997). And on meatpackers in Chicago, Roger Horowitz, *"Negro and White, Unite and Fight"* (Urbana: University of Illinois Press, 1997); and Rick Halpern and Roger Horowitz, *Meatpackers: An Oral History of Black Packinghouse Workers and Their Struggle for Racial and Economic Equality* (New York: Monthly Review Press, 1999). (I am indebted to Ethan Young for these references.)

18. Jacob Lawrence (1917–2000), only a few years Walker's junior, also began his artistic career with the help of the WPA's Federal Artists' Project. "The Migration of the Negro" series was completed in 1943. In many ways it is a complementary artistic testimony to *For My People.* It might be argued that Langston Hughes's proletarian poetry of the 1930s (that, under pressure, he later renounced in a 1949 article in *Phylon*) serves as companion testimony to these two previously mentioned black cultural projects. And all three should be "read" together.

19. For a discussion of African American militant labor politics in the South, see Robin D. G. Kelley, *Hammer and Hoe.* His chapter on the Share Croppers' Union, in particular, discusses gendered aspects of working-class life and struggle in the black South.

20. Jacqueline Jones notes the important distinction between black and white female workers. Even as white women were disproportionately represented on the shop floor in comparison to white men, after their migration north, black women found

most factory jobs completely closed to them. Instead, most black women found work in laundries or as domestics in the homes of middle- and upper-class white women.

21. Folklorist Roger D. Abrahams has commented upon how most African American folktale collecting has been done by whites, with notable exceptions such as Zora Neale Hurston's *Mules and Men.* He does not explore, however, how African American poets such as Langston Hughes, Sterling Brown, and Margaret Walker, writing at the same period in which much of the tale collecting occurred, were also responsible for disseminating much of these same folk materials. It is also important to note that Hughes, Brown, and Walker challenge the modern poetry canon as it has evolved with work that questions the canon's emphasis on Western "erudition" with the "folkways" important to black structures of feeling. See Abrahams's preface to *Afro-American Folk Tales: Stories from Black Traditions in the New World* (New York: Pantheon Books, 1985). See also Sterling A. Brown, *Southern Road* (1932; Boston: Beacon Press, 1974); and Langston Hughes, *The Weary Blues* (New York: Knopf, 1926).

22. Lawrence Levine characterizes these two seminal figures respectively as "the bad man who transgressed totally all of the moral and legal bounds of society and the strong, self-contained hero who violated not the laws or the moral code but the stereotyped roles set aside for black people in a white society" (407).

23. A plethora of musical renditions of the legend exist from the country blues of performers like Hurt in the 1920s to rhythm and blues performers like Lloyd Price in the 1950s. Even white performers such as Johnny Cash sang about "Staggerlee," as he was also called, in addition to Stack-a-lee, after its *proper* pronunciation, and Stacker Lee. In the early 1980s a white, British punk band, The Clash, opened a reggae-inspired tune, "Wrong-em Boyo" with the Stagolee legend. Rock music's indebtedness to black cultural tropes no doubt found inspiration for its own bad boy, outlaw images with the Stagolee legend. For a discussion of the Stagolee tale and its connections to American popular music see Greil Marcus's *Mystery Train.*

24. Lomax's interest in the Stagolee story focuses upon its use in the blues music idiom, which appropriated antebellum material and adapted it to this musical genre as it developed in the postslavery period. See his *The Land Where the Blues Began* (New York: Delta Books, 1993).

25. Walker's mention of "memorial day" is of course a reference to the aforementioned Memorial Day Massacre. Letter dated June 6, 1938, Richard Wright Papers, Beinecke Rare Book and Manuscript Library, Yale University.

26. For discussion of these two figures see Levine as well as John W. Roberts, *From Trickster to Badman: The Black Folk Hero in Slavery and Freedom* (Philadelphia: University of Pennsylvania Press, 1989).

27. Since folktales told about women seem overwhelmingly to detail domestic issues and romantic problems, it has been difficult to locate a possible source for "Kissie Lee." However, Lawrence Levine cites a fragment sent to Alan Lomax from a woman named

Willie George King of Louisiana. This fragment is interesting not only because of its articulation of female agency, it also contains elements of prowess associated with the hypermasculinized rock and roll music inspired by black performers such as Bo Diddley:

> There is nothing in the jungle is any badder than me.
> I am the baddest woman ever come out Tenisee;
> I sleep with a panther till the break of day;
> I caught a tiger-cat in the collar and I ask him what he had to say;
> And I wore a rattlesnake for my chain,
> And a Negro man for my fob. (402)

28. Another interesting "womens" text is "Molly Means," about a conjure woman. The conjurer tale has, however, received more critical attention, so I have chosen to reserve my space for the female outlaw whose exploits, for the most part, have been overlooked.

29. Zora Neale Hurston's collection *Mules and Men* contains prose narratives in which women's exploits are at the center. One tale does celebrate a female tough named "Ella Wall," but her "legend" appears to be filtered through the lyrics of masculine desire: "If you want good boody / [o]h, go to Ella Wall" (146). In this tale Hurston describes Ella pulling a blade inside a gambling house. For a discussion of women's blues see Hazel Carby, "It Jus' Bes that Way Sometimes," in *Feminisms,* ed. R. Warhol, 2nd ed. (New Brunswick, N.J.: Rutgers University Press, 1997); Angela Y. Davis, "I Used to Be Your Sweet Mama," in *Sexy Bodies;* and also Davis's *Blues Legacies and Black Feminism: Gertrude "Ma" Rainey, Bessie Smith, and Billie Holiday* (New York: Pantheon, 1998). Davis cites as "trailblazing" Daphne Duval Harrison's study *Black Pearls: The Blues Queens of the 1920s* (New Brunswick, N.J.: Rutgers University Press, 1988). Harrison's text is the first full-length study of women blues performers.

30. Walker commented a number of times that her "black" *American Tragedy, Goose Island,* prefigures Richard Wright's *Native Son.*

31. Kevin Mumford suggests the importance of "interzones," black/white sex districts in Chicago and New York in the early twentieth century. He connects them to a variety of sex and gender issues, including prostitution as part of the social impact of the Great Migration. He discusses racial difference within "commercialized sex," as he refers to it, but these "interzones" were greatly changed by the Depression. Cayton and Drake examine prostitution in the context of the impact of the Depression on Chicago's black belt.

32. Kevin Mumford also maintains that historical data suggests the existence of racial bias in the policing of prostitutes: "[B]lack women were easy prey to police, who possibly were under pressure to inflate the number of arrests. Black prostitutes were more likely to be convicted and, after conviction, more likely to receive maximum sentences. After serving their sentences, black prostitutes were less successful on probation than

were white women and more likely than white women to return to prostitution. Indeed, their rates of recidivism were higher" (94).

Afterword

1. In the category of "minor" one might include neglected poets with small output like Lola Ridge, Mina Loy, and Lorinne Niedecker, as well as rediscovered poets such as Eve Triem and Rose Drachler.

2. These are Robert Hass, John Hollander, Carolyn Kizer, Nathaniel Mackey, and Marjorie Perloff.

3. Lechlitner and Trent appear in Nekola and Rabinowitz's *Writing Red*. Trent appears in Cary Nelson's *Anthology of Modern American Poetry*. But Welch, whose last book *The Otherwise* was published posthumously in 1977, seems to have received not a single bit of attention since her death. While her output was slim, her poems are delicately wrought, powerful, and beautiful.

4. See chapter 7 of *The First Wave,* 170–210.

5. T. J. Clark's recent writing about this is worth noting: "Anarchism is an aspect of socialism (among many others) that those of us wishing socialism, or some comparable form of resistance, to survive will have to think about again, this time without a prearranged sneer" (9).

Bibliography

Aaron, Daniel. *Writers on the Left: Episodes in Literary Communism.* New York: Oxford University Press, 1961.

Auden, W. H. *Collected Poems.* New York: Random House, 1976.

Avrich, Paul. *Anarchist Portraits.* Princeton: Princeton University Press, 1988.

―――. *The Modern School Movement.* Princeton: Princeton University Press, 1980.

―――. *Sacco and Vanzetti: The Anarchist Background.* Princeton: Princeton University Press, 1991.

Bakhtin, M. M. *The Dialogic Imagination.* Ed. Michael Holquist. Trans. Caryl Emerson and Michael Holquist. Austin: University of Texas Press, 1981.

Bedau, Hugo A. *The Death Penalty in America.* Chicago: Aldine, 1964.

Bedau, Hugo, and Michael Radelet. *In Spite of Innocence: Erroneous Convictions in Capital Cases.* Boston: Northeastern University Press, 1992.

Bernikow, Louise, ed. *The World Split Open: Four Centuries of Women Poets in England and America, 1552–1950.* New York: Vintage, 1974.

Bird, Stewart et al. *Solidarity Forever: An Oral History of the I. W. W.* Chicago: Lake View, 1985.

Burke, Carolyn. *Becoming Mina Loy.* New York: Farrar, Straus, and Giroux, 1996.

Chaplin, Ralph. *Wobbly: The Rough and Tumble Life of an American Radical.* Chicago: University of Chicago Press, 1948.

Clark, T. J. *Farewell to an Idea: Episodes from a History of Modernism.* New Haven: Yale University Press, 1999.

Coiner, Constance. *Better Red: The Writing and Resistance of Tillie Olsen and Meridel LeSueur.* Urbana: University of Illinois Press, 1996.

Daley, James. Review of *Calling Western Union,* by Genevieve Taggard. *New Republic,* October 21, 1936, 324.

D'Attilio, Robert. "The Sacco and Vanzetti Case." *Dictionary of the American Left.* Ed. Mari Jo Buhl et al. Urbana: University of Illinois Press, 1992. 667–70.

Davis, Angela Y. "I Used to Be Your Sweet Mama." *Sexy Bodies: The Strange Carnalities of Feminism.* Ed. Elizabeth Grosz and Elspeth Probyn. London: Routledge, 1995.

Davis, Cynthia, and Kathryn West. *Women Writers in the United States: A Time Line of Literary, Cultural, and Social History.* New York: Oxford University Press, 1996.

Dimock, Wai Chee and Michael T. Gilmore, eds. *Rethinking Class: Literary Studies and Social Formations.* New York: Columbia University Press, 1994.

Drake, St. Clair, and Horace Cayton. *Black Metropolis: A Study of Negro Life in a Northern City.* New York: Harcourt, Brace, 1945.

Drake, William. *The First Wave: Women Poets in America, 1915–1945.* New York: Macmillan, 1987.

Dubofsky, Melvin. *We Shall Be All: A History of the Industrial Workers of the World.* Chicago: Quadrangle, 1977.

DuBois, W.E.B. *Darkwater: Voices from the Veil.* New York: AMS, 1969.

DuBois, W.E.B., and Martha Gruening. "The Massacre of East St. Louis." *Crisis,* September 1917, 219–38.

Ebert, Teresa L. *Ludic Feminism and After: Postmodernism, Desire, and Labor in Late Capitalism.* Ann Arbor: University of Michigan Press, 1996.

Erkkila, Betsy. *Wicked Sisters: Women Poets, Literary History, and Discord.* New York: Oxford University Press, 1992.

Flynn, Elizabeth Gurley. *Rebel Girl: An Autobiography.* New York: International Publishers, 1973.

Foley, Barbara. *Radical Representations: Politics and Form in U.S. Proletarian Fiction.* Durham, N.C.: Duke University Press, 1993.

Forche, Carolyn, ed. *Against Forgetting: Twentieth Century Poetry of Witness.* New York: W. W. Norton, 1993.

Foucault, Michel. *Discipline and Punish: The Birth of the Prison.* Trans. Alan Sheridan. New York: Pantheon, 1977.

Frankfurter, Marion Denman, and Gardner Jackson, eds. *The Letters of Sacco and Vanzetti.* New York: Octagon, 1980.

Friedman, Susan Stanford: *Psyche Reborn: The Emergence of H.D.* Bloomington: Indiana University Press, 1981.

Frost, Richard. *The Mooney Case.* Palo Alto: Stanford University Press, 1968.

Gates, Henry Louis Jr. "New Negroes, Migration and Cultural Exchange." *Jacob Lawrence: The Migration Series.* Ed. Elizabeth Hutton Turner. Washington, D.C.: Rappahannock Press, 1993.

Gilbert, James B. *Writers and Partisans: A History of Literary Radicalism in America.* New York: Columbia University Press, 1992.

Gilbert, Sandra, and Susan Gubar. *No Man's Land: The Place of the Woman Writer in the Twentieth Century.* New Haven: Yale University Press, 1988.

Giovanni, Nikki. *A Poetic Equation: Conversations between Nikki Giovanni and Margaret Walker.* Washington, D.C.: Howard University Press, 1974.

Glenn, Susan A. *Daughters of the Shtetl.* Ithaca, N.Y.: Cornell University Press, 1991.

Gold, Mike. "Go Left Young Writers!" *Mike Gold Reader.* New York: International Publishers, 1954.

Goldman, Emma. *Living My Life.* Vol. 1. New York: Dover, 1970.

Harrison, Alferdteen. "Looking Back: A Conversation with Margaret Walker." *Margaret Walker's "For My People": A Tribute.* Jackson: University Press of Mississippi, 1992.

Hedges, Elaine, and Shelley Fisher Fishkin, eds. *Listening to Silences: New Essays in Feminist Criticism.* New York: Oxford University Press, 1994.

Hurston, Zora Neale. *Mules and Men: Folklore, Memoirs, and Other Writing.* New York: Library of America, 1995.

Johnson, Helene. "A Southern Road." *Fire!!: A Quarterly Devoted to the Younger Negro Artists.* Ed. Wallace Thurman. 1926. Reprint, Metuchen, N.J.: Fire!! Press, 1982.

Jones, Jacqueline. *Labor of Love, Labor of Sorrow: Black Women, Work, and Family from Slavery Times to the Present.* New York: Vintage Books, 1985.

Josephson, Matthew. *Life among the Surrealists.* New York: Holt, Rinehart, and Winston, 1962.

Kalaidjian, Walter. *American Culture between the Wars: Revisionary Modernism and Postmodern Critique.* New York: Columbia University Press, 1993.

Kaplan, Cora. Special Topic Announcement. *PMLA* (October 1997): 1038.

Kelley, Robin D. G. *Hammer and Hoe: Alabama Communists during the Great Depression.* Chapel Hill: University of North Carolina Press, 1990.

Kozlenko, William. "Morphology of the Proletarian Movement." *Literary America* 1 (November 1934): 7.

Kreymborg, Alfred. "A Poet of Arms." *Poetry: A Magazine of Verse.* (March 1919): 335–40.

Kunitz, Stanley. *Living Authors: A Book of Biographies.* New York: H. H. Wilson, 1931.

———. *Twentieth Century Authors.* New York: H. H. Wilson, 1942.

LeSueur, Meridel. *Salute to Spring.* 1966. New York: International Publishers, 1983.

Levine, Lawrence. *Black Culture and Black Consciousness.* New York: Oxford University Press, 1975.

Loeb, Harold. *The Way It Was.* New York: Criterion, 1959.

Marcus, Greil. *Mystery Train: Images of America in Rock 'n' Roll Music.* New York: Dutton, 1976.

Miliband, Ralph. *Socialism for a Skeptical Age.* London: Verso, 1994.

Miller, Nina. *Making Love Modern: The Intimate Public Worlds of New York's Literary Women.* New York: Oxford University Press, 1998.

Monroe, Harriet. "A Symphony of the Cross." *Poetry: A Magazine of Verse* (April 1930): 36–41.

Morgan, Edmund, and Louis Joughin. *The Legacy of Sacco and Vanzetti.* New York: Harcourt, Brace, 1948.

Mumford, Kevin. *Interzones: Black/White Sex Districts in New York and Chicago in the Early Twentieth Century.* New York: Columbia University Press, 1997.

Nadel, Ira B. *Joyce and the Jews: Culture and Texts.* London: Macmillan, 1989.

Neel, Alice. *Paintings from the Thirties.* New York: Robert Miller Gallery, 1997.

Nekola, Charlotte, and Paula Rabinowitz, eds. *Writing Red: An Anthology of American Women Writers, 1930–1940.* New York: Feminist Press, 1987.

Nelson, Cary. "Literature as Cultural Studies: 'American' Poetry of the Spanish Civil War." *Disciplinarity and Dissent in Cultural Studies.* Ed. Cary Nelson and Dilip Parameshwar Gaonkar. New York: Routledge, 1996. 29–59.

———. "Poetry Chorus: Dialogic Politics in 1930s Poetry." *Radical Revisions: Rereading 1930s Culture.* Ed. Bill Mullen and Sherry Lee Linkon. Urbana: University of Illinois Press, 1996. 63–102.

———. *Repression and Recovery: Modern American Poetry and the Politics of Cultural Memory, 1910–1945.* Madison: University of Wisconsin Press, 1989.

———, ed. *Anthology of Modern American Poetry.* New York: Oxford University Press, 2000.

Nestor, Agnes. "A Day's Work Making Gloves." *Life and Labor* (May 1912): 137–39.

Olsen, Tillie. *Silences.* New York: Delta/Seymour Lawrence, 1978.

Orleck, Annelise. *Common Sense and a Little Fire: Women and Working-Class Politics in the United States, 1900–1965.* Chapel Hill: University of North Carolina Press, 1995.

Ostriker, Alicia. *Stealing the Language: The Emergence of Women's Poetry in America.* Boston: Beacon, 1986.

Pitts, Rebecca. "Tough, Reasonable, Witty." Review of *Calling Western Union,* by Genevieve Taggard. *New Masses* October 27, 1936: 22.

Porter, Katherine Anne. *The Never Ending Wrong.* Boston: Little, Brown, 1977.

Rabinowitz, Paula. *Labor and Desire: Women's Revolutionary Fiction in Depression America.* Chapel Hill: University of North Carolina Press, 1991.

Rexroth, Kenneth. "Thou Shall Not Kill." *In Defense of the Earth.* New York: New Directions, 1956.

Ridge, Lola. *Dance of Fire.* New York: Smith and Haas, 1935.

———. *The Ghetto and Other Poems.* New York: B. W. Huebsch, 1918.

———. Letter to Leonard Abbot. N.d. Carl Zigrosser Papers. Van Pelt Library, University of Pennsylvania.

———. Letter to David Lawson. 1923. Lola Ridge Papers. Sophia Smith Collection. Smith College.

———. Letter to Harold Loeb. March 1922. Harold Loeb Papers. Princeton University.

———. Letter to Harold Loeb. July 11, 1922. Harold Loeb Papers. Princton University.

———. *Red Flag.* New York: Viking Press, 1927.

―――. Review of *Circumference: Varieties of Metaphysical Verse,* ed. Genevieve Taggard. *New York Evening Post,* April 5, 1930, 11.

―――. *Sun-Up, and Other Poems.* New York: B. W. Huebsch, 1920.

―――. "Woman and the Creative Will." Ed. Elaine Sproat. *Michigan Occasional Papers in Women's Studies* (1981): 1–23.

Robinson, Lillian. *Sex, Class, and Culture.* New York: Methuen, 1986.

Rowbotham, Sheila. *Women, Resistance and Revolution.* New York: Pantheon, 1972.

Rudnitzky, Anna. "Time Is Passing." *Life and Labor* (April 1912): n. pag.

Rukeyser, Muriel. "Anne Burlak." Nekola and Rabinowitz. 138.

Scarry, Elaine. *The Body in Pain: The Making and Unmaking of the World.* New York: Oxford University Press, 1985.

Schenck, Celeste M. "Exiled by Genre: Modernism, Canonicity, and the Politics of Exclusion." *Women's Writing in Exile.* Ed. Mary Lynne Broe and Angela Ingram. Chapel Hill: University of North Carolina Press, 1989.

Schweik, Susan M. *A Gulf So Deeply Cut: American Women Poets and the Second World War.* Madison: University of Wisconsin Press, 1991.

Scott, Bonnie Kime, ed. *The Gender of Modernism: A Critical Anthology.* Bloomington: University of Indiana Press, 1990.

Sproat, Elaine. "Lola Ridge." *American Women Writers: A Reference Guide.* New York: Ungar, 1981. 475–76.

Stanford, Ann, ed. *The Women Poets in English: An Anthology.* New York: McGraw-Hill, 1972.

Taggard, Genevieve. "Bolshevik Sweethearts." Review of *Red Love,* by Alexandra Kollantay. *New Masses* (June 1927): 29.

―――. *Calling Western Union.* New York: Harper, 1936.

―――. *Circumferences: Varieties of Metaphysical Verse.* New York: Covici-Friede, 1930.

―――. *Collected Poems: 1918–1938.* New York: Harper, 1938.

―――. *For Eager Lovers.* New York: T. Seltzer, 1922.

―――. Interview with Martha Millet. *Daily Worker,* October 11, 1936, 13.

―――. Letter to Josephine Herbst, in William Drake, *The First Wave: Women Poets in America, 1915–1945.* New York: Macmillan, 1987. 180.

―――. *The Life and Mind of Emily Dickinson.* 1930. Reprint, New York: Harper, 1934.

―――. *Long View.* New York: Harper, 1942.

―――. *Origin: Hawaii.* Honolulu: Donald Angus, 1947.

―――. *A Part of Vermont.* East Jamaica, Vt.: River Press, 1945.

―――. "Plenty Pilikia." *Yale Review* 35 (September 1945): 48–60.

―――. *Slow Music.* New York: Harper and Brothers, 1946.

Takaki, Ronald. *A Different Mirror: A Multicultural History of the United States.* Boston: Little, Brown, 1993.

Tate, Claudia. "Margaret Walker." *Black Women Writers at Work.* New York: Continuum, 1983.

Terkel, Studs. "Horace Cayton." *Hard Times: An Oral History of the Great Depression.* New York: Pantheon, 1980.

Trent, Lucia. "Breed, Women, Breed." Nekola and Rabinowitz. 168.

United Committee to Aid Vermont Marble Workers. "Verbatim Report of Public Hearing, Town Hall, West Rutland, Vermont, February 29, 1936." Unpublished ms. Genevieve Taggard Book Collection. Baker Library, Dartmouth College.

Van Wienen, Mark. *Partisans and Poets: The Political Work of American Poetry in the Great War.* New York: Cambridge University Press, 1997.

Vorse, Mary Heaton. *Footnote to Folly.* New York: Farrar and Rinehart, 1935.

Wald, Alan M. *Writing from the Left: New Essays on Radical Culture and Politics.* London: Verso, 1994.

Walker, Margaret. *For My People.* New Haven, Conn.: Yale University Press, 1942.

———. *How I Wrote* Jubilee *and Other Essays on Life and Literature.* Ed. Maryemma Graham. New York: Feminist Press, 1990.

———. Letter to Richard Wright. June 6, 1938. Richard Wright Papers. Beinecke Rare Book and Manuscript Library, Yale University.

———. *This Is My Century: New and Collected Poems.* Athens: University of Georgia Press, 1987.

Walker, Nancy. "Wider than the Sky: Public Presence and Private Self in Dickinson, James, and Woolf." *The Private Self: Theory and Practice of Women's Autobiographical Writing.* Ed. Shari Benstock. Chapel Hill: University of North Carolina Press, 1988. 272–303.

Ward, Estolv Ethan. *The Gentle Dynamiter.* Palo Alto, Calif.: Ramparts Press, 1983.

Weinberger, Eliot. "The Modernists in the Basement and 'The Stars Above.'" *Works on Paper.* New York: New Directions, 1986. 159–75.

Welch, Marie de L. *The Otherwise.* San Francisco: Adrian Wilson, 1976.

———. "Skyscraper in Construction." *New Masses* (July 1928): 4.

———. *This Is Our Own.* New York: Macmillan, 1940.

Williams, William Carlos. *The Autobiography of William Carlos Williams.* New York: Random House, 1951.

Woolf, Virginia. *A Room of One's Own.* New York: Harcourt, Brace, and World, 1929.

Wright, Richard. Introduction. *Black Metropolis.* By St. Clair Drake and Horace Cayton. New York: Harcourt, Brace, 1945. xvii–xxxiv.

Index

Nancy Berke has taught English and women's studies at Hunter College, City University of New York. She was a Fulbright Lecturer at the University of Zagreb and visiting professor of American literature and culture at the University of Liège.